the family cookbook: **italian**

the family cookbook

by Charlotte Adams & Alvin Kerr

Special Consultant:

James Beard

———

Illustrations
by Helen Federico

Photography
by Arie deZanger

italian

A Ridge Press Book | Holt, Rinehart and Winston | New York

RIDGE PRESS:
Editor-in-Chief: Jerry Mason
Editor: Adolph Suehsdorf
Art Director: Albert Squillace
Project Art Director: Harry Brocke
Project Editor: Barbara Hoffbeck
Associate Editor: Ruth Birnkrant
Associate Editor: Moira Duggan
Art Associate: Mark Liebergall
Art Production: Doris Mullane

RESTAURANT ASSOCIATES:
Project Director: George E. Lang
Chef of The Trattoria: Giacomo Zoni
Chef of Mamma Leone's: Peter Pioli

Courtesy of ROSENTHAL STUDIO-HAUS, New York,
in lending objects for photographic still lifes is gratefully acknowledged.

contents

introduction

The cuisines of France and Italy have in common deserved reputations for excellence and high accomplishment. Yet the two differ greatly in approach. The French may work a kind of magic transformation on the foods they use (and which they choose often at the inspiration of other cuisines); in the process, ingredients frequently lose their singularity for the sake of the final glorious dish.

The Italians, on the other hand, unfailingly emphasize the true flavor of their ingredients. Each food is treated with respect for its unique individual contribution—and the results are notable.

I remember an experience in a rather small but elegant Roman restaurant, whose owner—a Venetian—told me one night as I arrived for dinner that I must taste a certain fish from the Adriatic, near Venice. It turned out that the owner had flown to Venice the day before and returned with the day's catch to serve to two or three parties of diners which were expected that evening. He did not trust the fish to come through commercial channels, but had got them himself—flying first class with the fish in his lap—to assure his guests perfect freshness and the best of flavors.

In Italy good eating and drinking is as natural as living. The intense honesty of fine Italian cookery makes eating a national joy wherever one travels in Italy. Nowhere else these days is regional produce so strongly stressed—not even in France.

There are three courses that, more than any others, prove the greatness of the Italian cuisine. One is the antipasti, another the minestre, in which I include soups and pastas, and the third is the desserts and ices. Recipes for many of these dishes may seem simple, but the ability to combine gastronomic elegance with simplicity is one of the high achievements of cooking. A dish of fettuccine with butter and cheese, for instance, can be memorable when all the necessary thought and technique are brought to bear to make it so. It is as simple as bread and milk, but it must be made from proper ingredients, timed perfectly, blended well, and served at once. It then is as great as a classic dish can be.

The repertoire of pastas contains many excellent combinations. Who but the Italians would have thought of mixing broccoli or cauliflower with perfectly cooked pasta for a superb flavor and texture contrast? Who else would have dreamed of the heady excitement of pasta sauced with a blending of fresh basil, olive oil, garlic, pine nuts, and cheese, as the Genovesi did when they invented pesto? That dish alone is enough to establish a cuisine.

Who prepares fish and shellfish better than this nation supplied with the bounty of the Mediterranean? I can remember few sights as vivid as the markets of Venezia, Livorno, and Napoli, where the fruit of the seas overflowed the stalls. There were superb scampi (which should be reserved for the towns where they originate, and not be allowed to wander—or to be counterfeited as they are in the United States), and thin razor clams. In almost any small seacoast village there is a cook who can prepare squid or *dentice* or fresh anchovies like a poet. And, as if that were not enough, the Italians take salt codfish from the faraway banks of Newfoundland and transpose it into dishes which are joys to the palate.

(I well recall a barman on the old liner *Independence.* He was a Triestino and a fine cook. Often he bade favored passengers to lunch in a small dining room near his bar. My great pleasure was a salad he made of salt codfish tenderly poached, thinly sliced waxy potatoes, onion slices, and parsley, the whole dressed with olive oil, lemon, salt, pepper, and a touch of garlic. It was supremely good, strikingly simple, and had the loving hands of a good cook in its construction.)

Who, since the days of ancient Rome, has explored more fully than the Italians the secrets of puréeing fruits and icing juices? Until you have had a proper granita di limone, or a granita di caffè, you have missed the exhilarating contrast of the cold, the bitter, and the sweet. And the creaminess of a fine Italian ice cream is something no other cuisine has even approximated. The French, the Americans—all have failed miserably trying to reproduce the superlative Italian ice creams, biscuits, and bombes. And I'm not being disloyal to anyone when I say this.

Italian cheeses are varied, interesting, and sometimes very great. Perhaps the supreme achievement of the Italian cheesemaker's art is Parmesan. Freshly cut from a wheel, it is one of the more satisfying cheeses one can put in the mouth. It is a great table cheese—which often amazes those whose acquaintance with it is limited to a shaker-top jar containing a rather stale cheese powder. Grating a freshly cut wedge of Parmigiano onto hot pasta releases a bouquet that is in itself a delightful gourmet experience. In the same way, the bland creaminess of a fine Fontina, melted and topped with shavings of a fresh white truffle, becomes a sensuous pleasure.

Other Italian favorites are caciocavallo, a deliciously peppery, dryish cheese; provolone; and the great blue cheese, Gorgonzola. Eaten with crusty bread or with a ripe pear, it has a superbly good flavor and creamy quality which make it distinctive among the blue cheeses of the world.

Italy also brings the cooking of cheeses to a noble height. The light texture of fine ricotta as used in cannelloni, or in that delicious cheese tart which one finds at certain periods of the year, or for the exquisite dessert with coffee, sugar, and rum, make this a cheese to reckon with.

One should accept Italian cooking as the homely, friendly, deliciously simple cookery it is. It is not *grande cuisine,* but it will be a welcome addition to anyone's cooking repertoire, with its honest approach to natural flavor and texture.

This cookery book, one of many dealing with Italian fare, differs from others in several ways. Its recipes extend far beyond the usual, and the authors have collaborated with the master chefs of Restaurant Associates to test and adapt them for the home kitchen. I am confident that anyone who tries them will be eminently well rewarded.

J.B.

1 | antipasti

On Italian menus, this is the course "before the pasta"—a dish to delight the eye and stimulate the appetite. It may consist of a simply prepared salad or vegetable, or something as elaborate as *zucchini ripieni* (stuffed zucchini) or *petto di vitello farcito* (stuffed breast of veal). In fact, many of the antipasto dishes are important enough to make an entire meal, at least by American standards.

In choosing the antipasto, one gives thought to color—the green of artichoke, the red of tomato, the deep purple of eggplant, to the texture and arrangement of thinly sliced salami or ham, to the fragrance of olive-oil flavored delicacies. Some foods will retain their simplicity, others will show time and imagination in the making. Whatever the choice, the purpose of the antipasto—as a piquant introduction to the meal to follow—should be fulfilled.

Clams with Oregano Filling | Vongole all'Origano

2 cups medium-dry bread crumbs	1 Tbl lemon juice
1 cup finely chopped parsley	½ tsp salt
1 tsp dried oregano	36 cherrystone clams on half shells
1 large clove garlic, mashed	Lemon wedges
¼ cup olive oil	Sprigs of parsley
2 Tbl butter	

In a mortar with a pestle or in a bowl with a wooden spoon, work to a paste the bread crumbs, parsley, oregano, garlic, olive oil, butter, lemon juice, and salt.

With a sharp knife free the clams from their retaining muscles, but do not remove them from the shells. Drain off juice. Spread each clam with 1 tablespoon of the paste and arrange them in a shallow baking pan. Set the pan in a 450-degree oven and let the fillings heat through for 10 minutes. Transfer the pan to a hot broiler and let fillings brown. Serve clams 6 to a serving with a wedge of lemon. Decorate plates with sprigs of parsley. Serves 6.

Eels in Marinade | Capitone Sotto Aceto

2 pounds eel, cleaned (page 130)	½ cup water
¾ cup olive oil	4 cloves garlic, mashed
2 Tbl flour	1 large bay leaf
1 medium onion, finely chopped	¼ tsp dried sage
1 large stalk celery, finely chopped	⅛ tsp white pepper
1½ cups red wine vinegar	1 tsp salt
1 cup white wine vinegar	1 Tbl finely chopped parsley
1 cup dry white wine	

Cut the eels in 3-inch lengths. In a large skillet heat the olive oil. Dust the eels lightly with the flour and cook them briskly in the oil, turning the pieces frequently to brown them evenly. Remove eels to a warm deep platter and keep warm. Strain oil from the skillet into a saucepan and reheat it. Add the onion and celery and cook them for 2 to 3 minutes, stirring them frequently to prevent their browning excessively.

Pour over them the two vinegars, the wine, and water, and add the garlic, bay leaf, sage, pepper, and salt. Let the marinade cook at simmer for 5 minutes to blend the flavors, and pour it over eels in platter, covering them completely. If marinade is insufficient, add more wine. When liquid has cooled, cover dish with plastic wrap and set it in refrigerator. The eels should marinate under refrigeration for 24 hours.

Transfer eels to a serving platter. Strain marinade over them and sprinkle them with the chopped parsley. Serves 6.

Mussels in Green Sauce | Cozze in Salsa Verde

1 cup dry white wine
1 cup water
48 mussels,
   scrubbed & bearded (page 130)

1 cup Green Sauce (page 274)
1 Tomato Rose (page 197)

Heat the wine and water in a large saucepan. Add the mussels and steam them, covered, over high heat until the shells open. Discard immediately any that do not open. Remove mussels and let them cool. Reserve shells to which they were secured. Discard other halves. In each of the reserved halves spread ½ teaspoon of green sauce. Place a cooled mussel over it and cover the mussel with another ½ teaspoon of sauce. Chill the prepared mussels in the shells. Arrange them in a bed of lettuce leaves on a large serving platter and decorate platter with the tomato rose. Serves 6.

Tomatoes Stuffed with Tuna Fish | Pomodori Ripieni al Tonno

6 large, ripe tomatoes
2 cans water-packed
   tuna fish, 7½-ounce size
½ cup thinly sliced scallions

½ cup thinly sliced celery
1 cup Mayonnaise (page 286)
1 Tbl finely chopped parsley
Salt & white pepper to taste

Cut off the tops of the tomatoes, and scoop out the pulp, leaving a durable shell. Place the shells upside down on a plate to drain. Remove the seeds from the pulp and discard them. Chop pulp finely. Drain and flake the tuna fish.

In a mixing bowl combine tomato pulp, tuna, scallions, celery, mayonnaise, and 1 teaspoon of the parsley. Season mixture with salt and white pepper to taste. Fill tomatoes with the mixture and sprinkle tops with the remaining parsley. Chill tomatoes thoroughly before serving them. Serves 6.

Squid with Genoa-Style Green Sauce | Calamari al Pesto

12 small squid (about 3 pounds)   **2 cups Green Sauce, Genoa-Style (page 275)**

Clean and steam the squid according to directions on pages 130 and 132. Cut the cooked squid into slices ½-inch thick. Remove the tentacles but leave them intact. Chill all of the squid thoroughly and dress with the sauce. Serves 6.

Stuffed Squid | Calamari Ripieni

24 squid	**1 tsp salt**
4 jumbo shrimp, shelled & de-veined	**¼ tsp white pepper**
2 canned roasted red peppers, coarsely chopped	**2 Tbl olive oil**
3 cloves garlic, peeled & coarsely chopped	**2 large cloves garlic, finely chopped**
¼ cup finely chopped parsley	**2 cups canned, peeled plum tomatoes**
½ cup soft bread crumbs	**¼ tsp oregano**
⅓ cup milk	**Salt**

Clean and steam the squid according to directions on pages 130 and 132. Coarsely chop 6 of the squid (set the remaining squid aside) and the shrimp. On a large chopping board combine the chopped squid, shrimp, peppers, garlic, and parsley. Using a knife, chop them until they are reduced almost to a paste. Transfer the mixture to a mixing bowl. Moisten the bread crumbs with the milk and blend them into the fish mixture along with the indicated quantities of salt and pepper, or more to taste. With a pastry bag, fitted with a large plain tube, pipe the prepared mixture

Colorful antipasti include Pearl Onions in Saffron, Pickled Vegetable Salad, cold meats, salads of chick-peas and seafood, and Stuffed Artichoke (on round platter), Skewered Shrimp (upper left), Pickled Trout (below shrimp), Stuffed Breast of Veal (upper right), Italian Ham and Melon (lower left), and various stuffed vegetables.

1. Chef greasing pan.

2. Fitting pie dough into pan.

3. Adding eggs to meat mixture.

4. Placing layer of meat in pan

5. Adding two rows of ham pieces.

6. Covering with spinach.

7. Slicing ends off hard-boiled eggs.

8. Making row of eggs.

9. Covering with meat mixture.

10. Adding rows of sweet red peppers.

11. Placing spinach down middle.

12. Shaping last of meat over al

13. Covering top with pie dough.

14. Crimping edges of dough.

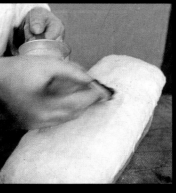

15. Painting with beaten egg.

16. Finished product at table.

equally into the remaining 18 cooked squid, filling them to within ½ inch of the top. Thread a toothpick through top of each squid to retain filling.

In a large saucepan heat the olive oil and in it cook the bits of garlic over low heat, stirring them until they take on a little color. Add the tomatoes, oregano, and salt to taste, and continue cooking for a few minutes to blend the flavors. Arrange the stuffed squid carefully in the sauce. Cover pan and cook them at bare simmer over very low heat for 25 minutes. Cooked at any greater degree of heat the squid may burst. Remove squid gently to a warm serving platter and remove toothpicks. Pour sauce over squid and serve them at once. This recipe provides 6 generous servings.

Pickled Trout | Trota in Carpione

1 cup olive oil	**2 large carrots, cut in fine julienne**
6 trout, about 8 ounces each, boned	**1½ cups dry white wine**
Flour	**1 bay leaf**
2 cloves garlic, mashed	**½ tsp salt**
2½ cups white wine vinegar	**4 peppercorns**
2 Tbl fresh sage leaves, chopped	**6 thin slices lemon**
(or 1 tsp dried sage, crumbled)	**2 Tbl finely chopped parsley**
2 large onions, thinly sliced	

Heat ½ cup of the olive oil in a large skillet. Dust the trout with flour and cook them in the oil over moderate heat for 6 minutes, or until they are lightly browned on both sides. Turn them just once, very carefully, so as not to break them. Remove trout and arrange them in a glass or enamel-coated baking pan large enough to accommodate them in a single layer. Reheat oil remaining in skillet and in it lightly brown the garlic. Remove pan from heat and carefully pour into it 1 cup of the vinegar. Add the sage and cook the mixture at simmer for 5 minutes.

In a large saucepan heat the remaining ½ cup of unused olive oil. Add the onions and carrots, and cook them, without browning, for 5 minutes. Carefully, to avoid spattering, pour over them the wine and the remaining vinegar. Add the bay leaf, salt, and peppercorns, and continue cooking, at simmer, for 10 minutes. Strain the mixture from skillet into

Versatile Meat Pie, Country Style, a colorful loaf of meats and vegetables encased in pastry, may be served as antipasto or as a luncheon entrée. For recipe, see page 22.

pan. Discard garlic and sage. Bring liquid to a boil and pour it, along with vegetables, over fish in baking pan. Place a slice of the lemon on each trout and surround it with a narrow band of the chopped parsley. Cool trout in the marinade and chill in refrigerator for 24 hours. Serve trout each with a little of the marinade and the parsley-ringed lemon slices as garniture. Serves 6.

NOTE: The trout may be prepared the same way with the bones left in.

Marinated Whitebait | Bianchetti Marinati

Olive oil & vegetable oil combined,
   for deep frying
1½ pounds whitebait
Flour
Salt & white pepper

2 cups white wine vinegar
½ cup dry white wine
2 cloves garlic, mashed
¼ tsp dried sage
1 Tbl finely chopped parsley

Fill a deep saucepan or fryer to no more than ½ its capacity with the combined oils and heat to 375 degrees.

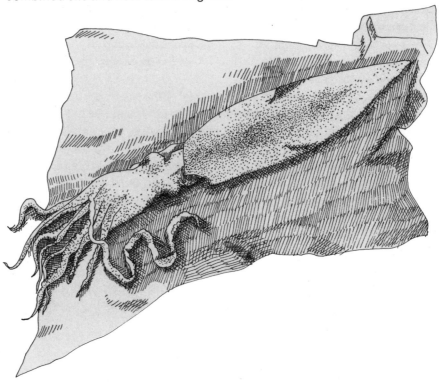

Wash the fish gently and dry them thoroughly on paper toweling. Season the flour generously with salt and white pepper and dredge fish with the mixture. Fry the floured fish in the hot oil for 3 minutes or until they are lightly browned. Drain and spread them in a deep platter or a glass baking dish.

In a saucepan heat together the vinegar and wine. Add the garlic and sage and cook at simmer until garlic is soft. Remove pan from heat and stir into the liquid ¼ cup of the combined oils in which fish were cooked. Strain the hot marinade over fish and let them cool in it. Chill them in the marinade for several hours or overnight. Drain fish, leaving about ¼ cup of the marinade (to keep fish moist) and transfer them to a serving dish. Sprinkle with the chopped parsley. Serves 6.

Stuffed Breast of Veal | Petto di Vitello Farcito

Broth:	
1 carrot	1 bay leaf
1 small onion	6 peppercorns
1 stalk celery	1½ tsp salt
	6 cups cold water

Combine all the ingredients in a large, deep saucepan. Bring the water to a boil and cook vegetables and herbs for 10 minutes. Keep broth warm over low heat.

Veal and Stuffing:	
Breast of veal, boned & trimmed	½ cup finely diced raw veal
¾ cup butter	¾ cup finely diced cooked ham
½ cup finely chopped onion	½ tsp oregano
1 cup chopped green pepper	10 eggs, well beaten
¾ cup chopped sweet red pepper	½ cup grated Parmesan cheese
	Salt & pepper

Cut a long, deep pocket lengthwise in the breast of veal. Heat the butter in a large skillet and, over high heat, lightly brown together the onion, peppers, and diced veal in it. Reduce heat to moderate and cook for 10 minutes. Add the ham and oregano, and heat them through. Stir in the eggs and cook them, continuing stirring, until they are soft-scrambled. Remove pan from heat and immediately blend the Parmesan cheese into the egg mixture. Season mixture with salt and pepper to taste and spread it evenly in the pocket cut in the breast of veal. Roll the filled meat into a long, firm sausage and wrap it in 4 layers of dampened cheesecloth. Secure meat in cloth by tying ends and several places along the length with kitchen twine. Place the roll in the prepared broth and cook it at simmer for 2 hours, or until it is tender, turning it occasionally so that it cooks evenly. Add boiling water as needed during cooking to keep level constant.

Take cooked roll from broth and remove cheesecloth. Serve roll warm or chilled, sliced to provide 10 to 12 servings as a main course. As antipasto, served chilled, it will provide 16 to 18 servings.

Meat Pie, Country Style | Torta Rustica di Carne

1 cup olive oil	**1 clove garlic, finely chopped**
2 large onions, thinly sliced	**4 cups finely chopped spinach**
2 pounds pork, coarsely ground	**(about 1 pound)**
1½ pounds beef, coarsely ground	**Vegetable shortening**
1 pound veal, coarsely ground	**1 recipe Pie Dough (page 72)**
1½ cups dry white wine	**1 slice cooked ham,**
1 Tbl salt	**5-inches square & 1-inch thick**
½ tsp white pepper	**5 hard-cooked eggs**
8 Tbl unflavored gelatine	**1 7-ounce can roasted**
2⅓ cups grated Parmesan cheese	**sweet red peppers, well drained**
6 large eggs	**Sprigs of parsley**
4 Tbl butter	**2 Tomato Roses (page 197)**

In a large saucepan heat the olive oil and in it cook the onions until they begin to take on color. Combine the ground meats. Add them to the onions and cook them over moderate heat for 40 minutes, stirring frequently so that they cook evenly. Transfer contents of the pan to a colander over a deep, heat-proof mixing bowl, and let them remain until all liquid and cooking oil seeps through. The mixture must be thoroughly drained, otherwise the pie filling will be soggy. Return meat and onions to saucepan, now wiped clean of any remaining oil, and add to them 1 cup of the wine, and the salt and pepper. Continue cooking for 5 minutes to blend the flavors and to heat the mixture through. Stir into it 6 tablespoons of the gelatine and 1⅓ cups of the grated cheese. Beat the mixture into 3 of the eggs, well beaten in a mixing bowl, adding it a very little at a time so as not to curdle the eggs. Set mixture aside for the moment.

In another saucepan heat the butter and in it very lightly brown the garlic. Add the spinach and cook it for 3 minutes or until it wilts, stirring it constantly. Stir in the remaining wine and continue cooking for 3 minutes longer. Blend in the remaining gelatine and grated cheese. In a mixing bowl beat 2 more eggs and slowly stir the spinach mixture into them. Set this preparation aside also.

Thickly coat with vegetable shortening a 10-cup-capacity loaf pan (11 by 5 inches and 3 inches deep). Prepare pie dough as directed in recipe, and roll ⅔ of it into a thin rectangle of a size to fit the prepared pan with an overhang of ½ inch all around. Line pan with that part of the dough, fitting it in snugly. Reserve remaining dough.

Over the bottom of the dough-lined pan firmly press 3 cups of the prepared meat mixture into an even layer. Cut the slice of ham into 5 sticks, each 1-inch wide. Cut 1 of the sticks in half. Align the sticks of ham in 2 rows, 2½ to a row, centered 1 inch apart down the length of the pan. Cover them with an even layer of ⅓ of the prepared spinach. Cut ¼-inch off each end of the hard-cooked eggs. Down the center of the spinach layer, between ham rows, arrange the hard-cooked eggs, end to end. Over them spread a firm even layer of another 3 cups of the prepared meats.

Split the red peppers lengthwise and arrange them equally in 2 rows, extending down the length on each side of the pan. Spread the remaining spinach evenly between those rows. Cover it all with the remaining meat mixture in a mound down the length, shaping it high in the center with the sides sloped down over peppers. Preheat oven to 350 degrees.

Roll out the remaining dough into a top crust for the pie. Brush overhanging edges of the lining dough with the remaining egg, well beaten. Fit on the top, pressing edges to secure the 2 crusts together. Brush top with beaten egg.

Bake the loaf in the preheated oven for 15 minutes or until pastry just begins to brown. Cover top loosely with foil and continue baking for

1 hour. Remove foil and bake pie for 15 minutes longer or until pastry is richly browned. Remove pan from oven. Cool pie in pan and chill it so in the refrigerator for 24 hours.

To unmold loaf, heat the oven to 200 degrees. Set pan in oven and let it remain for 15 minutes or until pastry loses its chill. It should not actually be warm. Remove pan and loosen sides of the pie by running a thin sharp knife around inside of pan, taking great care not to pierce pastry. Gently ease the pie sideways out of pan onto a serving platter, supporting the side of the loaf on your hand. Set the pie upright on platter. Chill it again until it is to be served. Surround base of pie with sprigs of parsley and decorate each side of platter with a tomato rose.

This recipe provides a party-size pie to be cut into 12 slices for a luncheon entrée or into 20 as antipasto. For a larger pie to provide about 18 entrée slices or 30 antipasto servings, as shown on page 18, increase all ingredients, including those for the dough, by ½ and use a 15- by 5-inch pan 4 inches deep. Baking time will be the same.

The pie may be kept under refrigeration for about 1 week. It should not be frozen.

Tripe Borgotaro Style | Trippa di Borgotaro

2 pounds tripe	1 bay leaf
2 Tbl olive oil	1 cup dry white wine
2 Tbl butter	3 medium tomatoes, peeled,
1 large onion, finely chopped	seeded & chopped
2 carrots, finely chopped	Salt & pepper
2 stalks celery, finely chopped	½ cup grated Parmesan cheese
1 clove garlic, mashed	Additional grated Parmesan cheese

Wash the tripe, put it in a saucepan, and cover with cold water. Bring water to a boil. Drain tripe, cover it again with cold water, and bring that to a boil. Cook tripe, covered, over moderate heat for 3½ hours. Drain tripe again. Freshen it with cold water, drain it once more, and cut it into strips ½-inch wide and 2-inches long.

In another saucepan heat together the olive oil and butter. Add the chopped vegetables, garlic, and bay leaf, and cook them slowly until the vegetables are soft but not brown. Blend into them the white wine and reduce it almost completely. Add the strips of tripe, the tomatoes, and salt and pepper to taste. Cover pan and continue cooking, at simmer, for 1 hour, stirring the mixture occasionally. If it becomes too dry, add a little more white wine during the cooking. Add the ½ cup grated Parmesan cheese and cook the mixture for 30 minutes longer. Remove and discard bay leaf. Transfer tripe and vegetables in equal portions to 6 individual casseroles. Sprinkle each lightly with additional grated cheese and brown the servings under a hot broiler. Serve them at once. Serves 6.

Tripe Friuli Style | Trippa alla Friulana

2 pounds tripe	Salt & pepper
2 Tbl butter	1 clove garlic
¼ pound salt pork, finely chopped	6 thick slices Italian bread
1 large onion, thinly sliced	¼ cup olive oil
¼ tsp dried rosemary	6 Tbl grated Parmesan cheese
3 cups Beef Broth (page 44), or more as required	2 Tbl finely chopped parsley

Wash the tripe thoroughly and cut it into thin strips. In a saucepan combine the butter and salt pork and heat them well. Add the onion and let the slices brown lightly. Stir into them the strips of tripe and the rosemary and cook over low heat for 5 minutes. Heat the beef broth in a small saucepan and pour it over the tripe and onions. Cover pan and cook tripe for 3½ hours or until strips are tender; add more broth, if needed. Season them with salt and pepper to taste after the first ½ hour of cooking. Add more beef broth as needed to provide the cooked tripe with about 1 cup of sauce.

Cut the clove of garlic and rub the cut sides over both sides of the bread. Brush slices generously on both sides with the olive oil and brown them well under a hot broiler. Place a slice of bread in each of 6 serving plates and cover them with equal portions of the tripe and sauce. Sprinkle servings each with 1 tablespoon of the grated cheese and 1 teaspoon of the chopped parsley. Serves 6.

Italian Ham and Melon | Prosciutto e Melone

18 2-inch slices melon, peeled   **18 paper-thin slices prosciutto**

Wrap each slice of melon in a slice of prosciutto, winding the ham around the piece diagonally from end to end. Serve the prosciutto and melon with wedges of lime or lemon and with black pepper to be ground to taste. Serves 6.

NOTE: Fresh figs also go well with prosciutto.

Hot Dipping Sauce | Bagna Cauda

½ cup olive oil   **8 anchovy fillets, mashed**
2 large cloves garlic, well mashed   **1 medium white truffle**
1½ cups butter

In a saucepan heat the olive oil and in it gently cook the garlic until it is very soft but not brown. Remove garlic and discard it. Add the butter and let it melt. Do not let it brown. Immediately add the mashed anchovies, blending them in thoroughly. Grate into the mixture the white truffle and let it just heat through.

Serve this hot, apportioned among 6 small heat-proof bowls as individual servings of a dipping sauce for an assortment of such prepared raw vegetables as broccoli buds, cauliflower flowerets, sticks of celery and carrot, scallions, and radishes, or vegetables combined with cubes of cooked meats. Serves 6.

Stuffed Artichokes | Carciofi Ripieni

6 medium artichokes	¼ tsp marjoram
Lemon juice	10 anchovy fillets, in small pieces
8 quarts water	⅛ tsp white pepper
2 tsp salt	⅓ cup white wine
½ cup olive oil	3 cups crisp bread crumbs
1 large onion, finely chopped	¼ cup capers
8 strips bacon,	Antipasto Dressing (page 284)
finely chopped (about 1 cup)	½ cup medium-size Croutons
2 stalks celery, finely chopped	(page 75)
6 large mushrooms, finely chopped	6 thin slices lemon
¼ tsp oregano	

Pull off small leaves at base of artichokes and discard them. Trim off stems flush with bottoms so that the globes will stand upright. Cut a slice about ¾-inch deep off the top of artichokes and, with a scissors, snip off the thorn-like ends of leaves. Rub all of the cuts with lemon juice to prevent discoloring.

Heat the water, seasoned with the salt, to boiling in a large kettle. Add artichokes. Cook, uncovered, at a gentle boil for 30 minutes or until tender. Artichokes are properly cooked when a leaf can be drawn easily from the globe and the bottoms are tender when pierced with the tines of a cooking fork. Drain artichokes upside down in a colander set over the kettle. When they are cool enough to handle, work your fingers into the centers of the globes and pull out the light green leaves. Discard them. With a ball cutter or a spoon scrape out chokes, the feathery coverings over the bottoms, and discard those also. Make certain that all the little "feathers" are out, but take care not to scrape off any of the choice tender pulp which is the artichoke heart.

Prepare a stuffing by first thoroughly heating the olive oil in a saucepan. Add the onion and cook it over low heat until it is lightly browned and soft. Blend into it the bits of bacon. When they are heated through add the celery, and continue cooking until it is very soft. Add the chopped mushrooms and when they have rendered their juice and the liquid evaporates, stir into the mixture the oregano, marjoram, chopped anchovies, pepper, and wine. When they are well combined, blend the bread crumbs and capers into the mixture and let them heat through.

Fill artichokes completely with the prepared mixture and brown tops under a hot broiler. Moisten artichokes by dribbling a little of the antipasto dressing between the leaves, but not over the filling. Distribute a few of the croutons also between the leaves. Place a thin slice of lemon on top of each artichoke. Serve artichokes warm or cooled. Serves 6.

Artichokes Roman Style | Carciofi alla Romana

6 artichokes
½ cup finely chopped parsley
2 cloves garlic, finely chopped
1 Tbl finely chopped
   fresh mint leaves
   (or ½ tsp dried mint)
6 anchovy fillets, in small pieces

4 tsp capers, finely chopped
1 cup bread crumbs
⅛ tsp white pepper
½ cup olive oil
½ cup white wine
¼ cup lemon juice

Prepare the artichokes, except for the stuffing, as for Stuffed Artichokes (above). For the stuffing (actually more a seasoning mixture) combine in a bowl the parsley, garlic, mint leaves, anchovies, capers, bread crumbs, white pepper, and ¼ cup of the oil. In a separate bowl beat together the remaining olive oil, the wine, and lemon juice. Sprinkle the hollows of the artichokes each with ⅙ of the bread-crumb mixture. Arrange artichokes upright in a baking pan and dribble the leaves of each equally with the wine blend. Bake artichokes at 400 degrees for 15 minutes. Cool artichokes and serve them chilled. Serves 6.

Broccoli in Oil and Lemon | Broccoli all'Olio e Limone

2 bunches broccoli
4 cups water
2 tsp salt
1 cup olive oil

⅓ cup strained lemon juice
1 clove garlic, mashed
1 Tbl chopped parsley
Salt & pepper

Split the broccoli into stalks of uniform size and wash and trim them. Pare the stalks up about 2 inches from the bottom so that they will cook evenly with the buds.

Heat the water in a large saucepan and season it with the salt. Arrange the stalks of broccoli in layers, alternating stalk and bud ends. Cover pan and steam them for 15 minutes or just until stalks are tender. Do not overcook. Drain stalks and freshen them immediately in cold water. Drain again, and chill.

In a mixing bowl combine the olive oil, lemon juice, garlic, parsley, and salt and pepper to taste. Arrange the chilled stalks of broccoli in a deep rectangular dish and pour the dressing over them. Chill broccoli thoroughly in the dressing, basting it from time to time. Remove and discard garlic. Serves 6.

Eggplant Sicilian Style | Melanzane alla Siciliana

3 medium eggplants
¼ cup red wine vinegar
3 cloves garlic, finely chopped
3 Tbl finely chopped parsley

½ tsp dried oregano
½ tsp salt
⅛ tsp white pepper
½ cup olive oil

Pierce the eggplants in several places with the tines of a fork and place them in a lightly oiled baking pan in a very hot oven (450 degrees) for 15 minutes. Turn eggplants frequently to prevent their burning. Remove them from oven and, when they are cool enough to handle, peel them. You should be able to remove the peels with your fingers. Wrap eggplants, 1 at a time, in several thicknesses of paper toweling and squeeze out as much of the liquid as possible. Cut eggplants into large irregular cubes and place in a serving bowl.

In a mixing bowl combine the vinegar, garlic, parsley, oregano, salt, and white pepper. Blend the olive oil into them. Pour this dressing over the eggplant cubes in the serving bowl and stir to coat them evenly. Serve chilled or at room temperature. Serves 6.

Marinated Eggplant | Melanzane Marinate

2 large eggplants	1 Tbl fresh basil leaves
Salt	(or ½ tsp dried basil)
Flour	¼ tsp white peppercorns, crushed
3 cups olive oil	1 Tbl salt
¼ cup red wine	3 anchovy fillets,
½ cup red wine vinegar	cut into small pieces
¼ cup lemon juice	2 Tbl capers
1 Tbl fresh mint leaves	
(or 1 tsp dried mint)	

Cut each eggplant, unpeeled, into 9 slices. Sprinkle slices lightly on both sides with salt and dust them on both sides with flour. In a skillet heat ¼ of 1 cup of the olive oil and sauté eggplant slices in it, a few slices at a time, browning them lightly on both sides. Add as much more of the remains of the cup of oil as may be needed to complete cooking. Drain slices well on paper toweling.

In a mixing bowl prepare a marinade by thoroughly combining the remaining 2 cups of olive oil with all of the remaining ingredients except the anchovies and capers. Place 2 to 3 tablespoons of the marinade in a deep platter and sprinkle it with a few bits of anchovies and ½ teaspoon of the capers. Arrange over the coating ½ of the eggplant slices, overlapping them slightly. Pour over them ½ of the remaining marinade and sprinkle them with ½ each of the remaining anchovy bits and capers. Cover them with the remaining eggplant, overlapping those slices somewhat also. Pour over them the remaining marinade and distribute over them the remaining bits of anchovies and capers. Chill the slices in the marinade for 24 hours. The eggplant slices should be almost completely covered with marinade. If they are not, turn slices from time to time so that they will be uniformly seasoned. Drain slices well before serving them. Serves 6.

Eggplant Relish | Caponata alla Siciliana

**2 medium eggplants
(about 2 pounds)**
Salt
½ cup olive oil
1 medium onion, finely chopped
2 large stalks celery, sliced thinly
½ cup dry white wine

1 Tbl sugar
¼ cup white wine vinegar
**½ cup Fresh-Tomato Purée
(page 281)**
⅓ cup capers
8 large pitted green olives, sliced
White pepper & salt

Trim off the ends of the eggplants and cut the vegetables, unpeeled, into ¾-inch cubes. Spread the cubes in a glass baking dish or on a platter and sprinkle them lightly with salt. Let them remain for 20 minutes or until much of the liquid has been drawn from them. Drain cubes and pat them dry between sheets of paper toweling. In a saucepan heat the olive oil and in it brown the eggplant cubes lightly. Remove them to a colander over a mixing bowl to drain. In the oil remaining in saucepan cook the onion and celery over low heat until they begin to soften but are not brown. Pour the wine over them and let them steam, covered, for a few minutes until the liquid evaporates. Return eggplants to saucepan and combine them with the onion and celery.

In a mixing bowl dissolve the sugar in the vinegar. Blend the vinegar and the fresh-tomato purée into eggplant mixture. Add the capers, olives, and pepper and salt to taste, and let it all heat through. Cool these 6 servings of Eggplant Relish before presenting them as antipasto or as a main course accompaniment.

Stuffed Escarole | Scarola Ripiena

2 quarts water
1 Tbl salt
24 large unbroken
    leaves of escarole, washed
⅓ cup olive oil
1 medium onion, finely chopped
6 ounces sweet Italian sausage,
    skinned
6 ounces lean veal

6 ounces lean beef,
    finely ground with sausage & veal
1¼ cups Chicken Broth (page 44)
¼ cup dry white wine
¼ tsp anise seeds, crushed
2 eggs, well beaten
¼ cup grated Parmesan cheese
Salt & pepper
6 Tbl Antipasto Dressing (page 284)

Add the salt to water in a large saucepan and heat it. Add the escarole leaves and poach them at simmer for 10 minutes. Drain them and freshen them immediately in cold water. Drain them again. Pat leaves dry between sheets of paper toweling, taking care not to puncture or tear them.

In a deep skillet heat the olive oil and in it cook the onions until they are soft but not brown. Combine the ground meats with the onions and cook them over moderate heat until they are lightly browned. In a small saucepan heat the broth and wine together, and stir them into the meat mixture. Add the crushed anise seeds and cook mixture at simmer, with pan covered, for 30 minutes or until the liquid is almost completely reduced. Let meat cool and blend into it the eggs and cheese. Season mixture with salt and pepper to taste. Preheat oven to 350 degrees.

Lay 6 of the escarole leaves on a flat surface, smooth sides up and somewhat separated. Cover them each evenly with another leaf. The remaining 12 leaves are intended as replacements for leaves that may be torn or punctured during cooking. If they are not needed, stack them, roll them together, and cut the roll into very fine shreds. Set them aside.

In the center of each pair of leaves place ⅙ of the prepared meat mixture. Fold the 2 leaves as one, envelope fashion, enclosing filling completely. Arrange stuffed leaves seam sides down in an oiled baking pan and bake them in the preheated oven for 20 minutes. Remove from oven and cool and chill them.

On a serving platter shape the shredded escarole leaves into 6 nests. Place a stuffed envelope of leaves in each nest and dress them equally with antipasto dressing. Serves 6.

Marinated Mushrooms | Funghi Marinati

2 pounds button mushrooms
1 medium green pepper
4 leeks
1 small sweet red pepper,
   fresh or canned
1 cup olive oil

2 Tbl white wine
2 Tbl lemon juice
½ tsp coriander seeds, crushed
½ tsp mustard seeds, crushed
Salt & pepper

Wash and thoroughly dry the mushrooms and trim off the stems flush with the caps. Do not pull out the stems or the caps will collapse. (Reserve stems, wrapped in heavy paper, under refrigeration for future uses.)

Core the green pepper and slice it into short julienne strips. Slice the white parts of the leeks only into thin slivers about 1-inch long. Cut the red pepper into short julienne strips. In a large saucepan heat the olive oil. Add the green pepper, leeks, and red pepper, and cook them over low heat until they are soft but not brown. Add the mushrooms and continue cooking until they are well coated with oil. Pour over them the wine and lemon juice and let the combined ingredients heat through. Add the seeds, and salt and pepper to taste. Increase heat to high for 1 minute. Remove pan from heat and let the mushrooms cool in the marinade. Transfer them to a glass bowl, cover them with the marinade, and chill them thoroughly. This recipe provides 6 to 8 servings.

Pickled Mushrooms | Funghi al Limone

2 pounds small button mushrooms
2 large cloves garlic, crushed
½ cup olive oil
⅓ cup lemon juice, strained
⅓ cup dry white wine

2 bay leaves
6–8 peppercorns
1½ tsp salt
Sprigs of parsley

Wash the mushrooms lightly and dry them well. Cut them down through the stems into thin slices.

In a large skillet lightly brown the garlic in the olive oil heated almost to the smoking point. Press the garlic with a fork as it cooks. Remove garlic cloves and discard them. Reduce heat somewhat, add the mushrooms, and cook them briskly for a few minutes, stirring gently until the slices take on a little color. Pour over them the lemon juice and wine and add the bay leaves, peppercorns, and salt. When the liquid is hot, turn off heat and cover pan for 1 minute. Uncover pan and let mushrooms cool. Transfer them, together with the marinade, to a glass bowl and chill them thoroughly.

Drain mushrooms, heap them on a serving platter, and decorate dish with sprigs of parsley. Serves 6.

Stuffed Mushrooms | Funghi Ripieni

18 large mushrooms
3 Tbl butter
1½ cups medium-fine bread crumbs
¼ cup finely chopped parsley
½ tsp dried oregano

1 small clove garlic, finely chopped
1 tsp paprika
⅓ cup grated Parmesan cheese
¼ cup olive oil
Salt & pepper

Wash the mushrooms lightly and dry them well. Remove stems and chop them finely. Heat the butter in a small skillet and cook the mush-

room stems in it until they render all their juice and the liquid evaporates. Preheat oven to 400 degrees. In a mixing bowl thoroughly combine the cooked mushroom stems along with any remaining butter, the bread crumbs, parsley, oregano, garlic, paprika, grated cheese, olive oil, and salt and pepper to taste. Fill mushrooms equally with the prepared stuffing. Arrange caps, stuffed sides up, in an oiled shallow baking pan. Set pan in the preheated oven and bake mushrooms for 15 minutes or until stuffing is heated through. Do not overbake or they will begin to render juice and become soggy. Serve the mushrooms hot or cold, 3 to a serving. Serves 6.

Stuffed Onions | Cipolle Ripiene

6 medium onions, peeled	1 cup Fresh-Tomato Purée
8 cups boiling hot water	(page 281)
1 Tbl salt	¼ cup dry white wine
⅓ cup olive oil	¼ cup soft bread crumbs
6 ounces lean beef	3 Tbl grated Parmesan cheese
4 ounces lean veal	1 egg, beaten
4 ounces prosciutto	Salt & pepper
2 ounces Italian-style salami, finely ground with beef, veal & prosciutto	

With a ball cutter scoop out the centers of the onions leaving shells each about ⅜-inch thick. Chop the centers finely and set them aside for the moment. Arrange the onion shells in a single layer in a deep skillet and gently pour the boiling water over them. Dissolve the tablespoon of salt in the water. Set pan over very low heat and blanch onions, with pan covered (the water should not even simmer), for 10 minutes. Remove onions and drain well. When they are cool enough to handle remove a little more of each center, carefully easing it out with your fingers to leave unbroken shells ¼-inch thick. Arrange shells in a lightly oiled baking pan.

Heat the oil in a skillet and in it lightly brown the chopped parts of the onions. Add the combined ground meats and sauté them over moderate heat, stirring to brown them evenly. Blend into the meat and onions the tomato purée and wine, and cook the mixture, covered, for 30 minutes or until the liquid has been completely absorbed. Let mixture cool and stir into it the bread crumbs, grated cheese, and beaten egg. Add salt and pepper to taste. Preheat oven to 350 degrees.

Fill onions equally with the mixture, heaping it high in the shells. Bake the stuffed onions for 15 minutes. Serve them chilled or hot.

Pearl Onions in Saffron | Cipolline allo Zafferano

1 cup dry white wine	**4 cups tiny white onions, peeled**
½ tsp saffron in threads	**1 tsp salt**
½ cup olive oil	**⅛ tsp white pepper**

Bring the wine to a boil in a stainless steel or enamel-coated saucepan and immediately remove pan from heat. Stir the threads of saffron into the hot wine and let them steep for 5 minutes. In another saucepan heat the olive oil. Add the onions and stir them in the oil, coating them well. Do not let them brown. Pour over them the hot wine, add the salt and pepper, and cook them so, over low heat, for 15 minutes, stirring them gently from time to time with a wooden spoon. Remove pan from heat and let onions cool in the liquid. Drain onions, but leave a tablespoon or two of the marinade to keep them moist. Transfer them to a serving bowl and chill thoroughly. Serves 6.

Stuffed Red Peppers | Peperoni Rossi Ripieni

6 medium-size, sweet red peppers	**¼ tsp dried basil**
2 large cloves garlic, mashed	**¼ tsp dried oregano**
6 anchovy fillets, in small pieces	**1½ cups medium-soft bread crumbs**
2 large tomatoes, peeled,	**½ cup grated Parmesan cheese**
** seeded & finely chopped**	**⅛ tsp white pepper**
¼ cup finely chopped parsley	**Salt**
3 Tbl capers, finely chopped	**Olive oil**

Place the peppers on a baking sheet under a hot broiler and leave them until the skins are well blistered. Turn the peppers frequently to prevent their burning. Remove peppers from broiler and, with a clean cloth, rub off the skins. Cool peppers, core them, and scrape out the white pulp and seeds.

Prepare a stuffing by working the garlic and anchovies to a paste in a mortar with a pestle or in a bowl with a wooden spoon. Combine the paste with the tomatoes, parsley, capers, basil, and oregano, and chop the mixture with a knife until it is reduced almost to a paste. Blend into it the bread crumbs, cheese, white pepper, and salt to taste. Press stuffing lightly into peppers, filling them almost to the top. Arrange peppers in a well-oiled baking pan and bake them at 350 degrees for 20 minutes. Remove peppers from oven and cool them. Brush with olive oil, to keep them from wrinkling and drying out, and chill them thoroughly. Serves 6.

Stuffed Green Peppers | Peperoni Verdi Ripieni

6 large green peppers	¼ pound lean veal, ground
2 thin slices prosciutto	½ tsp oregano
(about 2 ounces)	⅓ cup dry white wine
½ cup olive oil	1 baby eggplant
1 medium onion, finely chopped	1 egg, beaten
1 clove garlic, mashed	½ cup grated Parmesan cheese
1 large stalk celery, finely chopped	½ cup fine dry bread crumbs
¼ pound lean pork, ground	½ cup pine nuts
¼ pound lean beef, ground	Salt & pepper

Cut a slice from the top of each pepper. Remove the stem and chop the slice finely. Remove white membrane and seeds from peppers. Set whole peppers and the chopped tops aside. Chop the prosciutto slices finely.

In a large saucepan heat the oil and in it cook the onion and garlic until they are soft but not brown. Add the prosciutto, celery, and the chopped green pepper, and let them brown lightly. Combine the meats with the vegetables, stirring mixture until meats are well browned. Add the oregano and wine. Cover pan and continue cooking for 15 minutes, stirring mixture several times. Remove pan from heat and let mixture cool completely. Preheat oven to 350 degrees.

Peel the eggplant and cut it into small cubes (there should be about ½ cup). Blend the beaten egg, grated cheese, and bread crumbs into the cooled mixture. Finally add the pine nuts and eggplant cubes, stirring mixture to distribute them evenly throughout. Add salt and pepper to taste.

Fill the peppers with the prepared mixture and arrange them in an oiled baking pan. Set pan in the preheated oven and bake peppers for 30 minutes, or until they are tender. Serve them hot. Serves 6.

Pickled Vegetable Salad | Giardiniera

1 large green pepper	⅔ cup water
1 carrot	2 bay leaves
1 small head cauliflower	3 or 4 cloves
1 white turnip	1 Tbl salt
2 stalks celery	½ cup tiny onions,
1 small head of fennel	fresh boiled or drained canned
1 sweet red pepper,	½ cup small green olives
fresh or drained canned	½ cup drained canned peperoncini
3 cups white wine vinegar	(see Glossary)

Core and seed the green pepper and cut it lengthwise into strips about 1-inch wide. Scrape the carrot and cut it into slices about ⅛-inch thick. Wash and trim the cauliflower and separate it into flowerets. Peel the turnip and cut it into 12 wedges. Scrape the stalks of celery, split them lengthwise, and cut them into 2-inch slices. Trim the head of fennel and cut it lengthwise into thin slices. Cut the red pepper into thin strips.

In a stainless steel or enamel-coated saucepan combine the green pepper, carrot, cauliflower, turnip, celery, fennel, and red pepper. In another stainless steel or enamel-coated saucepan heat together the vinegar, water, bay leaves, cloves, and salt, and pour the mixture over the vegetables. Set that pan over moderate heat and cook the vegetables at simmer for 10 minutes. Gently combine the onions, olives, and peperoncini with the vegetables and let them heat through. Re-

move pan from the heat and let the pickled vegetables cool. Chill them thoroughly, for at least 24 hours, in the marinade in a glass bowl. Drain the vegetables before serving them. Serves 6.

Trattoria Stuffed Tomatoes | Pomodori Ripieni alla Trattoria

6 large tomatoes
2 Tbl olive oil
1 medium onion, finely chopped
2 Tbl white wine vinegar
2 Tbl red wine vinegar
1 cup Tomato Sauce (page 282)
⅛ tsp dried marjoram
⅛ tsp dried basil

⅛ tsp dried thyme
⅛ tsp dried sage
2 7½-ounce cans chunk tuna fish, drained
½ tsp chopped parsley
½ tsp salt
⅛ tsp white pepper
Sprigs of parsley

Cut a slice from the top of each tomato to include stem. Scoop out pulp and remove seeds. Chop pulp and reserve it. Arrange the tomato shells upside down on a platter and let them drain.

Heat the olive oil in a skillet and cook the onion in it until it is lightly browned. Add the reserved tomato pulp and continue cooking, over low heat, until it is reduced to a paste. Blend into it the 2 vinegars, tomato sauce, and herbs, and let them heat through. Gently stir into them the chunks of tuna fish and add the parsley and the indicated amounts of salt and pepper or more to taste. Cook ingredients for 2 to 3 minutes to blend the flavors. Cool the mixture and fill the prepared tomatoes equally with it. Chill stuffed tomatoes and serve them each decorated with a sprig of parsley. Serves 6.

Minted Zucchini | Zucchini Scapece

6 medium zucchini	**⅓ cup white wine vinegar**
(about 1½ pounds)	**¼ cup strained lemon juice**
Flour	**½ cup Chicken Broth (page 44)**
Bland cooking oil for deep frying	**3 Tbl fresh mint leaves, bruised**
1 Tbl olive oil	**(or 1 tsp dried mint, crushed)**
1 very small onion, finely chopped	**½ tsp salt**
⅓ cup white wine	**⅛ tsp white pepper**

Scrub the zucchini, trim off the ends, and cut them into slices ½-inch thick. Dredge the slices well with flour. In a deep saucepan or fryer heat sufficient cooking oil for deep frying to 375 degrees. Cook the zucchini in it, a few slices at a time, until they are lightly browned. Drain them thoroughly and arrange them in a deep platter or glass baking dish.

Heat the olive oil in a saucepan and sauté the onion in it until it is soft but not brown. Add the wine, vinegar, lemon juice, and chicken broth and bring liquid to a boil. Remove pan from heat and add the mint, salt, and pepper. Let the leaves steep in the liquid for 5 minutes. Reheat the marinade, if necessary (it should be warm), and strain it over the slices of zucchini. The slices should be completely covered with marinade. If they are not, add proportionate quantities of wine, broth, and lemon juice, as needed, heated together. Let zucchini marinate in the liquid under refrigeration for 24 hours. Drain zucchini and serve chilled. Serves 6.

Stuffed Zucchini | Zucchini Ripieni

6 medium zucchini
  (about 1½ pounds)
1 Tbl salt
3 Tbl butter
4 medium-size fresh mushrooms,
  finely chopped
3 Tbl olive oil
1 medium onion, finely chopped
2 inner stalks celery,
  very finely chopped

⅓ cup dry white wine
1 large canned, roasted red pepper,
  finely chopped
½ cup Fresh-Tomato Purée
  (page 281)
¼ tsp dried oregano
Salt & pepper
½ cup medium-dry bread crumbs
⅓ cup grated Parmesan cheese
Small clusters of parsley leaves

Wash the zucchini well, trim off ends, and split lengthwise. Place zucchini halves in a large heat-proof bowl. Sprinkle them with the salt and cover them with boiling water. Let them remain so for 5 minutes. Drain zucchini well. Scoop out pulp, leaving a firm shell. Finely chop and reserve pulp.

In a skillet heat the butter and in it cook the mushrooms over moderately high heat until they render their juice. Reduce heat somewhat and continue cooking until the liquid evaporates almost completely. Transfer mushrooms to a mixing bowl.

Pour the olive oil into the skillet and heat it. Add the onion and celery and cook them gently until they are lightly browned and soft. Stir into them the wine and continue cooking until the liquid is well reduced. Add the reserved zucchini, roasted pepper, tomato purée, oregano, and salt and pepper to taste, and let mixture bubble for a moment or two. Preheat oven to 400 degrees. Combine the mixture, along with the bread crumbs and grated cheese, with the mushrooms in the mixing bowl. Use the mixture to fill the prepared halves of zucchini.

Arrange filled halves in an oiled baking pan in the preheated oven and bake them for 12 minutes. Serve zucchini halves, 2 to a serving, each decorated with a small cluster of parsley leaves. Serves 6.

2 | soups

When soup comes to an Italian table, it arrives as a replacement for pasta, for Italian meals do not generally include both. When they do, soup and pasta are one, which is to say soup with pasta, or *pasta in brodo.* This is hearty and filling and one of the more common Italian dishes.

In many Italian restaurants, soup is found under *ministre,* a catch-all category that sometimes includes pasta (but not antipasti).

The soups of Italy are robust and surprising. Nothing from the garden is alien to them. As each vegetable matures, it finds its way into the various pots on the stove, but especially the soup pot. This is true even of salad greens, such as escarole.

Fish lovers are also favored by this course. In nearly every port town in Italy, the visitor will find a distinctive fish soup, a concoction featuring local fish or shellfish, and made savory with seasonings that are themselves regional specialties.

How To Clarify Broth

In a stainless steel or enamel-lined saucepan combine each 2 cups of cool broth with the crushed shell and lightly beaten white of 1 egg. Set pan over low heat and bring liquid to a boil, beating it constantly with a whisk. When it boils up, remove pan from heat, and let broth settle for 10 minutes. Soak a piece of clean, close-woven cloth, such as sheeting, in cold water and wring it out well. Line a sieve with the wet cloth and strain the clarified broth through it into a glass or porcelain bowl. Do not force broth through; let it take its time.

Beef Broth | Brodo di Manzo

4 pounds beef with bone	**1 bay leaf**
4 quarts cold water	**¼ tsp peppercorns**
1 cup chopped carrots	**2 sprigs parsley**
1 cup chopped celery	**1 large tomato, quartered**
1 cup chopped onion	**2 tsp salt**

In a large saucepan combine the beef and bone with all of the other ingredients except the salt. Set pan over low heat, bring liquid to a boil, and skim it. Cook, covered, at simmer for 2 hours. Add the salt and continue cooking for 2 hours longer. Strain broth and clarify it, if required (above). Reserve beef for other uses. Discard bones, vegetables, and herbs. This recipe will provide 2 quarts of broth which may be served as is, or used as the basis for sauces and other soups.

Chicken Broth | Brodo di Gallina

1 fowl, weighing about 4 pounds	**1 bay leaf**
4 quarts cold water	**¼ tsp peppercorns**
1 cup chopped carrots	**2 sprigs parsley**
1 cup chopped celery	**1 large tomato, quartered**
1 cup chopped onion	**2 tsp salt**

Clean, skin, and remove the fat from the fowl. Cut it into pieces and place it in a large saucepan with all of the other ingredients except the salt. Set pan over low heat, bring liquid to a boil, and skim it. Cook chicken, covered, at simmer for 2 hours. Add the salt and continue cooking for 1 hour longer. Strain broth and clarify it, if required (page 44). Reserve chicken for other uses. Discard vegetables and herbs. This recipe will provide 2 quarts of broth which may be served as is, or used as the basis for sauces and other soups.

Fish Broth | Brodo di Pesce

1 pound fresh fish bones	Stems only of 3 sprigs parsley
½ pound small pieces	4 peppercorns
of assorted bland fish	½ tsp salt
1 medium onion, thinly sliced	½ cup dry white wine
1 carrot, thinly sliced	6 cups cold water
1 stalk celery, thinly sliced	

Combine all the ingredients in a large saucepan over low heat and bring liquid to a boil. Cover pan and cook broth at simmer for 45 minutes, skimming it several times during cooking. Strain broth through a fine sieve and clarify it (page 44). This recipe will provide about 4 cups of broth, to be used as a basis for soups and sauces. Cooled and in a covered container it will keep, under refrigeration, for about 1 week. Frozen, it may be safely stored for about a month.
NOTE: If requested in advance, a fish market will supply fish bones and fish trimmings.

Broth for Poaching Fish | Brodo per Pesce

6 cups cold water	2 Tbl vinegar
1 medium onion, sliced	1 bay leaf
1 small carrot, sliced	5 or 6 peppercorns
1 stalk celery, sliced	2 tsp salt

In a large saucepan combine all of the ingredients and cook them at simmer for 15 minutes. This recipe will provide sufficient broth to poach 2 pounds shrimp or 12 lobster tails.

Beef Soup with Little Meatballs | Zuppa di Polpettine

¾ **pound lean beef, ground**
¼ **cup grated Parmesan cheese**
2 Tbl fine dry bread crumbs
2 Tbl finely chopped parsley
1 clove garlic, very finely chopped

1 egg, beaten
Salt & pepper
10 cups Beef Broth (page 44)
¼ **pound vermicelli**
Grated Parmesan cheese

In a mixing bowl combine the ground beef, cheese, bread crumbs, parsley, and garlic. Blend into mixture the beaten egg and season it with salt and pepper to taste. Form meat mixture into tiny marble-size balls. Bring broth to simmer in a large saucepan over low heat. Add the vermicelli and cook it for 5 minutes. Add the little meatballs and continue cooking for 5 minutes longer, or until the pasta is cooked *al dente* and the meatballs are cooked through and tender. Serve the soup in bowls, apportioning pasta and meatballs equally. Pass the grated cheese separately. Serves 6.

Luigian Bread Soup | Zuppa di Pane alla Luigia

1 1-pound loaf Italian white bread
1 cup olive oil
8 cups Chicken Broth (page 44)

2 eggs
1 cup grated Parmesan cheese
Salt & white pepper

Break the bread into medium-size pieces and spread them in a shallow baking pan. Set pan in a 200-degree oven and let bread heat through without browning for 30 minutes. Remove pan and let bread remain at room temperature overnight, after which time it will be of required dryness. Transfer the pieces to a large bowl and pour over them the olive oil and the broth. Cover bowl, set it in the refrigerator, and let bread soak overnight. By morning it will be reduced to a thick paste. Beat it with a wooden spoon until it is very smooth. If it is too thick to be the proper consistency for soup, beat in a little more broth. Set pan over low heat and cook it at bare simmer for 30 minutes, stirring it frequently to maintain the smoothness.

In a mixing bowl thoroughly combine the eggs and cheese, and blend the mixture gradually into the bread purée. Season soup with salt and white pepper to taste. Reheat it gently without boiling and serve it at once. Serves 6.

Cream of Broccoli Soup | Crema di Broccoli

1 pound firm broccoli, about ⅔ bunch	2 Tbl flour
7 cups Chicken Broth (page 44), heated	⅛ tsp ground coriander seeds
6 Tbl butter	Salt & white pepper
1 medium onion, thinly sliced	2 egg yolks
	1 cup heavy cream

Wash the broccoli thoroughly. Trim off about ½ cup of small flowerets and cook them in 1 cup of the broth for 10 minutes or just until they are tender. Drain the flowerets and set them aside in a bowl. Add broth remaining from cooking the flowerets to the 6 cups.

Trim stalk ends of the broccoli, and chop stalks and buds coarsely. In a large saucepan heat the butter over moderate heat, and in it cook the onion until it is very lightly browned. Add the broccoli and stir it until it is well coated with butter and heated through. Sprinkle the vegetables with the flour and blend in the heated broth. Add the ground coriander and salt and white pepper to taste. Cover the pan, reduce heat, and cook vegetables at simmer for 1 hour or until they are very tender. Strain broth through a fine sieve and force vegetables through, or purée them in a blender. Reheat broth and puréed vegetables.

In a mixing bowl blend the egg yolks and cream. Gradually beat into them 2 cups of the hot soup. Combine the mixture with the remaining soup in the pan. Heat soup without boiling and serve it with a tablespoon of cooked broccoli flowerets in each serving. Serves 6.

Mother's Special Broth with Filled Pasta |
Tortellini in Brodo della Mamma

2 Tbl butter	1½ cups grated Parmesan cheese
2 Tbl olive oil	3 eggs, beaten
6 ounces lean veal, diced	⅛ tsp ground nutmeg
6 ounces raw chicken meat, diced	Salt & pepper
2 ounces prosciutto	Pasta Dough with Semolina
(2 or 3 paper-thin slices)	(page 65)
2 ounces mortadella sausage	9 cups Chicken Broth (page 44)
(2 or 3 slices)	

In a skillet heat the butter and olive oil together and in it cook the veal and chicken together until well browned. Combine them with the prosciutto and mortadella, both coarsely chopped, and put the mixture through the fine blade of a food chopper. Grind meats again. In a mixing bowl blend the ground meats, Parmesan cheese, and eggs, and season them with the nutmeg and salt and pepper to taste.

Prepare tortellini with the pasta dough following instructions on page 71, and fill the little pasta shapes with the meat mixture. Bring the chicken broth to a boil in a large saucepan over moderate heat. Add tortellini, a few at a time so as not to stop the boiling, and cook them for 10 minutes or to desired degree of doneness. Serves 6.

Cabbage Soup | Minestra di Cavoli

¼ cup olive oil	Salt & pepper
1 medium onion, coarsely chopped	1 small head cabbage
1 small clove garlic, finely chopped	(about 1½ pounds),
3 medium tomatoes, peeled,	cored & shredded
seeded & coarsely chopped	

10 cups Beef Broth (page 44)	1 large potato,
1 bay leaf	peeled & cut into medium dice
2 whole cloves	2 Tbl finely chopped parsley
¼ tsp oregano	Grated Parmesan cheese

In a large saucepan heat the olive oil and in it lightly brown the onion. Add the garlic and merely heat it through. Combine the tomatoes with the onion and garlic and cook them for 2 to 3 minutes to blend the flavors. Stir in the broth. Combine the bay leaf, whole cloves, and oregano, and tie them in cheesecloth. Immerse the bag in the broth. Add salt and pepper to taste. Bring the liquid quickly to boil and let it bubble for 1 or 2 minutes. Reduce heat to low and skim liquid. Cover pan and simmer broth for 30 minutes. Add the cabbage and potato. Re-cover the pan and continue cooking for 20 minutes longer. Remove the cheesecloth bag containing the herbs and spice and discard it. Add the chopped parsley and cook soup for 10 minutes longer. Correct the seasoning, adding more salt, if necessary. Serve soup hot with an accompaniment of freshly grated Parmesan cheese to be added to the individual servings as desired. Serves 6.

Chick-Pea Soup | Minestra di Ceci

1 cup chick-peas	¼ tsp white pepper
4 cups cold water	2 whole cloves
¼ cup olive oil	8 cups Beef Broth
1 medium onion, coarsely chopped	or Chicken Broth (page 44)
1 clove garlic, finely chopped	1 stalk celery, coarsely chopped
2 cups canned plum tomatoes,	Salt
with juice	2 Tbl finely chopped parsley
1 bay leaf	Grated Parmesan cheese
¼ tsp dried oregano	

Soak the beans for at least 12 hours in a mixing bowl with enough cold water to cover them. Drain beans, transfer them to a large saucepan, and cover them with 4 cups fresh cold water. Cook beans, covered, over moderate heat for 1½ hours, or until they are tender but still firm. Drain beans, reserving the cooking liquid.

Heat the olive oil in a large saucepan and cook the onion in it until lightly browned. Add the garlic and when it has taken on a little color, stir in the plum tomatoes with their juice and the dried herbs and spices. Let the mixture heat through. Stir into it the broth and the bean cooking liquid and add the celery. Season the mixture with salt to taste. Cover pan and cook ingredients over moderate heat for 1 hour. Add the parsley and the beans. Reduce heat and cook soup at simmer for 30 minutes longer. Serve the soup accompanied by the Parmesan cheese, to be added to individual servings as desired. Serves 6.

Chicken Soup, Pavia Style | Zuppa alla Pavese

6 thick slices Italian bread	**10 cups Chicken Broth**
4 Tbl softened butter	**(page 44), heated**
8 Tbl grated Parmesan cheese	**Salt & white pepper**
6 eggs	

Butter the slices of bread evenly with the softened butter and coat them each with 2 teaspoons of the grated cheese. Brown the cheese-topped slices lightly under a hot broiler. Put a slice of the prepared bread in each of 6 soup plates and break an egg carefully on top of each slice. Gently pour the hot broth equally over each egg (thereby cooking it slightly) and around each slice of bread. Sprinkle servings each with 2 teaspoons of the remaining cheese and serve soup immediately. Serves 6.

Roman Egg-Drop Soup | Stracciatella alla Romana

4 eggs
¼ cup grated Romano
   or Parmesan cheese
4 tsp semolina

8 cups Chicken Broth (page 44)
2 Tbl finely chopped parsley
Salt & white pepper

In a mixing bowl beat the eggs thoroughly. Separately, in a small bowl, work the cheese and semolina to a smooth paste with a little of the beaten egg. Combine the paste with the remaining beaten egg.

In a large saucepan heat the broth until it steams but does not boil. Pour the egg mixture into it in a thin but steady stream, beating it in vigorously as it enters the broth. Remove pan from heat and continue beating for 2 to 3 minutes, or until the egg separates into strands. Stir the parsley into soup. Season soup with salt and white pepper to taste and serve it at once. Serves 6.

Escarole Soup, Sicilian Style | Zuppa di Scarola alla Siciliana

1 pound escarole
4 slices lean bacon
1 tsp olive oil
2 cloves garlic, mashed
8 cups Chicken Broth (page 44)

1 cup vermicelli in bits
1 cup diced cooked chicken
Salt & pepper
Grated Parmesan cheese

Wash and drain the escarole and cut it into ¼-inch slices. Set it aside for the moment. In a small skillet sauté the bacon in the olive oil until it is thoroughly cooked but not crisp. Remove the slices, drain them, and cut them into small squares. Reheat the fat in skillet and in it lightly brown the garlic. In a large saucepan combine garlic and bacon, and add the chicken broth. Set pan over low heat and bring broth to simmer. Add the sliced escarole and cook it, uncovered, for 10 minutes. Add the vermicelli and continue cooking for 10 minutes longer. The pasta at this point will be cooked *al dente*. If a softer pasta is desired, continue cooking, testing the pasta at 1-minute intervals until desired degree of doneness is achieved. Add the diced chicken and let it heat through. Season soup with salt and pepper and serve it with the grated cheese. Serves 6.

Fish Soup I | Zuppa di Pesce I

12 littleneck clams
12 mussels
½ cup olive oil
1 medium onion, thinly sliced
1 large clove garlic, mashed
4½ cups Chicken Broth (page 44)
2 cups canned,
    peeled plum tomatoes,
    coarsely chopped
1 baby lobster (about 1 pound)

1 pound mackerel, cleaned
1 pound red snapper, cleaned
Black pepper
Cayenne pepper
Salt
6 thick slices Italian bread, toasted
1 clove garlic, cut
2 Tbl butter, melted
2 Tbl finely chopped parsley

Thoroughly scrub the clams and mussels, and remove the mussel beards. In a large saucepan heat the olive oil and in it lightly brown the onion and garlic. Stir in ½ cup of the chicken broth and bring it to boil. Add the clams and mussels and steam them, covered, over high heat until the shells open. Discard immediately any that do not open. Lower heat to moderate. Shell the opened clams and mussels and reserve them. Strain into the saucepan any juice remaining in shells. Remove garlic from saucepan and discard it. Add the remaining chicken broth and the tomatoes and bring liquid to simmer.

Remove the lobster claws and crack them. Cut lobster through shell, and the fish into slices about 2 inches thick. Remove all traces of the lobster stomach and intestinal vein. Combine fish slices and lobster, including claws, with ingredients in saucepan. Season soup with a good grinding of black pepper and a few grains of cayenne pepper and cook it for 15 minutes or until fish flakes easily when tested with the tines of a fork. Add the reserved shelled clams and mussels and let them just heat through. Further cooking will toughen them. Correct the seasoning, adding salt, if necessary.

Rub the slices of toasted bread well with the cut clove of garlic and brush them with the melted butter. Place a slice of toast in each of 6 soup plates and apportion soup equally among them. Sprinkle each serving with 1 teaspoon of the chopped parsley and serve soup at once. Serves 6.

Fish Soup II | Zuppa di Pesce II

3 small squid (about ¾ pound)
1½ pounds cleaned halibut
18 small shrimp (about ¾ pound)
3 Tbl olive oil
1 small onion, finely chopped
6 large tomatoes (about 3 pounds)
¼ cup dry white wine
12 littleneck clams, scrubbed clean

6 cups Fish Broth (page 45)
⅛ tsp dried oregano
1 small bay leaf
Salt & pepper
4 Tbl butter
1 clove garlic, mashed
6 thick slices Italian bread

Clean the squid (page 130) and cut them into 1-inch pieces. Cut the halibut into 1-inch slices. Shell and de-vein the shrimp. In a skillet heat the olive oil and in it slowly cook the squid and onion for 15 minutes without letting them brown excessively.

Peel and core the tomatoes and cut them into small segments. In a large saucepan heat together the tomatoes and wine. Add the clams and steam them, covered, over high heat until the shells open. Discard immediately any that do not open. Remove clams, shell them, and set them aside. Strain into the pan any juice remaining in shells, and add the fish broth. Reduce heat to low and add squid and onion, along with any remaining oil in which they were cooked, the oregano, bay leaf, and salt and pepper to taste. Cover pan and continue cooking for 30 minutes or until squid are almost tender. Add the halibut. Cook ingredients for another 10 minutes and add the shrimp. Cook soup for 5 minutes longer or until squid are completely tender and the halibut flakes easily when tested with a fork. Add the reserved shelled clams and let them just heat through. Remove and discard bay leaf.

In a skillet heat the butter and in it lightly brown the garlic. Add the bread and brown the slices well on both sides. Remove and drain them. Place a slice in each of 6 soup plates and surround the slices with equal portions of the steaming hot soup. Serves 6.

Cream of Mushroom Soup | Crema di Funghi

⅓ cup dried Italian mushrooms
   (about ½ ounce)
12½ cups Chicken Broth (page 44)
3 Tbl butter
1 Tbl olive oil
1 medium onion, thinly sliced

1 pound fresh mushrooms
¼ cup flour
1 bay leaf
Salt & white pepper
3 egg yolks
1½ cups heavy cream

Wash the dried mushrooms and soften them for about 15 minutes in ½ cup of the chicken broth, warmed. In a large saucepan combine the butter and olive oil and heat them. Add the onion and cook it until it is soft and takes on a little color. Coarsely chop the fresh mushrooms, reserving 1 or 2 mushrooms for later use. Add the chopped mushrooms (there should be about 3 cups), and when they begin to render their juice blend in the flour. Stir in gradually the remaining 12 cups of chicken broth and the softened dried mushrooms along with their remaining broth. Add the bay leaf and salt and white pepper to taste. Cover pan and cook soup at simmer for 1 hour, stirring it occasionally. Line a fine sieve with several thicknesses of cheesecloth and strain the soup through it into another saucepan, pressing the solids to extract all possible liquid. Discard solids.

In a mixing bowl thoroughly combine the egg yolks and cream and blend the mixture, a little at a time, into the strained broth. Reheat soup without boiling. Slice the reserved mushrooms thinly. Serve soup in warm soup cups and garnish each serving with 2 or 3 slices of the raw mushrooms. Serves 6.

Lentil Soup, Florentine Style |
Minestra di Lenticchie alla Fiorentina

1 cup lentils
1 tsp salt
⅓ cup oil
1 medium onion, coarsely chopped
3 leeks, white parts only, sliced

1 bay leaf
¼ tsp white pepper
8 cups Beef Broth (page 44)
1 medium potato,
   peeled & coarsely chopped

1 clove garlic, finely chopped
2 cups canned plum tomatoes,
    with juice
1 stalk celery, coarsely chopped

½ cup coarsely chopped
    spinach leaves, firmly packed
Salt
Grated Parmesan cheese

Cover the lentils with cold water in a mixing bowl and soak overnight. Drain the soaked lentils and put them in a deep saucepan with enough fresh cold water to cover them and add the teaspoon salt. Set pan over low heat and bring water to a boil. Cook lentils, covered, at simmer for 1 hour. Drain them again, reserving 2 cups of the cooking liquid.

    In a large saucepan heat the oil and in it cook the onion, leeks, and garlic until they are very lightly browned. Blend into them the partially cooked lentils and the reserved liquid, the tomatoes with their juice, celery, bay leaf, and white pepper. Heat the mixture through and stir the broth into it. Bring the mixture back to boil. Cover pan, reduce heat, and cook soup at simmer for 1 hour or until lentils are tender. Add the potato and continue cooking for 15 minutes. Add the spinach and cook soup for a final 5 minutes longer. Season it with salt to taste. This recipe will provide 8 generous servings to be accompanied by freshly grated Parmesan cheese.

Onion Soup | Zuppa di Cipolle

6 Tbl butter	Salt & pepper
2 Tbl olive oil	6 thick slices Italian white bread,
12 medium onions (about 2 pounds),	toasted
very thinly sliced	Additional olive oil
10 cups Beef Broth (page 44)	6 Tbl grated Parmesan cheese

In a large saucepan heat together the butter and olive oil. When they are sizzling hot add the onions and brown them well, stirring them constantly. Blend the broth into them and season it with salt and pepper to taste. Cover pan and cook soup at simmer for 45 minutes.

Apportion soup equally among 6 flame-proof serving bowls. Brush the slices of toast on both sides with olive oil and float a slice in each bowl of soup. Sprinkle the slices each with 1 tablespoon of the Parmesan cheese. Place the bowls of soup on a tray under a hot broiler until cheese browns. Serves 6.

Cream of Pea Soup | Crema di Piselli

2 cups dried green peas	2 large tomatoes, peeled,
¼ cup olive oil	seeded & coarsely chopped
1 large onion, finely chopped	1 bay leaf
3 stalks celery, finely chopped	10 cups Chicken Broth (page 44)
1 large potato,	2 egg yolks
peeled & coarsely chopped	⅔ cup light cream
	Salt & white pepper

Rinse the peas thoroughly in cold water. Place them in a bowl, cover with fresh cold water, and let them soak overnight.

Heat the olive oil in a large saucepan and in it cook the onion until it begins to brown. Add the celery, potato, tomatoes, and bay leaf, and let them heat through. Drain the peas and add them, along with the chicken broth, to the vegetables in saucepan. Bring liquid slowly to a boil and skim it. Cover pan and continue cooking, at simmer, for 1½ hours or until peas are soft. Remove and discard bay leaf. Strain soup through a fine sieve into a bowl and force vegetables through, or purée them a little at a time in an electric blender, with as much of the liquid as may be needed to facilitate the blending.

Heat the purée slowly in the saucepan just to the boiling point. In a mixing bowl blend the egg yolks and cream and beat into them, a little at a time, 1 cup of the heated purée. Add the mixture to the remaining purée in saucepan and continue to heat soup without boiling. Season soup with salt and white pepper to taste. This quantity of soup is sufficient for 6 to 8 servings.

Tripe Soup, Parmesan Style | Minestra di Trippa alla Parmigiana

2 pounds fresh honeycomb tripe	2 leeks, white parts only
2 whole cloves	4 medium potatoes, peeled
2 medium onions	1 clove garlic, mashed
1 carrot	1 tsp salt
2 stalks celery	2 cups shredded cabbage
3 or 4 peppercorns	3 Tbl finely chopped parsley
¼ pound fat salt pork, minced	⅓ cup grated Parmesan cheese

Wash the tripe thoroughly. Cut it into narrow strips about 1-inch long and put them in a large saucepan with enough cold water to cover them well. Set pan over low heat and bring water slowly to a boil. Drain the strips of tripe, cover them again, this time with boiling water to a height of at least 1 inch above their surface. Stick the cloves into 1 onion. Add that onion, the carrot, 1 stalk of the celery, and the peppercorns. Cover pan and cook tripe for 4½ hours. Drain it and set it aside for the moment. Strain the cooking liquid, return it to the saucepan, and reheat it.

In a skillet partially try out the salt pork. Slice the remaining onion and separate the slices into rings. Add the onion rings and cook them over moderate heat until they are lightly browned. Slice the leeks and the potatoes into narrow strips about 1-inch long. Set the potatoes aside. Cut the remaining stalk of celery into short narrow strips and add them, the garlic, and the strips of leeks. Cook them just until they wilt and are well coated with the pork fat, about 2 minutes. Drain off the remaining fat in the skillet and add the sautéed vegetables and reserved tripe to the heated liquid in saucepan. Add the salt and continue cooking for 45 minutes. Add the cabbage and cook it for 10 minutes. Add the potatoes and complete the cooking after 10 minutes more or when the potatoes are tender. Stir the parsley into soup during the last moment or two of the cooking. Correct the seasoning, adding more salt, if needed. Serve soup very hot, sprinkled with the Parmesan cheese. Serves 6.

Vegetable Soup | Zuppa di Verdura

1 Tbl olive oil
5 Tbl butter
1 clove garlic, peeled & halved
3 medium potatoes, peeled & diced
2 medium onions, thinly sliced
2 carrots, peeled & thinly sliced
4 stalks celery, thinly sliced

4 large tomatoes, peeled,
 seeded & coarsely chopped
8 cups Chicken Broth (page 44)
Salt & pepper
½ cup shelled fresh peas
Grated Parmesan cheese

In a large saucepan heat the olive oil and butter. Add the clove of garlic and brown the halves well. Remove and discard them. Add the potatoes, onions, carrots, and celery and stir them until they are heated through and well coated with the seasoned fat. Add the tomatoes and continue cooking until they are soft. Stir in the broth and bring it quickly to boil. Add salt and pepper to taste. Reduce heat and cook soup at simmer for 20 minutes or until vegetables are tender, but still firm. Add the peas and

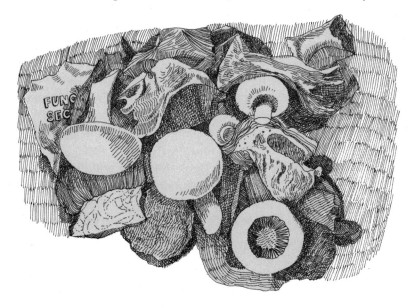

continue cooking for 10 minutes longer or until they are tender. Serve soup very hot and offer the grated cheese separately to be added to individual tastes. Serves 6.

Vegetable Soup, Florentine Style |
Minestrone di Verdura alla Fiorentina

½ cup dried white beans
6 cups cold water
1 Tbl salt
2 medium onions
2 medium zucchini
1 small stalk broccoli
   (about ¼ pound)
2 carrots, peeled
2 stalks celery
2 small potatoes, peeled

⅓ cup olive oil
2 small tomatoes,
   peeled & quartered
½ tsp dried basil
6 cups boiling water
Salt & pepper
⅓ cup long-grain rice
⅓ cup shell macaroni
¼ cup grated Parmesan cheese

Remove and discard any imperfect beans. Wash the rest, cover them with cold water, and let them soak overnight. Drain beans and combine them in a deep saucepan with 6 cups fresh cold water seasoned with the tablespoon of salt. Cook beans, covered, at simmer for 2 hours, or until they are very tender. Drain beans again, reserving 1 cup of the cooking liquid, and force them through a fine sieve, or reduce them to a purée in an electric blender, adding a little of the cooking liquid, if necessary, to facilitate the blending.

Coarsely chop the onions, zucchini, broccoli, carrots, celery, and potatoes, and cook them for 3 minutes in the olive oil heated in a large saucepan. Add the tomatoes and cook for 2 minutes. Stir the puréed beans into the sautéed vegetables along with the reserved cooking liquid, the basil, and boiling water. Season vegetables with salt and pepper to taste. Cook them, covered, at simmer for 30 minutes, or until all of them are tender. Meanwhile, cook the rice in 1½ cups boiling water for 12 minutes and drain. Add the shell macaroni, the partially cooked rice, the ¼ cup of Parmesan cheese, and continue cooking for 8 to 10 minutes, or until grains of rice are tender and pasta has reached desired degree of doneness. Serve the 8 to 10 servings of this hearty soup with accompaniment of additional Parmesan cheese.

Vegetable Soup with Parmesan Cheese |
Minestrone al Parmigiano

½ cup dried kidney beans
½ cup dried pea beans
4 cups cold water
¼ cup olive oil
1 medium onion, finely chopped
2 leeks, white parts only,
    thinly sliced
1 clove garlic, finely chopped
2 cups canned,
    peeled plum tomatoes with juice
10 cups Chicken Broth
    or Beef Broth (page 44)
2 stalks celery, thinly sliced
2 large carrots,
    peeled & cut in julienne strips
1 bay leaf
¼ tsp dried basil
    (or 2 leaves fresh basil)
¼ tsp dried oregano

2 whole cloves
2 Tbl salt
¼ tsp white pepper
⅓ cup rice
4 large, tender cabbage leaves,
    shredded
6 escarole leaves, coarsely chopped
⅛ cauliflower,
    trimmed & flowerets separated
1 medium white turnip,
    coarsely chopped
1 medium zucchini,
    sliced moderately thin
1 medium potato,
    peeled & cut into medium dice
⅓ cup shelled fresh peas
⅓ cup ditalini (see Glossary)
2 Tbl finely chopped parsley
Grated Parmesan cheese

Put the kidney beans and pea beans in separate saucepans, cover them each with 2 cups of the cold water, and let them soak overnight. Cook beans, at simmer, in water in which they were soaked, the kidney beans for 20 minutes, the pea beans for 30 minutes. Drain and set aside.

Heat the olive oil in a large saucepan. Add the onion, leeks, and garlic and cook them over low heat until they are soft but only lightly browned. Blend in the tomatoes with the juice and when mixture is heated through stir into it the broth and add the celery, carrots, and partly cooked beans. Combine the bay leaf, basil, oregano, and cloves, tie them in cheesecloth, and immerse the bag in the broth. Add the salt and white pepper. Bring liquid slowly to boil and skim it. Cover pan and cook combined ingredients for 30 minutes. Stir in the rice and when it has cooked for 10 minutes add the cabbage and escarole leaves, the cauliflower, and turnip. When liquid returns to boil, skim it again and add to it the zucchini, potato, and peas. Continue cooking for 10 more minutes. Remove cheesecloth bag with its enclosed herbs and spice and discard it. Stir in the ditalini and complete the cooking when the pasta is tender, after about 8 minutes more. Sprinkle soup with the chopped parsley and correct the seasoning, adding more salt if necessary. Serve soup steaming hot with the grated cheese passed separately. This recipe provides 8 to 10 generous servings.

A Soup for Winter | Minestra Invernale

½ **pound escarole**
½ **pound spinach**
½ **cup olive oil**
4 **thin slices bacon,**
    coarsely chopped
2 **cloves garlic, mashed**
1 **medium onion, thinly sliced**

6 **scallions, thinly sliced**
1 **cup cooked red kidney beans**
1 **cup cooked pea beans**
9 **cups Chicken Broth (page 44)**
Salt & pepper
Grated Parmesan cheese

Trim the escarole and spinach. Wash the leaves well and dry them between sheets of paper toweling. Heat the olive oil in a large saucepan and in it simmer the bacon until the bits are thoroughly cooked and lightly browned but not crisp. Remove bacon and set it aside in a small bowl. Add the cloves of garlic to oil in saucepan and brown them well. Remove cloves and discard. Add the onions and scallions to the hot oil and cook them until they are lightly browned. Drain off oil and combine the cooked beans with the onions and scallions in the saucepan. Stir into them the chicken broth and add the cooked bacon. Cut the escarole into thick pieces and stir them, along with the spinach leaves, into the stock. Cook soup, uncovered, over moderate heat for 15 minutes or until the greens are tender. Season soup with salt and pepper to taste and sprinkle the 6 servings, which this recipe provides, with freshly grated Parmesan cheese.

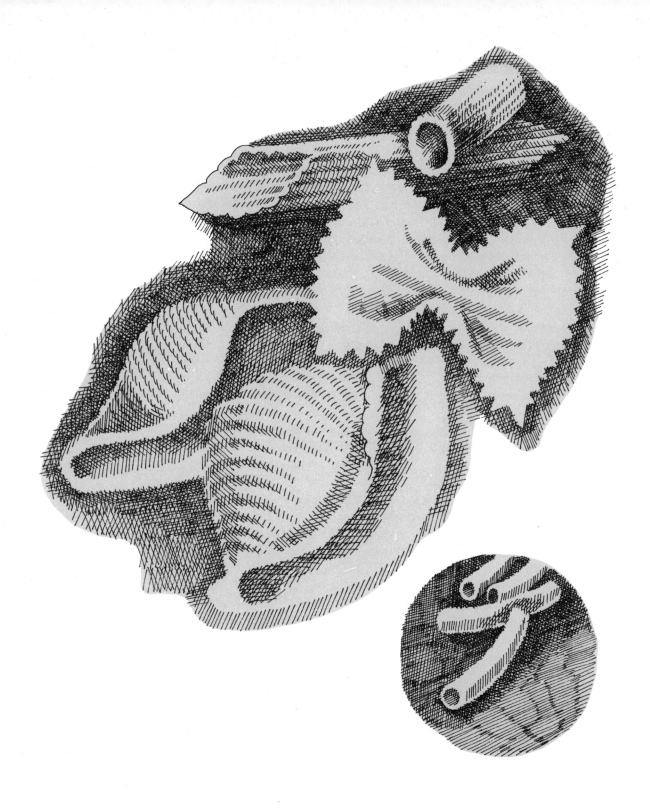

3 | pasta

A certain signora who cooks for a *pensione* in Italy is reputed in fifty years of service never to have served pasta the same way twice. True or not, the story does make a point, two in fact. First, it stresses the importance of pasta to the Italian palate. And second, incredible as it may seem, it indicates the endless creativity possible when a good cook is unfettered by rules.

Pasta may be dressed merely with butter and cheese, or ingeniously adorned with truffles, sweetbreads, broccoli, sausage—and so, deliciously, on and on. One has only to think of pasta and a boundless horizon of possible embellishments presents itself.

Commercial macaroni and spaghetti products come in all imaginable sizes and shapes. Although they are all made from the same dough, Italians insist that each has a flavor distinctly its own. The proof of that we leave to you. For the distinctive flavor of homemade pasta, follow the instructions on page 65. It requires surprisingly small effort for a very large reward.

fresh pasta

How to Cook Pasta

If pasta is to be the main course, 4 ounces of the raw product will, when cooked, provide a generous serving. As a first course allow about half that amount per serving, and if the pasta is intended only to accompany a main course, 1 ounce per serving should suffice.

Cook pasta in a very large saucepan, even if the amount is small. For each ¼ pound of pasta to be cooked heat 4 cups cold water to a brisk boil, and never let the boiling subside. Season water with 1 teaspoon salt and add to it ¼ teaspoon butter or oil. Lower the pasta, a few strands at a time, into the boiling water, being careful not to add so much that the boiling is arrested. When pasta has softened and is swirling around in the water, add the next few strands, and so on until the required amount has been added to the boiling water. Cook pasta, uncovered, to degree of doneness desired, but know that the preferred texture is *al dente,* which is to say just cooked enough still to be "bite-able." If, however, your personal preference is for pasta somewhat softer than that, have it your way—as long as it is not reduced to mush. Five minutes or less, depending upon the thickness of the pasta, may be sufficient for *al dente,* but you can be certain only by testing it. Remove a strand and pinch it, or better still actually bite it. If, after 5 minutes, it is still insufficiently cooked, test it again 1 minute later and continue testing it at 1-minute intervals until an acceptable degree of doneness is achieved. These suggestions apply primarily to the spaghetti and macaroni varieties of pasta.

The moment the pasta is done, drain it quickly, but not completely dry. Retain a little of the water to keep the strands separated. It is neither necessary nor advisable to rinse the pasta. Serve it at once, while it is still hot, with the sauce of the moment. If pasta must be kept for a time, return it to the pot (but not to the water) and blend into it a tablespoon or so of melted butter. Cover the pan, set it in a warm oven (not over 200 degrees, however)—but for no more than thirty minutes.

About the sauce: Pasta can suffer from too much as well as too little. One half cup is about right for each cooked ¼ pound of raw pasta. Less than ⅓ cup is austere. And don't count on the sauce to warm the pasta or vice versa. Both should be equally hot.

2 cups semolina   **4 eggs**
1 cup all-purpose flour

Sift the semolina and all-purpose flour together onto a pastry board or into a bowl. Make a well in the center of the mound and put the eggs into it. Work eggs into flour to produce a stiff but malleable mass, adding more flour if necessary to make it so. Knead dough for about 5 minutes or until it is smooth and elastic. Let it rest, covered, for 5 minutes. Roll dough and cut it to size required for specific types of pasta. Serves 6.

Green Pasta Dough with Semolina | Pasta Verde di Semolino

6 ounces trimmed spinach leaves   **3 eggs**
2 cups semolina   **2 Tbl warm water**
1 cup all-purpose flour

Thoroughly wash the spinach leaves and drain them by shaking off the water. Cook spinach briskly in a saucepan, in just the water that clings to the leaves, for 3 minutes or until leaves wilt. Drain it. When it is cool enough to handle, wrap it in several thicknesses of cheesecloth and squeeze out as much of the remaining liquid as possible. Force spinach through a fine sieve or purée it in an electric blender.

Proceed as for regular semolina pasta dough, working spinach into flour along with remaining ingredients to produce a stiff but malleable dough. Kneaded, as directed, and allowed to rest for 5 minutes, it may be rolled and cut to size required for specific types of pasta. This quantity is sufficient for 6 servings.

Pasta Dough with All-Purpose Flour | Pasta di Farina

3 cups flour   **3 eggs**
1 tsp salt   **1 egg yolk**
1 Tbl olive oil

Sift the flour and salt together onto a pastry board or into a bowl. Make a well in the center of the mound and put into it the olive oil, whole eggs, and yolk. Work them into flour to produce a stiff but malleable mass, adding more flour if necessary. Knead dough until it is quite elastic. Shape it into a ball and let it rest, covered, for 30 minutes.

This recipe provides about 1¼ pounds of dough for use as required for specific preparations.

Green Pasta Dough with All-Purpose Flour |
Pasta Verde di Farina

6 ounces trimmed spinach leaves	1 Tbl olive oil
3 cups flour	3 eggs
1 tsp salt	1 egg yolk

Thoroughly wash the spinach leaves and drain them well by shaking off the water. Place leaves in a saucepan over moderate heat and cook them until they wilt, about 3 minutes, in just the water that clings to them. Drain spinach and, when it is cool enough to handle, wrap it in several thicknesses of cheesecloth and squeeze out as much of the remaining liquid as possible. Force spinach through a fine sieve or purée it in an electric blender. Proceed as in recipe above, working spinach into flour along with remaining ingredients. Kneaded and allowed to rest for 30 minutes, the dough is ready for use as required in specific recipes. Provides enough pasta for 6 servings.

Dough for Ravioli | Pasta per Ravioli

2 cups all-purpose flour	4 eggs
1 cup semolina	

Sift the all-purpose flour and semolina together onto a pastry board or into a bowl. Make a well in the center of the combined flours and put the eggs into it. Work eggs and flour together to produce a dough that is stiff but malleable, adding more flour, if necessary, to make it so. Knead dough for 5 minutes or until it is smooth and elastic. Let it rest, covered, for 5 minutes before rolling and cutting it as required.

Pasta dough, made from a few simple
ingredients, can be shaped in a seemingly infinite
variety of shapes, sizes, and lengths.

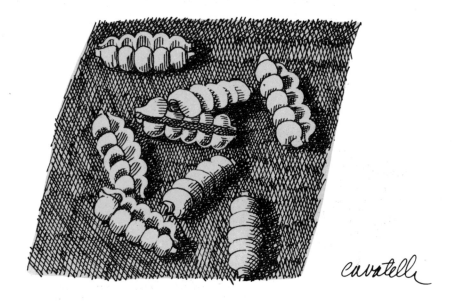

cavatelli

How to Roll and Cut Dough for Various Pasta

Fettuccine
Divide dough into 2 equal parts and roll each into a rectangle of tissue-paper thinness. Dust them lightly with semolina and fold each loosely down the length into 2½-inch widths. Cut them crosswise into slices ¼-inch thick. Unfold them immediately onto a pastry board or onto a large clean cloth and let these noodle ribbons dry for 30 minutes before using them.

Ravioli
Divide dough into 6 equal parts and roll each into a sheet 10 inches square and about ⅛-inch thick. Dust them lightly with semolina. Using the dull edge of a table knife lightly mark off each sheet into 16 squares of 2½ inches each. Do not cut them through.

Manicotti
Divide dough into 6 equal parts and roll each into a tissue-paper-thin sheet 9 inches wide and 10 inches long. Cut each sheet in half across the width and each half into 3 strips each measuring 3 inches by 5 inches, thus producing 36 strips.

Spaghetti, cooked to perfection—that is,
al dente—in plenty of boiling water; here the pasta
is ready to be sauced and served.

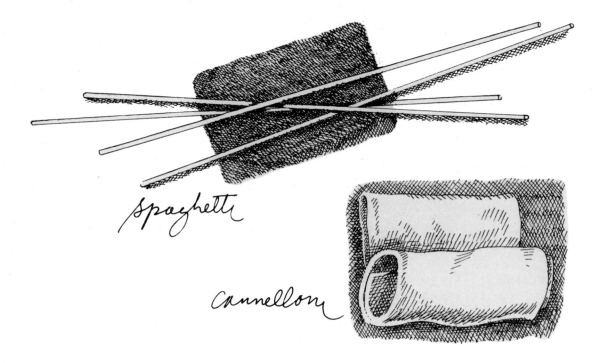

spaghetti

cannelloni

Cannelloni
Divide dough into 3 parts. Roll each part into a sheet 10 inches square and cut them each into 4 equal-size squares to provide 12 squares.

Tagliatelle
Roll and fold dough as for Fettuccine and cut lengths into slices ⅛-inch thick. Unroll them immediately onto a pastry board or large clean cloth and let these noodle ribbons dry for 30 minutes before using them.

Tagliatini
Proceed as for Fettuccine, but cut the folded dough into very fine noodles, 1/16-inch, or less, thick.

Lasagne

Divide dough into 6 parts and roll each into a sheet 8 inches square. Cut the sheets each into 4 strips and dust them lightly with semolina. Spread them on a clean cloth, cover them with another, and let dry for 1 hour.

Tortellini

Roll dough into a paper-thin circular sheet. Using a cookie cutter, cut dough into rounds each 1½ inches in diameter. Do not let them dry at this point. Fill and shape them as directed in specific recipes. Cut remaining bits of dough into tiny squares. Sprinkle them over a pastry board and let them dry for 30 minutes. Reserve them for use as noodles for soup or in other pasta preparations.

tortellini

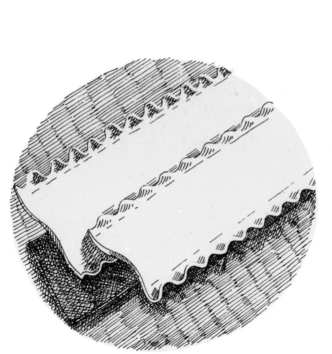

lasagne ricce

doughs and bread

Dough for Pizza | Pasta per Pizza

2 envelopes dry yeast
4 cups lukewarm water
9 cups flour
1 Tbl sugar

1 Tbl salt
¼ tsp white pepper
¼ cup olive oil

In a small bowl soften the yeast in ½ cup of the lukewarm water and combine it in a larger bowl with the dry ingredients and as much of the remaining warm water, or more, as may be needed to make a dough that
is soft but not sticky. Work into it the olive oil and knead dough vigorously
for 10 minutes or until it is quite elastic. Place dough in a slightly oiled
bowl. Brush top of dough also with a little oil and cover it lightly with a
cloth. Set bowl in a draft-free place and let dough rise until it has doubled
in bulk. This may take about 1½ hours. Press the risen dough down and
divide it into 10 pieces of equal size. Roll the pieces each into a ball and
let them rise for 15 minutes.

To prepare dough for baking, stretch each ball into a round about
¼-inch thick and of a size to fit a lightly oiled 8- or 9-inch round pan.
Spread dough with ingredients indicated in specific recipe. Makes 10 individual pizzas.

Pie Dough | Pasta per Torte

4 cups flour
1 tsp salt
9 Tbl chilled butter
9 Tbl well-chilled
  vegetable shortening

1 tsp olive oil
2 egg yolks
Approximately ¼ cup, more or less,
  iced water

Into a mixing bowl sift the flour with the salt, and blend into it the butter
and shortening, working with your fingers gently but thoroughly. The mixture should be the consistency of coarse meal. Blend in the olive oil and
egg yolks, and add the iced water, about a teaspoon at a time, to produce
a dough that will just hold together and is not sticky. Depending upon the
absorbency of the flour and the humidity of the day, you may need as
little as 3 tablespoons of water to slightly more than ¼ cup. Form dough

into a ball, wrap it in waxed paper or plastic wrap, and chill it in the refrigerator (not in the freezer compartment) for about 20 minutes. Use dough as required. This recipe will provide enough dough, rolled to a thickness of about ⅛ inch, to line 2 9-inch pie pans and provide top crusts, as well.

To Line Pan with Dough:
Roll dough of required thickness and size onto rolling pin and lay it gently down over pan. Lift edges of dough and work it carefully down into pan, fitting it in evenly but slightly thicker on sides. Trim off edges by rolling the rolling pin over top of pan. Using your fingers, force dough from sides of pan up about ⅛ inch over rim. Crimp this edge or not, as required. Chill dough briefly in pan before filling and baking it.

Italian Bread | Pane

Dough for Pizza (page 72)	1 egg, beaten
Cornmeal	Sesame seeds (optional)

Prepare pizza dough following basic instructions, but use only 6 cups of the flour and about 3 cups of the water, plus all of the remaining ingredients. Recipe provides 3 medium-size loaves of bread.

When dough has risen as required, press it down and let it rise again until it has once more doubled in bulk. Press it down again and divide it into 3 equal parts. Shape each part into a round loaf about 7 inches in diameter. Lightly oil a baking sheet, sprinkle it with cornmeal, and arrange loaves on it. Set baking sheet in a warm place and let loaves rise for 30 minutes. Cut a cross about ¼-inch deep into top of each loaf and let loaves rest 10 minutes longer. Preheat oven to 400 degrees. Brush loaves with the beaten egg and, if desired, sprinkle with sesame seeds. Bake loaves in the preheated oven for 30 minutes or until they are golden brown and test done. To test, tap loaves with your fingers; if loaves sound hollow, they are baked. Remove and place on a wire rack to cool.

This quantity of dough may be used also for small long loaves suitable for hero sandwiches. It will provide 6 such loaves. Before brushing them with the beaten egg slash the tops diagonally in 2 places about ¼-inch deep. Bake loaves at 400 degrees for 30 minutes or until they test

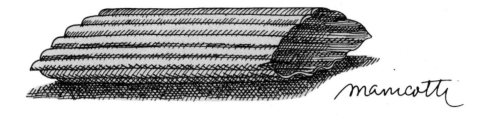

done. For crisper crusts brush long or round loaves with white of egg and 1 teaspoon cold water beaten together, or with cold water only.

Breadsticks | Grissini

Dough for Pizza (page 72)   **1 tsp olive oil**
1 egg   **¼ tsp salt**

Prepare pizza dough following basic instructions, but use only 1 envelope yeast (softened in ¼ cup lukewarm water) and ⅓ of each of the remaining ingredients.

Divide dough into 24 equal parts. Roll each part between the palms of your hands to a thickness of about ¼ inch. The rolls will be about 10 inches long. Arrange them on a lightly oiled baking sheet about 1 inch apart and let them rise, lightly covered, for 15 minutes. Preheat oven to 350 degrees. With a knife make 3 equidistant shallow indentations across each roll. In a small mixing bowl beat together the egg, olive oil, and salt, and brush the rolls of dough with it. Bake them in the preheated oven for 20 minutes or until they are golden in color. For crisper breadsticks brush with cold water only.

Variations:
1. Brush the rolls of dough with lightly beaten egg white only and sprinkle with sesame seeds.
2. Combine the flour for the pizza dough with ⅓ cup grated Parmesan cheese.
3. Brush the rolls of dough lightly with olive oil flavored with garlic and sprinkle with salt.

Garlic Croutons | Crostini all'Aglio

1 slice white bread, ½-inch thick **1 clove garlic, mashed**
3 Tbl butter

Cut the bread into ½-inch cubes and put them in a baking pan in a 250-degree oven for 15 minutes or until they are well dried and lightly browned. In a skillet over low heat melt the butter. Add the garlic and sauté until golden. Remove garlic and discard. Add the dried cubes of bread and stir them gently until they have absorbed all of the butter. Cool cubes before using them. Provides about 1 cup of croutons.

dumplings

Italian Dumplings with Cream | Gnocchi alla Panna

1 cup flour **⅓ cup shredded mozzarella cheese**
3 Tbl farina **1 whole egg, beaten**
4 egg yolks **Fine dry bread crumbs**
½ tsp sugar **Olive oil**
½ tsp salt **Bland cooking oil**
1 cup milk **1½ cups heavy cream**
1½ cups grated Parmesan cheese

In the top pan of a double boiler combine the flour, farina, egg yolks, sugar, salt, and milk. Set pan over, but not touching, simmering water, and cook mixture, stirring it frequently for 10 minutes or until it is very thick and smooth. Remove pan from over heat and blend into the mixture ½ the grated cheese and all of the mozzarella. Lightly oil a platter and spread the batter on it ½-inch thick. Cover platter with waxed paper or plastic wrap and chill the batter until it is very firm. Cut it into 1-inch squares. Coat squares with the beaten egg and dredge them well with bread crumbs.

   In a deep saucepan or fryer heat for deep frying sufficient quantities of the oils, combined in equal proportion. Fry the squares at 360 degrees, a few at a time, until they are moderately browned. Drain them on paper

agnolotti

toweling and keep them warm on a serving platter in an oven no warmer than 150 degrees.

In a saucepan slowly cook the cream until it is reduced to ¾ cup. Blend into it the remaining grated cheese. Serve the dumplings with the accompanying sauce passed separately. Serves 6.

Potato Dumplings | Gnocchi di Patate

1¼ cups mashed cooked potatoes	3 quarts simmering water
1 cup flour	Country-Style Sauce (page 272)
1 egg, beaten	Grated Parmesan cheese
2 Tbl salt	

In a mixing bowl smoothly combine the potatoes, flour, egg, and ½ teaspoon of the salt. Shape the mixture into finger-thick rolls about 1-inch long. Poach them for 5 minutes in the simmering water seasoned with the remaining salt. Drain dumplings well and serve hot with separate servings of country-style sauce and freshly grated Parmesan cheese.

Potato Dumplings Montano | Gnocchi di Patate alla Montano

1 cup flour	**Flour**
2 cups mashed cooked potatoes	**1 cup grated Parmesan cheese**
Salt	**4 Tbl butter, melted**

Thoroughly combine the flour, potatoes, and salt to taste. Shape the mixture into small rolls about 1-inch thick and 1½-inches long and dredge lightly with flour. Poach them for 3 minutes, or just until they are heated through, in barely simmering water lightly seasoned with salt. Preheat oven to 375 degrees. Drain the dumplings well and arrange them in layers in a baking dish, sprinkling the layers equally with the grated cheese and melted butter. Cover dish and bake dumplings for 5 minutes in the preheated oven. Serve hot. This recipe provides 6 servings.

Baked Farina Dumplings | Gnocchi di Semolino al Forno

4 cups water	**6 Tbl butter**
1 tsp salt	**2 eggs, beaten**
1 cup farina	**⅔ cup grated Parmesan cheese**

In a saucepan season the water with the salt and bring it to a boil. Slowly stir in the farina and cook it, at simmer, for 3 minutes, stirring it constantly. Remove pan from heat and add 2 tablespoons of the butter and the beaten eggs to the farina, beating constantly to produce a smooth mixture. Spread it ½-inch thick on a lightly buttered platter and let it cool completely. Preheat oven to 375 degrees. Cut the firmly set mixture into rounds 1½ inches in diameter and arrange them overlapping slightly in a shallow baking dish. Sprinkle with the remaining butter, melted, and the grated cheese. Bake them for 5 minutes in the preheated oven and brown them under a hot broiler. Serve them at once. This recipe provides 6 servings.

Ricotta Dumplings | Gnocchi di Ricotta

1½ cups ricotta cheese
⅓ cup grated Parmesan cheese
6 Tbl butter, softened
3 eggs, beaten
⅓ cup flour
3½ tsp salt

⅛ tsp white pepper
¼ tsp ground nutmeg
3 quarts simmering water
Melted butter
Country-Style Sauce (page 272)

In a mixing bowl combine the cheeses, softened butter, eggs, flour, ½ teaspoon of the salt, and the pepper and nutmeg. Stir them vigorously to produce a smooth mixture. Chill it for at least 2 hours. Drop the batter by teaspoonsful onto a lightly floured pastry board and, with your fingers, gently roll the mounds, coating them with flour and shaping them into rolls about 1-inch long.

Poach the rolls for 8 minutes in the simmering water seasoned with the remaining salt. Stir them occasionally, very gently, to keep them separated. Drain dumplings thoroughly and arrange on a warm serving platter. Brush lightly with melted butter and serve immediately with an accompaniment of country-style sauce passed separately, or with 1 cup hot browned butter combined with 1 cup freshly grated Parmesan cheese. This recipe provides 6 light entrée servings.

rotelle

pasta dishes

Stuffed Pasta Rolls, Florentine Style | Cannelloni alla Fiorentina

½ small chicken
Pasta Dough, plain or with semolina
   (pages 65, 66)
1 Tbl olive oil
1 Tbl butter
1 small onion, chopped
1 small clove garlic, mashed
1 small carrot, chopped
1 stalk heart of celery, chopped
1 small bay leaf
⅛ tsp oregano

⅛ tsp thyme
½ cup dry white wine
3 ounces spinach leaves,
   washed & drained
   (about 1 cup packed)
1⅔ cups grated Parmesan cheese
½ tsp salt
⅛ tsp white pepper
1 egg, beaten
2¼ cups cream
2 egg yolks

Cook and bone the chicken, but do not remove the skin. Cut the pasta for cannelloni (page 70). Set chicken and pasta aside.

Heat the olive oil and butter in a skillet and in it cook the onion and garlic until they are soft but not brown. Add the carrot, celery, and herbs, and let the vegetables brown lightly. Add the chicken meat with skin and heat through. Blend in the wine and continue until it is reduced to about ½ its volume. Finally, add the spinach and cook it until it is almost dry. Remove pan from heat and put mixture through the fine blade of a food chopper. In a mixing bowl combine the ground mixture, ⅓ cup of the grated cheese, and the salt and pepper or more to taste. Thoroughly beat in the beaten egg. Set this filling aside for the moment. Preheat oven to 350 degrees.

Cook the prepared squares of pasta dough, for 3 to 4 minutes only, as directed (see How to Cook Pasta). Cool quickly by plunging into ice cold water. Drain well on a clean cloth or paper toweling. Along 1 edge of each square place 2 generous tablespoons of prepared filling. Roll squares firmly, enclosing filling securely and taking care that it is completely contained. Brush a baking pan with olive oil and in it arrange the filled rolls, seam sides down. Set pan in another pan partially filled with hot water in the preheated oven. Bake rolls so for 10 minutes. Cover them loosely with foil and continue baking for 5 minutes longer. Remove pan from oven and transfer rolls to 6 individual heat-proof serving dishes.

Heat the cream in a saucepan. Pour it slowly into the egg yolks, beating constantly. Blend in 1 cup of the remaining grated cheese, a little at a time, continuing the beating to produce a smooth sauce. Dress each serving of the pasta with ½ cup of the sauce, 2 tablespoons around the cannelloni and the remainder over them. Sprinkle each with a little of the remaining grated cheese. Set dishes under a hot broiler for just a few seconds to brown cheese. Serve cannelloni at once. Serves 6.

Noodles Boschetto | Fettuccine alla Boschetto

Pasta Dough with Semolina　　**5 Tbl olive oil**
**　(page 65)**　　　　　　　　**5 Tbl butter**
2 medium heads escarole　　**1 clove garlic, very finely chopped**
4 quarts water　　　　　　　**Salt & white pepper**
1 Tbl salt　　　　　　　　　**6 Tbl grated Parmesan cheese**

Cut the pasta dough for fettuccine (page 69).

　Trim off the escarole leaves and wash them well. In a large saucepan season the water with the tablespoon of salt and bring it to a boil. Add escarole leaves and cook 15 minutes over moderate heat. Drain leaves well and pat dry between sheets of paper toweling. Chop leaves finely.

　In a large skillet heat the olive oil and butter and in them cook the garlic just until the bits begin to brown. Stir in escarole, season with salt and white pepper to taste, and cook for 5 minutes, stirring to blend it with the oil, butter, and garlic.

　Cook the fettuccine as directed (see How to Cook Pasta). Drain well. Place in a warm serving bowl, pour the sauce over, and sprinkle with the grated cheese. Serve at once. This recipe provides 6 servings.

Grandmother's Noodles | Fettuccine della Nonna

Pasta Dough with Semolina　　**8 medium tomatoes, peeled,**
**　(page 65)**　　　　　　　　**　seeded & coarsely chopped**
3 Tbl olive oil　　　　　　　**¼ tsp dried rosemary**
3 Tbl butter　　　　　　　　**Salt & pepper**
2 medium onions, finely chopped　**⅓ cup grated Parmesan cheese**
1 pound tender lean beef,
**　finely ground**

Cut the pasta dough for fettuccine (page 69).

In a deep skillet heat the olive oil and butter together and in them cook the onions until they are soft but not brown. Add the meat and brown it and onions together, mashing meat with a fork. Stir in the tomatoes and add the rosemary, and salt and pepper to taste. Cover pan and cook sauce over low heat for 2 hours or until it is smooth. Stir it frequently.

Cook the fettuccine (see How to Cook Pasta). Drain well. In a warm serving bowl blend the prepared sauce into the noodles and sprinkle with the grated cheese. Serves 6.

Fettuccine Trattoria Style | Fettuccine alla Trattoria

Pasta Dough with Semolina
   (page 65)
8 Tbl butter
2 cups heavy cream

3 egg yolks
2 cups grated Parmesan cheese
Salt & white pepper

Cut the pasta dough for fettuccine (page 69) and cook it as directed (see How to Cook Pasta). Drain well. Place fettuccine in a warm serving bowl and gently stir in 2 tablespoons of the butter, melted. Keep warm.

In a saucepan melt the remaining butter but do not let it foam. Stir the cream into it and let it heat through. In a bowl lightly beat the egg yolks and stir into them, a very little at a time, the heated butter and cream. Return mixture to saucepan and reheat it without letting it boil. Blend into it 1 cup of the grated cheese and add salt and white pepper to taste. When cheese is well incorporated into the cream, pour sauce over fettuccine in serving bowl. Stir sauce and remaining cheese into the noodles and serve them immediately. Serves 6.

Special Fettuccine | Fettuccine Speciali

¼ pound Italian sweet sausage
1 Tbl butter

Fettuccine Trattoria Style (above)

Skin and crumble the sausage and brown it well in the butter. Sprinkle the bits of sausage over the prepared Fettuccine Trattoria Style in a serving bowl. Serve the noodles at once.

Fettuccine with Cauliflower | Fettuccine con Cavolfiore

Pasta Dough with Semolina
   (page 65)
1 small cauliflower
½ cup olive oil
1 medium onion, finely chopped
1 clove garlic, mashed
½ pound Italian sweet sausage,
   skinned & crumbled

⅓ cup dry white wine
4 medium tomatoes, peeled,
   seeded & coarsely chopped
1 Tbl finely chopped Italian parsley
¼ tsp dried oregano
Salt & pepper
Grated Parmesan cheese

Cut the pasta dough for fettuccine (page 69).

    Wash and trim the head of cauliflower and separate it into small flowerets. Set aside. In the olive oil, heated in a saucepan, cook the onion and garlic until they are soft but not brown. Add the sausage and lightly brown them all together. Stir in the wine and when it is reduced to ½ its volume, add the tomatoes and continue cooking until they are reduced almost to a paste. Add the cauliflower, parsley, oregano, and salt and pepper to taste. Cover pan and continue cooking over low heat for 30 minutes or until pieces of cauliflower are tender.

    Cook the fettuccine as directed (see How to Cook Pasta). Drain and place in a warm serving bowl. Cover fettuccine with the cauliflower sauce and serve immediately. Pass freshly grated Parmesan cheese separately to be added as desired to the 6 servings provided by this recipe.

Fettuccine and Chick-Peas | Fettuccine con Ceci

Pasta Dough with Semolina
   (page 65)
1½ cups dried chick-peas,
   soaked 24 hours & drained
2 quarts boiling water
2 tsp salt
⅓ cup olive oil
2 medium onions, thinly sliced

2 small cloves garlic, mashed
2 medium tomatoes, peeled,
   seeded & chopped
1 Tbl finely chopped Italian parsley
¼ tsp dried rosemary, crumbled
Salt & pepper
½ cup grated Parmesan cheese

Cut the pasta dough for fettuccine (page 69).

In a large saucepan cover the chick-peas with the boiling water, seasoned with the salt, and cook them at simmer for 2 hours or until they are tender. Drain peas, reserving the remaining liquid, if any (it may be all absorbed). Set them aside for the moment.

In a large saucepan heat the olive oil and in it lightly brown the onions and garlic together. Add the tomatoes, parsley, and rosemary and cook until the tomatoes are soft.

Force ½ the reserved chick-peas through a fine sieve or purée them in an electric blender. Combine the purée, along with remaining whole chick-peas and reserved cooking liquid, with the tomato mixture, and continue cooking at simmer for 15 minutes, stirring frequently. Season sauce with salt and pepper to taste.

Cook the fettuccine (see How to Cook Pasta). Drain well. Stir fettuccine into the chick-pea sauce and let them heat through. Transfer fettuccine and chick-peas to a warm serving bowl and sprinkle with the grated cheese. This recipe provides 6 servings.

Green Lasagne | Lasagne Verdi

Green Pasta Dough with Semolina (page 65)	**1 egg, well beaten**
Butter	**¼ tsp ground nutmeg**
6 cups Bolognese Sauce (page 268)	**1⅓ cups grated Parmesan cheese**
2 cups medium Béchamel Sauce (page 270)	**Additional grated Parmesan cheese**

Cut the dough for lasagne (page 71).

Cook the strips of pasta as directed (see How to Cook Pasta) for 5 minutes only. Drain them thoroughly. Use an 8-inch square baking pan, 2 inches deep, and butter it well. Combine 3 cups of the Bolognese sauce, all of the Béchamel sauce, the egg, and ground nutmeg.

Spread ⅔ cup of the combined sauces over the bottom of the prepared pan and fit 4 of the strips of pasta neatly over it. Cover them with successive layers of ⅔ cup of the combined sauces, 3 tablespoons of the grated cheese, and 4 strips of the pasta, using all of the remaining ingredients and finishing with a layer of the combined sauces sprinkled with cheese. Let the lasagne rest at room temperature for 1 hour to allow it to settle. Bake it, lightly covered with foil, at 400 degrees for 30 minutes, removing the foil after 20 minutes to let the top brown lightly. Remove pan from oven and let lasagne rest for 10 minutes before cutting it into 6 portions. Serve the green lasagne with the remaining Bolognese sauce, heated, and with additional grated cheese, both of which should be passed separately.

NOTE: The lasagne will improve in flavor and cut more neatly if it is prepared a day in advance and reheated.

Baked Manicotti | Manicotti al Forno

½ **recipe Pasta Dough,**	½ **cup grated Parmesan cheese**
white or green,	**1 cup ricotta cheese**
plain or with semolina	**2 Tbl finely chopped Italian parsley**
(pages 65–66)	**1 egg, beaten**
⅔ **cup mozzarella cheese**	**Salt & white pepper**
1 thin slice prosciutto	**2 cups Tomato Sauce (page 282)**
(about 1 ounce)	**Additional grated Parmesan cheese**

Cut the pasta for manicotti (page 69). Cook the manicotti, for 3 to 4 minutes only, as directed (see How to Cook Pasta). Drain and immediately immerse, for 1 minute only, in a bowl of lightly salted ice cold water. Drain again and arrange in a single layer on a clean cloth. Cover lightly and set aside for the moment.

Put the mozzarella cheese and the prosciutto through the fine blade of a food chopper. In a mixing bowl thoroughly combine that mixture with the remaining 2 cheeses, the parsley, and egg. Season with salt and white pepper to taste. Preheat oven to 350 degrees.

Place 2 tablespoons of the mixture at one end of each pasta strip. Roll strips gently to enclose fillings. Spread ½ cup of the tomato sauce in a baking dish. Arrange pasta rolls in it and cover with the remaining sauce. Bake manicotti in the preheated oven for 20 minutes or until sauce bubbles and fillings are set. Serve immediately with additional grated Parmesan cheese to be added as desired. This recipe provides 18 filled manicotti with sauce, sufficient for 6 servings.

Green Lasagne—layers of wide noodles and rich sauce—is served simply and effectively with crisp salad and a glass of Chianti.

Dough for Ravioli (page 66)
½ cup cooked spinach
   (about 4 ounces raw)
3 Tbl ricotta cheese

⅓ cup grated Parmesan cheese
¼ cup fine dry bread crumbs
1 egg, beaten
Salt & pepper

Cut and mark dough for ravioli (page 69).

Drain the spinach and chop it finely. Thoroughly drain ricotta cheese and press it through a sieve. In a mixing bowl smoothly combine the spinach, cheeses, bread crumbs, and egg, and season the mixture with salt and pepper to taste.

Arrange 3 of the prepared ravioli sheets, marked sides up, on a flat surface. In the center of each marked square place 1 teaspoon of the prepared filling. Cover filled sheets each evenly with 1 of the remaining square sheets of dough, marked sides up. With your fingers press down firmly along markings to seal fillings securely each in its own square. With a pastry wheel or a sharp knife, cut the little squares apart.

Spread ravioli on a pastry board and let them dry for 30 minutes. Cook them, 16 at a time, in a large deep saucepan in 3 quarts rapidly boiling water seasoned with 1 tablespoon salt. They will cook *al dente* in 6 to 7 minutes. For softer pasta increase cooking time, testing each minute after 6 minutes, until an acceptable degree of doneness is achieved. Drain ravioli and serve with a sauce of your choice or simply with melted butter and freshly grated Parmesan cheese. Serves 6.

Meat-Filled Ravioli | Ravioli Ripieni di Carne

Dough for Ravioli (page 66)
3 Tbl olive oil
1 small onion, coarsely chopped
3 ounces lean beef, diced
6 ounces lean veal, diced
1 small bay leaf
¼ cup dry white wine

¼ cup cooked spinach leaves,
   well drained
2 Tbl grated Parmesan cheese
1 egg, beaten
Salt & pepper
Country-Style Sauce (page 272)

Cut and mark dough for ravioli (page 69).

Cannelloni, well-loved stuffed pasta rolls,
may be filled with a variety of foods. Ingredients pictured
are combined in the Florentine version.

In a skillet heat the olive oil and in it lightly brown the onion and meats together. Add the bay leaf and wine and cook over low heat until the liquid is completely absorbed. Add the spinach and continue cooking for 3 minutes or until any liquid rendered evaporates. Remove and discard bay leaf. Cool the mixture. Put it through the fine blade of a food chopper and combine it in a mixing bowl with the grated cheese, egg, and salt and pepper to taste.

Arrange 3 of the prepared ravioli sheets marked sides up on a flat surface. In the center of each marked square place 1 teaspoon of the prepared meat filling. Cover those sheets each evenly with 1 of the remaining square sheets of dough, marked side up. With your fingers press down firmly along markings to seal filling securely each in its own square. With a pastry wheel or a sharp knife, cut squares apart.

Spread ravioli on a pastry board and let them dry for 30 minutes. Cook them, 16 at a time, in a large deep saucepan in 3 quarts rapidly boiling water seasoned with 1 tablespoon salt. They will cook *al dente* in 6 to 7 minutes. For softer pasta increase cooking time, testing each minute after 6 minutes, until an acceptable degree of doneness is achieved. Drain ravioli, and serve them, 8 to a serving, with the country-style sauce, or with other sauce of your choice, or simply with melted butter and freshly grated Parmesan cheese. Serves 6.

Shepherd's Ravioli | Ravioli del Pastore

Dough for Ravioli (page 66)
3 ounces mortadella sausage, finely chopped
3 ounces Italian-style salami, finely chopped
½ cup shredded mozzarella cheese
3 Tbl grated Parmesan cheese
1 egg, beaten
Salt
Bland cooking oil

Prepare the dough for ravioli, using an additional 3 tablespoons of olive oil. Cut and mark the dough (page 69).

In a mixing bowl smoothly combine the meats, cheeses, and egg, and season the mixture with salt to taste.

Arrange 3 of the ravioli sheets, marked sides up on a flat surface. In the center of each marked square place 1 teaspoon of the prepared fill-

ing. Cover each filled sheet evenly with 1 of the remaining square sheets of dough, marked side up. With your fingers press down firmly along markings to seal fillings securely each in its own square. With a pastry wheel or a sharp knife cut the little squares apart. Spread ravioli on a pastry board and let them dry for 30 minutes.

In a deep saucepan or a fryer heat sufficient bland cooking oil for deep frying to 350 degrees and in it fry ravioli, a few at a time, until they are golden brown in color and crisp. Drain them on absorbent paper. This recipe provides 48 ravioli, sufficient for 6 servings.

Ravioli with Potato Stuffing | Ravioli Ripieni di Patate

Dough for Ravioli (page 66)
1 Tbl butter
1 scallion, white part only,
   finely chopped
1 Tbl tomato paste
1 tsp finely chopped parsley
¼ cup Chicken Broth (page 44)
¾ cup mashed cooked potatoes

2 Tbl fine dry bread crumbs
3 Tbl grated Parmesan cheese
1 egg, beaten
Salt & pepper
3 quarts water
1 Tbl salt
Country-Style Sauce (page 272)

Cut and mark the dough for ravioli (page 69).

In a skillet heat the butter and in it cook the scallion until it is lightly browned. Add the tomato paste, parsley, and chicken broth and continue cooking until liquid is almost entirely absorbed. Remove pan from heat and blend in the potatoes, bread crumbs, grated cheese, egg, and salt and pepper to taste. Cool mixture completely.

Arrange 3 of the prepared ravioli sheets, marked sides up, on a flat surface. In the center of each marked square place 1 teaspoon of the prepared filling. Cover filled sheets each evenly with 1 of the remaining square sheets of dough, marked side up. With your fingers press down firmly along markings to seal fillings securely each in its own square. With a pastry wheel or a sharp knife cut the little squares apart.

Spread ravioli on a pastry board and let them dry for 30 minutes. Cook them, 16 at a time, in the water at a rapid boil, seasoned with the tablespoon of salt, in a large deep saucepan. They will cook *al dente* in 6 to 7 minutes. For softer pasta increase cooking time, testing each minute after 6 minutes, until an acceptable degree of doneness is achieved. Drain ravioli and serve them with country-style sauce. Serves 6.

Chicken and Sausage Filling for Ravioli |
Ripieno di Pollo e Salsiccia per Ravioli

1 breast of chicken
   (about ½ pound)
2 links Italian sweet sausage
   (about ¼ pound)

1 tsp flour
¼ cup dry white wine
1 large tomato, peeled,
   seeded & finely chopped

1 Tbl butter
1 Tbl olive oil
1 small onion, finely chopped
1 clove garlic, mashed
1 small bay leaf

1 Tbl finely chopped parsley
Salt & pepper
1 egg
Fine dry bread crumbs

Bone the chicken breast and grind it finely. Skin the sausage links and grind them finely.

In a skillet heat together the butter and olive oil and cook the onion and garlic in them until they are soft. Blend in the ground meats, browning the mixture well and mashing it with a fork to prevent its becoming lumpy. Add the bay leaf. Sprinkle mixture with the flour and stir into it the wine, tomatoes, parsley, and salt and pepper to taste. Cover skillet and continue cooking over low heat for 30 minutes, stirring occasionally. Remove pan from heat and let mixture cool. Beat into it the egg and blend in just enough bread crumbs to produce a filling that is firm but not dry. Remove and discard bay leaf. This recipe provides enough filling for 48 ravioli, sufficient for 6 servings.

Stuffed Pasta Coronets, Bolognese Style |
Tortellini alla Bolognese

Pasta Dough with All-Purpose Flour
   (page 65)
6 ounces cooked lean pork
3 ounces cooked veal
¼ pound prosciutto
3 ounces mortadella
1 small bay leaf

2 Tbl butter
⅔ cup grated Parmesan cheese
1 egg
Salt & pepper
1 cup heavy cream
2 cups Bolognese Sauce (page 268)
Additional grated Parmesan cheese

Cut the pasta dough for tortellini (page 71).

Combine the meats and put them, along with the bay leaf, through the fine blade of a food chopper. In a skillet heat the butter and in it brown the ground mixture lightly. Remove pan from heat and blend in the grated cheese, egg, and salt and pepper to taste. Let mixture cool.

In the center of each round of the prepared pasta place a generous ¼ teaspoon of the meat mixture and fold the round in half over it. Press

elbow macaroni

edges together firmly to secure fillings. Gently fold the half rounds, bringing curved edges to the straight, and wind the resulting strips around your index finger to form tiny coronets. Secure ends by pressing them together. Cook filled pasta (see How to Cook Pasta), for 6 minutes only. Drain well. Preheat oven to 400 degrees.

Pour the cream into a baking dish and arrange the coronets in it. Cover with the Bolognese sauce and sprinkle lightly with a little additional grated Parmesan cheese. Bake pasta in the preheated oven for 15 minutes or until top is well browned. This recipe provides 6 very generous servings.

Bucatini with Bacon and Tomatoes |
Bucatini alla Pancetta e Pomodoro

½ pound bacon, cut in small pieces	1 tsp chopped fresh basil (or ¼ tsp dried basil)
2 Tbl olive oil	Salt & freshly ground black pepper
1 large clove garlic, finely chopped	1½ pounds bucatini (see Glossary)
8 very ripe tomatoes, peeled, seeded & chopped	¾ cup grated Parmesan cheese
	1 Tbl chopped parsley

Put the bacon in a large unheated skillet without additional fat and try it out over low heat until it is cooked through, but not crisp. Drain off the rendered fat. Add the olive oil, heat it, and in it cook the bits of garlic just until they are soft. Blend in the tomatoes, basil, and salt and pepper to taste, and cook, uncovered, over medium heat for 30 minutes or until tomatoes are very soft.

Meanwhile, cook the bucatini pasta (see How to Cook Pasta), drain, and keep hot. Apportion the hot bucatini in 6 individual serving dishes and pour sauce over them. Sprinkle equally with the grated cheese and parsley.

Cavatelli with Ricotta Cheese | Cavatelli con Ricotta

1½ pounds cavatelli (see Glossary)	Pepper
5 Tbl butter	1 Tbl chopped parsley
¾ pound ricotta cheese	½ cup grated Parmesan cheese
6 ounces prosciutto,	
cut in small julienne	

Cook the cavatelli (see How to Cook Pasta), drain, and keep hot. In a small saucepan melt 2 tablespoons of the butter and stir the ricotta cheese into it. Warm it gently. In a warm serving dish combine the hot pasta with the remaining butter, melted. Blend in the warm ricotta, the prosciutto, and a good grinding of pepper. Sprinkle cavatelli with the parsley and grated cheese and serve at once. This recipe provides 6 servings.

Farfalle with Sausage, Amatriciana Style |
Farfalle con Salsiccia all'Amatriciana

¼ cup olive oil	1 bay leaf
¼ pound salt pork,	½ cup red wine
in small julienne	3 cups canned,
18 Italian sweet sausages	peeled plum tomatoes
(about 2 pounds)	½ tsp dried oregano
1 medium onion, finely chopped	Salt & pepper
1 clove garlic, finely chopped	4 cups farfalle (see Glossary)
1 medium green pepper,	1 Tbl finely chopped parsley
cut in small julienne	

In a saucepan heat the olive oil and in it lightly brown the salt pork. Add the sausages and cook them slowly, turning frequently to brown evenly on all sides. Add the onion, garlic, green pepper, and bay leaf and, when the vegetables are soft (after about 5 minutes), stir in the wine. When it is almost completely absorbed, add the tomatoes, oregano, and salt and pepper to taste. Continue cooking, still over low heat, for 20 minutes. Remove and discard bay leaf.

Cook the farfalle as directed (see How to Cook Pasta). Drain pasta well. Spread about ½ cup of the sauce in a warm serving dish and arrange pasta over it. Place sausages over pasta. Pour the remaining sauce over them and sprinkle it with the parsley. Serve farfalle and sausages hot. This recipe provides 6 servings.

Farfalle with Anchovies | Farfalle con Acciughe

1 cup olive oil
8 anchovy fillets, mashed to a paste
2 cups dry coarse bread crumbs

1½ pounds farfalle (see Glossary)
1 Tbl finely chopped parsley

In a skillet heat ½ cup of the olive oil. Blend the mashed anchovies into it and let them steep in the oil over very low heat for 3 minutes. In a separate skillet heat the remaining olive oil and in it brown the bread crumbs. Drain them and transfer them to a warm serving bowl. Keep them warm.

Cook the farfalle (see How to Cook Pasta). Drain and place in a warm serving bowl. Pour the anchovies and oil over the hot pasta, stir in parsley, and serve at once. Pass the bread crumbs separately to be sprinkled over individual servings as desired.

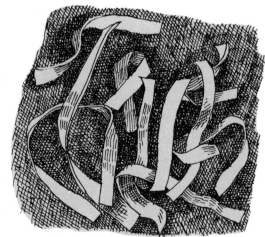

fettuccine

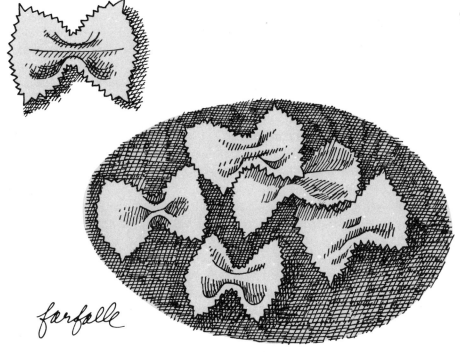

farfalle

Spiral Spaghetti, Carrara Style | Fusilli all'Uso di Carrara

1½ pounds fusilli (see Glossary)	**2 cups ricotta cheese, sieved**
6 links Italian sweet sausage	**Salt & white pepper**
(about ¾ pound)	**1 cup grated Parmesan cheese**
1 Tbl olive oil	**1 Tbl finely chopped parsley**

Cook the spaghetti (see How to Cook Pasta), drain, and keep it hot. Skin and crumble the sausage links. Heat the oil in a skillet. Add the sausage meat and cook slowly until the bits are well browned. Drain off all remaining fat. Remove pan from heat and stir in the sieved ricotta cheese. Season with salt and white pepper to taste.

In a warm serving bowl blend into the hot fusilli the Parmesan, parsley, and sausage and ricotta mixture. Serve at once. This recipe provides 6 servings.

Spiral Spaghetti Rossi | Fusilli alla Rossi

¼ pound veal	1½ pounds fusilli (see Glossary)
6 ounces beef	6 ounces mushrooms, thinly sliced
Salt & pepper	¼ pound prosciutto,
6 Tbl butter	cut in small pieces
½ cup dry white wine	1 Tbl finely chopped parsley
2½ cups Tomato Sauce (page 282)	

Put the raw meats through the fine blade of a food chopper together and season them with salt and pepper to taste. In a large deep skillet heat 3 tablespoons of the butter and in it brown the chopped meat well, mashing with a wooden spoon to eliminate any lumps. Stir in the wine and when it is completely absorbed blend in the tomato sauce. Cover skillet and cook mixture for 30 minutes or until it is smooth. Meanwhile, cook the spaghetti (see How to Cook Pasta), drain, and keep hot.

In a separate skillet heat the remaining butter. Add the mushrooms and prosciutto, and brown them quickly but lightly. Combine them with the sauce and cook for a few minutes to blend the flavors. Pour over the hot pasta in a warm serving dish and sprinkle with the parsley. This recipe provides 6 servings.

Spiral Spaghetti and Vegetables | Fusilli con Verdura

3 medium potatoes (about 1 pound)	1 large onion, finely chopped
1 small head cabbage	¼ tsp dried sage
1 Tbl salt	⅔ cup grated Parmesan cheese
3 quarts water	½ pound Bel Paese cheese,
1 pound fusilli (see Glossary)	thinly sliced
6 Tbl butter	

Peel and cube the potatoes. Core and shred the cabbage. Add the salt to the water in a large saucepan and in it, at a rolling boil, cook potatoes and cabbage for 10 minutes. Add the spiral spaghetti and continue cooking until pasta is *al dente,* about 5 minutes longer. Drain vegetables and pasta. In a skillet heat the butter and brown the onion in it. Remove pan from heat and blend in the sage and grated cheese. Set aside for the

maruzzelle

moment. Preheat oven to 450 degrees.

Butter a deep baking dish and in it spread ⅓ of the vegetables and pasta. Cover them with ½ of the slices of Bel Paese. Over that spread ½ of the onion mixture and, in order, ½ of the remaining vegetables and pasta, the rest of the Bel Paese and the onion mixture, and the remaining vegetables and pasta. Bake the layered fusilli in the preheated oven for 5 minutes. Allow it to rest for a few minutes before cutting it into squares to provide 6 servings.

Narrow Noodles with Squid | Linguine con Calamari

3 squid	**2 cups Marinara Sauce (page 277)**
1½ pounds linguine (see Glossary)	**Dried oregano (optional)**
⅓ cup olive oil	**Salt & pepper**
1 medium onion, finely chopped	**1 Tbl finely chopped Italian parsley**
2 Tbl dry white wine	

Clean the squid and steam them (pages 130, 132), and cut them into small pieces. Cook the linguine as directed (see How to Cook Pasta), drain, and keep it hot.

Heat the olive oil in a saucepan and lightly brown the onion in it. Add squid and merely heat them through. Stir in the wine and marinara sauce. Add oregano to taste, if desired, keeping in mind that the marinara sauce is already well seasoned with the herb. Continue cooking at simmer for 5 minutes to blend the flavors. Season sauce with salt and pepper to taste and stir the parsley into it. Combine sauce with pasta in a warm serving bowl and serve it at once. This recipe provides 6 servings.

Macaroni Cremona Style | Maccheroni alla Cremonese

⅓ cup Italian dried mushrooms (about ½ ounce)	⅛ tsp nutmeg
	Salt & pepper
8 Tbl butter	1 pound elbow macaroni
4 large chicken livers	1 cup grated Parmesan cheese
½ pair sweetbreads	2 cups Tomato Sauce (page 282)
¼ pound cooked ham, chopped	2 cups thin Béchamel Sauce
1 medium white truffle	(page 270)

Soften the mushrooms in warm water for 30 minutes and drain them. Cut them into small pieces and set aside. In a skillet heat 1 tablespoon of the butter and in it cook the chicken livers until they are lightly browned and firm. Remove the chicken livers, cut them into small pieces, and add them to the mushrooms.

Parboil the sweetbread (for directions, see Sauce with Sweetbreads, page 276) and finely chop it. In the skillet heat 3 more tablespoons of the butter and in it quickly, but lightly, brown the sweetbread. Add the mushrooms, chicken livers, and ham, and the truffle, chopped, and cook them for a few minutes to blend the flavors. Season the mixture with the nutmeg and salt and pepper to taste.

Meanwhile, cook the macaroni *al dente* (see How to Cook Pasta) and drain. Preheat oven to 375 degrees. Butter a large deep baking dish with 1 tablespoon of the butter and in it arrange 3 series of layers, each series composed of ⅓ of the macaroni, grated cheese, remaining butter (in bits), tomato sauce, and meat mixture, in that order. Bake the macaroni in the preheated oven for 20 minutes or until the meat topping is well browned. Serve the Macaroni Cremona Style hot and pass the Béchamel sauce separately, to be added to individual servings to taste. This recipe provides 6 servings.

Macaroni with Pine Nuts | Maccheroni con Salsa di Pignoli

1½ pounds macaroni
2 cups pine nuts
¾ cup dry-roasted peanuts
1 clove garlic, grated
½ tsp dried marjoram

1 Tbl finely chopped parsley
½ tsp salt
1 cup ricotta cheese
½ cup olive oil
Grated Parmesan cheese

Cook the macaroni (see How to Cook Pasta), drain, and keep hot. Roll the pine nuts and peanuts to a powder with a rolling pin or pulverize them in an electric blender. Thoroughly combine them in a mixing bowl with the garlic, marjoram, parsley, salt, and ricotta cheese. Beat in the olive oil, a little at a time. In a skillet heat the mixture gently and pour it over the hot macaroni in a warm serving bowl. Accompany the 6 servings provided by this recipe with freshly grated Parmesan cheese passed separately.

Macaroni and Meat Pie | Torta di Maccheroni e Carne

Pie Dough (page 72)
3 Tbl olive oil
¾ pound maccheroncelli
   (see Glossary)
½ pound veal, finely ground
½ pound beef, finely ground

3 cups Tomato Sauce (page 282)
1 cup grated Parmesan cheese
Salt & pepper
4 eggs
½ cup heavy cream

Roll out ⅔ of the prepared dough into a round slightly less than ¼-inch thick. Brush a deep 10-inch pie pan with a little of the olive oil and line pan with the rolled dough, leaving an overhang about ½ inch all around. Reserve remaining dough.

    Cook the maccheroncelli (see How to Cook Pasta), drain, and keep hot. Heat the remaining olive oil in a skillet. Combine the ground meats, add them to skillet, and brown well, mashing them with a fork to eliminate any lumps. In a mixing bowl combine browned meats, maccheroncelli, tomato sauce, cheese, and salt and pepper to taste. Spread mixture evenly in the pan lined with the pie dough. Blend 3 of the eggs into the cream and pour it over the pie filling. Brush edges of dough with the remaining egg, beaten. Preheat oven to 350 degrees.

Roll out remaining dough to provide a top crust and fit it over filling. Press edges of the 2 crusts together to seal them. Trim off excess. Bake pie in the preheated oven for 30 minutes or until pastry is well browned. Serve pie cut in wedges to provide 6 servings.

Pasta Shells with Mushrooms | Maruzzelle con Funghi

½ cup olive oil
1 clove garlic, peeled & flattened
1½ pounds fresh mushrooms,
    washed & sliced
2 large tomatoes, peeled,
    seeded & finely chopped

Salt & pepper
1 Tbl finely chopped parsley
1 cup grated Parmesan cheese
1 pound maruzzelle (see Glossary)

In a large skillet heat the olive oil and in it lightly brown the garlic. Remove and discard it. Add the mushrooms to the oil and cook them briskly, stirring constantly, until the slices are lightly browned. Add the tomatoes and cook over moderate heat for 20 minutes. Season with salt and pepper to taste. Blend in the parsley and the grated cheese.

Cook the maruzzelle (see How to Cook Pasta) and drain them well. Stir cooked pasta into sauce and serve at once. This recipe provides 6 servings.

Rigatoni Sicilian Style | Rigatoni alla Siciliana

1½ pounds rigatoni (see Glossary)
1 medium eggplant
Flour
1 egg, beaten
½ cup olive oil

3 cups heavy cream
1½ cups grated Parmesan cheese
½ cup Tomato Sauce (page 282)
3 egg yolks
Salt & white pepper

Cook the rigatoni (see How to Cook Pasta). Drain well and set aside for the moment.

Peel the eggplant and cut it in small julienne. Dredge eggplant in flour and coat with the beaten egg. Brown lightly in the olive oil heated

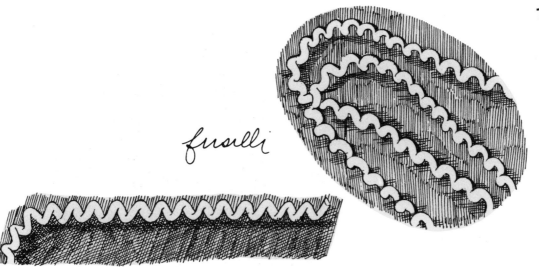

fusilli

in a skillet. Drain on paper toweling.

Preheat oven to 400 degrees. Scald the cream in a saucepan. Blend into it 1 cup of the grated cheese. Add the eggplant and tomato sauce. Cool the mixture and stir the egg yolks into it. Season it with salt and white pepper to taste. Add the rigatoni, stirring them in gently so as not to break them. Turn mixture into a deep baking dish and sprinkle it with the remaining grated cheese. Bake it in the preheated oven for 15 minutes. Serve rigatoni and sauce at once. This recipe provides 6 servings.

Stuffed Rigatoni | Rigatoni Ripieni

1 pound rigatoni (see Glossary)	**1 Tbl finely chopped Italian parsley**
6 ounces lean beef, finely ground	**2 eggs**
6 ounces lean pork, finely ground	**1 cup grated Parmesan cheese**
6 ounces veal, finely ground	**Salt & pepper**
⅔ cup fine dry bread crumbs	**4 cups Bolognese Sauce (page 268)**

Cook the rigatoni as directed (see How to Cook Pasta), but for 5 minutes only. Drain and immediately immerse in ice cold water for 1 minute to

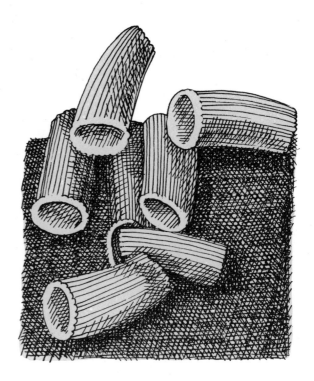

rigatoni

keep it firm and make it easier to handle. Drain well and set aside for the moment.

Preheat oven to 350 degrees. In a mixing bowl combine the meats, bread crumbs, parsley, eggs, ½ cup of the grated cheese, and salt and pepper to taste. Stuff rigatoni (equally) with the mixture. In a baking dish arrange a single layer of stuffed pasta. Cover with 2 cups of the Bolognese sauce. Over that arrange another layer of pasta and cover it with the remaining sauce. Sprinkle with the remaining grated cheese.

Cover pan lightly with foil and bake pasta in the preheated oven for 1 hour. Remove foil and continue baking for 15 minutes longer. Serve rigatoni and sauce from the baking dish. This recipe provides 6 servings.

Spaghetti with Meatballs | Spaghetti con Polpette

¾ pound veal, finely ground
¾ pound lean beef, finely ground
2 eggs, lightly beaten
2 Tbl finely chopped parsley
1 clove garlic, finely chopped
1½ tsp salt
Freshly ground pepper
¾ cup soft white bread crumbs
6 Tbl milk

⅓ cup olive oil
1 medium onion, finely chopped
4 cups canned, peeled
    plum tomatoes, crushed
1 tsp finely chopped fresh basil
    (or ¼ tsp dried basil)
2 Tbl tomato paste
1½ pounds spaghetti
Grated Parmesan cheese

In a mixing bowl thoroughly combine the meats, eggs, parsley, garlic, ¾ teaspoon of the salt, pepper to taste, and the bread crumbs moistened with the milk. Shape the mixture into 12 balls of equal size. In a large skillet heat the olive oil and in it brown the meatballs well on all sides. Transfer them to a warm side dish and keep them warm.

Lightly brown the onion in the oil remaining in the skillet. Add to it the tomatoes, basil, the remaining salt, and pepper to taste. Cook the tomatoes at simmer for 30 minutes. Blend into them the tomato paste. Return meatballs to pan and let them heat through in sauce.

Meanwhile, cook the spaghetti as directed (see How to Cook Pasta), drain it, and keep it hot.

Pour sauce over prepared spaghetti in a warm serving dish and arrange meatballs over it. Serve the spaghetti and meatballs with grated Parmesan cheese passed separately. Serves 6.

Spaghetti with Cauliflower | Spaghetti con Cavolfiore

1 medium head cauliflower
6 medium tomatoes
    (about 2 pounds)
⅓ cup olive oil
1 clove garlic, peeled & crushed

⅔ cup water
Salt & white pepper
1 Tbl finely chopped Italian parsley
1½ pounds spaghetti
Grated Parmesan cheese

Wash, trim, and finely chop the head of cauliflower. Peel, seed, and finely chop the tomatoes. Heat the olive oil in a saucepan and in it brown the clove of garlic. Remove garlic and discard it. Add tomatoes and water, and bring liquid to simmer. Add cauliflower and salt and white pepper to taste. Cover pan and cook vegetables over moderately low heat for 1 hour or until they are very soft. Force them through a fine sieve. Return the resulting purée to the saucepan and continue cooking for 20 minutes longer or until sauce is thick and smooth. Blend the chopped parsley into it.

Meanwhile, cook the spaghetti as directed (see How to Cook Pasta), drain, and keep it hot. Dress the spaghetti, in a warm serving bowl, with the sauce and serve it at once. Serve freshly grated Parmesan cheese separately, to be added to individual servings to taste. Serves 6.

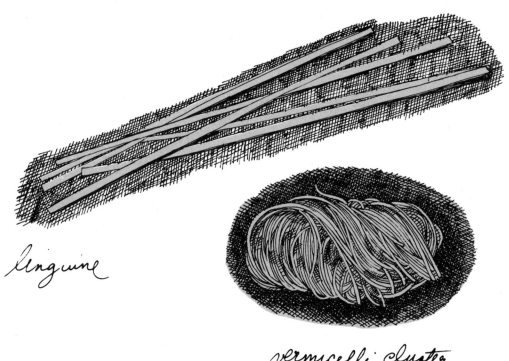

linguine

vermicelli cluster

Spaghetti Carbonara | Spaghetti alla Carbonara

8 slices bacon	¼ tsp crumbled dried red peppers
1 cup medium cream	(without seeds)
2 eggs	Salt
2 egg yolks	1½ pounds spaghetti
½ cup grated Parmesan cheese	6 Tbl butter, melted

Cut the bacon crosswise into ¼-inch strips. Cook bacon slowly without additional fat in a skillet over moderate heat until strips are crisp. Remove bacon strips and drain on paper toweling. Crumble them into a bowl and set aside. Drain off all but 1 tablespoon of fat remaining in skillet and blend the cream into that remainder. Heat it gently without boiling, then cool it. In a mixing bowl beat together the cream, eggs, egg yolks, cheese, red peppers, and salt to taste.

Cook the spaghetti as directed (see How to Cook Pasta) and drain it. Blend the sauce, melted butter, and reserved bacon into the hot spaghetti. This recipe provides 6 servings.

Spaghetti Caruso Style | Spaghetti alla Caruso

2 Tbl olive oil	¼ pound fresh mushrooms,
1 medium onion, thinly sliced	thinly sliced
3 cups canned,	Salt & pepper
peeled plum tomatoes	1½ pounds spaghetti
1 small bay leaf	1 pound chicken livers
¼ tsp dried oregano	2 Tbl dry white wine
4 Tbl butter	1 Tbl finely chopped parsley
	Grated Parmesan cheese

Heat the olive oil in a saucepan and brown the onion lightly in it. Add the tomatoes, bay leaf, and oregano and cook, covered, at simmer for 20 minutes.

In a skillet heat 2 tablespoons of the butter. Add the mushrooms and cook briskly until the slices begin to take on color. Combine mushrooms with tomatoes and continue cooking for 10 minutes. Season with salt and pepper to taste.

bucatini

Meanwhile, cook the spaghetti as directed (see How to Cook Pasta), drain, and keep hot.

Cut the chicken livers in halves and remove membranes. Heat the remaining butter in the skillet and in it sauté livers until they are lightly browned and firm. Add them to tomato mixture. Blend the wine into the cooking glaze remaining in skillet and stir it into sauce. Continue cooking for 1 minute or just long enough to allow livers to absorb the tomato-mushroom flavor. Combine sauce with spaghetti in a warm serving bowl and sprinkle with chopped parsley. Serve spaghetti and sauce immediately with an accompaniment of freshly grated Parmesan cheese passed separately. This recipe provides 6 servings.

Spaghetti Parmesan Style | Spaghetti alla Parmigiana

⅓ cup olive oil	Salt & pepper
1 clove garlic, finely chopped	1½ pounds spaghetti
4 large tomatoes, peeled, seeded & coarsely chopped	6 ounces mozzarella cheese, shredded
2 Tbl finely chopped parsley	½ cup grated Parmesan cheese
2 tsp finely chopped fresh basil (or ½ tsp dried basil)	

In the olive oil, heated in a saucepan, sauté the garlic until it takes on a little color. Add the tomatoes, parsley, basil, and salt and pepper to taste, and cook, covered, over moderate heat for 15 minutes.

Meanwhile, cook the spaghetti as directed (see How to Cook Pasta), drain it, and keep it hot. Preheat oven to 400 degrees.

Spread the prepared spaghetti in a lightly oiled baking dish and pour the sauce over it. Combine the cheeses and sprinkle them evenly over sauce. Set pan in the preheated oven and let it remain until cheeses melt and are lightly browned. Serve spaghetti at once. This recipe provides 6 servings.

Spaghetti Pompeian Style | Spaghetti alla Pompeiana

½ cup Italian dried mushrooms	½ pound prosciutto, in fine julienne
6 large tomatoes (about 3 pounds)	½ cup dry white wine
3 Tbl olive oil	Salt & pepper
2 Tbl butter	1½ pounds spaghetti
1 medium onion, finely chopped	¾ cup grated Parmesan cheese

Soften the mushrooms in warm water, drain, and chop them finely. Peel, seed, and finely chop the tomatoes. Set mushrooms and tomatoes aside. In a saucepan heat the olive oil and butter and cook the onion in the oil until it is soft but not brown. Combine the prosciutto with the onion and let them brown lightly together. Stir in the wine and bring to a boil. Add the chopped mushrooms and tomatoes, and continue cooking over moderate heat, with pan covered, for 30 minutes or until the sauce thickens. Stir occasionally. Season it with salt and pepper to taste.

Meanwhile, cook the spaghetti as directed (see How to Cook Pasta), drain, and keep it hot.

Blend the sauce and grated cheese into the spaghetti in a warm serving bowl. Serve the pasta at once. This recipe provides 6 servings.

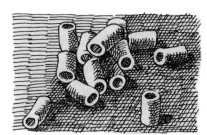

ditalini

Spaghetti Sicilian Style | Spaghetti alla Siciliana

1 large eggplant	1 tsp finely chopped fresh
¾ cup olive oil	basil leaves (or ¼ tsp dried basil)
2 cloves garlic, peeled & flattened	Salt & pepper
8 large tomatoes	1½ pounds spaghetti
(about 3½ pounds)	1½ cups grated Parmesan cheese

Peel the eggplant and slice it thinly. Arrange eggplant slices in 1 layer in a large broiler pan and brush them lightly on 1 side with some of the olive oil. Set pan under a hot broiler and let slices brown. Turn them, brush with olive oil, and brown that side also. Keep slices warm.

In a large saucepan heat the remaining olive oil (there should be about ⅓ cup) and in it brown the cloves of garlic. Remove and discard them. Peel, seed, and chop the tomatoes. Add the tomatoes, basil, and salt and pepper to taste, and cook them until they are reduced to a thick purée.

Meanwhile, cook the spaghetti as directed (see How to Cook Pasta), drain it, and keep it hot.

Blend the sauce into the prepared spaghetti in a deep serving platter and sprinkle it with ½ cup of the grated cheese. Arrange over it the eggplant slices, overlapping them. Serve Spaghetti Sicilian Style hot and pass the remaining grated cheese separately. Serves 6.

Pasta and Beans | Pasta e Fagioli

2 Tbl olive oil	1 leek, thinly sliced
1 large onion, finely chopped	2 Tbl finely chopped parsley
1 clove garlic, mashed	1 bay leaf
4 cups Chicken Broth (page 44)	¼ tsp dried oregano
1½ cups pea beans,	Salt & pepper
soaked overnight & drained	½ cup spaghetti,
2 cups canned,	broken in 1-inch lengths
peeled plum tomatoes	Grated Parmesan cheese
2 stalks celery, thinly sliced	

Heat the olive oil in a large saucepan. Add the onion and garlic and cook them until they begin to take on color. Stir in the chicken broth, beans, tomatoes, celery, leek, 1 tablespoon of the parsley, herbs, and salt and pepper to taste. Cook for 1 hour or until beans are tender but still retain their shape.

Meanwhile cook the spaghetti pieces as directed (see How to Cook Pasta), drain, and keep hot.

When beans are tender add spaghetti and continue cooking for 2 minutes or until pasta is heated through. Transfer spaghetti and vegetables to a warm serving dish and sprinkle with the remaining parsley. Serve pasta and beans hot with a separate serving of freshly grated Parmesan cheese. This recipe provides 6 servings.

Ziti Catania Style | Ziti alla Catanese

1 pound ziti (see Glossary)
2 Tbl butter
6 ounces fresh mushrooms, sliced
3 cups heavy cream
3 egg yolks

¼ pound mozzarella cheese, shredded
1⅓ cups grated Parmesan cheese
Salt & white pepper

Cook the ziti (see How to Cook Pasta), drain, and keep hot. In a skillet heat the butter. Add the mushrooms and brown them lightly. Preheat oven to 400 degrees.

In a saucepan over low heat scald the cream. With pan off heat,

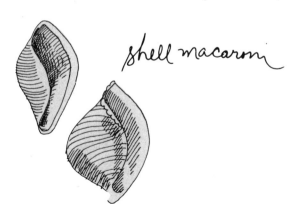

shell macaroni

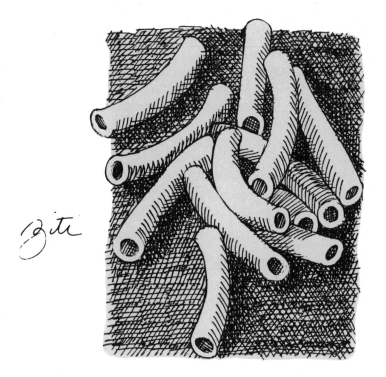

stir the egg yolks vigorously into cream. Blend in the mozzarella and 1 cup of the grated cheese. Season sauce with salt and white pepper to taste. Add mushrooms and gently stir in the cooked ziti. Transfer mixture to a deep baking dish and sprinkle with the remaining grated cheese. Bake in the preheated oven for 15 minutes or until sauce bubbles and top is brown. Serve hot. This recipe provides 6 servings.

Ziti with Fennel | Ziti con Finocchi

6 heads fennel
4 quarts water
4 tsp salt
1 pound ziti (see Glossary)
⅓ cup olive oil
1 medium onion, finely chopped

3 medium tomatoes, peeled,
   seeded & chopped
Salt & pepper
½ cup grated Parmesan cheese
1 Tbl finely chopped parsley

Wash and trim the heads of fennel. Cook the fennel for 15 minutes over moderate heat in a large saucepan with the water, seasoned with the salt, at boil. Remove fennel. Reserve liquid in saucepan. Drain fennel thoroughly, squeezing to remove as much moisture as possible. Chop drained fennel coarsely. Set it aside in a bowl and keep it warm.

Reheat the cooking liquid in the saucepan and in it cook the ziti *al dente,* about 6 minutes, or to the degree of doneness preferred (see How to Cook Pasta). Remove and place in a warm serving bowl with ¼ cup of the liquid. Cover and keep warm in a 150-degree oven. Reserve an additional 1 cup of the liquid to be used in the sauce.

Heat the olive oil in a deep skillet and in it very lightly brown the onion. Add the reserved cup of liquid, the tomatoes, and salt and pepper to taste. Cover skillet and cook vegetables over moderate heat for 10 minutes. Remove cover and continue cooking for 10 minutes longer. Combine the sauce with the ziti and fennel. Sprinkle with the grated cheese and parsley. Serve at once. Serves 6.

Pasta with Broccoli | Pasta con Broccoli

1 bunch broccoli
   (about 1½ pounds)
1½ pounds pasta of choice
¾ cup olive oil

1 clove garlic, mashed
Salt & pepper
1 cup grated Parmesan cheese

Wash the broccoli and trim off leaves and tough ends of stalks. Cook stalks upright in a minimum of lightly salted water in a covered saucepan for 15 minutes or until they are tender but firm. Drain broccoli and chop it coarsely.

Cook the pasta as directed (see How to Cook Pasta), drain, and keep hot.

Heat the olive oil well in a large skillet and cook the garlic in it until it softens, mashing it apart with a wooden spoon. Add broccoli and sauté it over moderate heat for 10 minutes, stirring to brown the pieces lightly and evenly. Season with salt and pepper to taste. Combine it with the pasta in a warm serving bowl and blend in the grated cheese. This recipe provides 6 servings.

4 | rice and polenta

As Southern Italy eats pasta, the people of the North prefer rice and the corn dish, *polenta.* While these grains are indigenous to a great area, they appear in resourcefully different interpretations from one locality of the North to the next.

Rice becomes *risotto* in a variety of preparations: with fennel or zucchini, with sweetbreads or chicken livers, molded as a complement to game birds, or glamorized—as in Milan—with saffron.

Polenta in Italy is not, as its translation into English unfortunately suggests, merely mush, but rather a delectable cornmeal combined with just the right amount of liquid, carefully stirred over gentle heat to produce a most satisfying accompaniment to the main dish, or a stellar attraction in itself.

Boiled Rice | Riso Bollito

One-third cup of raw rice, cooked in boiling water, will produce an average serving. Rice, so cooked, more than doubles in volume. For each 6 servings, therefore, cook 2 cups rice in at least 3 quarts (12 cups) rapidly boiling water, each 4 cups seasoned with 1 teaspoon salt, 14 to 20 minutes, depending upon the degree of doneness desired.

It is not usually necessary to wash packaged rice. Simply add it a little at a time, so as not to interrupt the boiling, and cook it uncovered, stirring it once or twice during the first 5 minutes. A little olive oil floated over the water will help prevent its boiling over. Test rice for doneness after the first 14 minutes of cooking by pressing a grain or two between your fingers. If rice feels slightly resistant at the center of the grains, it is *al dente,* properly cooked for most Italian-style preparations. For softer rice, continue cooking a little longer, testing after each additional minute. Do not overcook it. Rice cooked in smaller quantities of liquid and/or combined with other ingredients usually requires longer cooking over lower heat.

Drain boiled rice well and spread it in a shallow baking pan in a warm oven (not over 250 degrees) to dry somewhat. Serve the rice unadorned, as a main course accompaniment, or use it as required in the preparation of specific recipes.

Baked Rice | Risotto al Forno

1 cup dried Italian mushrooms	2 cups Chicken Broth (page 44)
¼ cup olive oil	1 Tbl finely chopped parsley
2 Tbl butter	Salt & pepper
1 medium onion, finely chopped	2 cups rice
2 small cloves garlic, peeled	⅓ cup grated Parmesan cheese
2 stalks celery, finely chopped	⅓ cup pitted black olives,
2 medium carrots, grated	finely chopped
2 cups canned,	⅓ cup pitted green olives,
peeled plum tomatoes	finely chopped

Soften the dried mushrooms in warm water. Drain and chop them finely.

Set them aside for the moment. In a skillet heat together the olive oil and butter and in them lightly brown the onion. Add the garlic, celery, and carrots, and cook them until they begin to take on a little color. Stir into them the tomatoes and continue cooking until all rendered juices evaporate. Remove and discard garlic. Add the chopped mushrooms, chicken broth, parsley, and salt and pepper to taste, and let mixture heat through.

In a large saucepan cook the rice for just 15 minutes, covered deeply with boiling water, each 2 cups seasoned with ½ teaspoon salt. Preheat oven to 350 degrees. After 15 minutes drain rice thoroughly and combine it in a casserole with the vegetable mixture. Bake rice, covered, in the preheated oven for 25 minutes or until broth is absorbed and grains of rice are tender. Sift the grated cheese over the rice and let it brown lightly, with casserole uncovered. Sprinkle top with the chopped olives, combined, and serve rice hot from casserole. Serves 6.

Rice Pilaff | Riso Pilaf

1 medium onion, finely chopped	**1 bay leaf**
¼ cup olive oil	**1 clove garlic, peeled**
2 cups rice	**Salt & pepper**
6 cups Chicken Broth, (page 44)	**4 Tbl butter**

Preheat oven to 325 degrees. In a heat-proof casserole over moderate heat lightly brown the onion in the olive oil. Add the rice, stirring it until the grains are well coated with the oil and begin to turn opaque. Heat the broth, stir it into the rice and add the bay leaf, garlic, and salt and pepper to taste, keeping in mind that broth is already salted. Bring broth to a boil and let it bubble for a moment or two. Fit heavy foil over casserole and place the lid tightly over it. Transfer casserole to the preheated oven and cook rice for 30 minutes or until grains are dry and tender. Add the butter, stirring it in lightly until it is absorbed. Serves 6.

Milanese-Style Rice: Prepare rice as for Rice Pilaff, substituting butter for the olive oil and using only 4 cups of chicken broth plus 2 cups of dry white wine with ⅛ teaspoon powdered saffron dissolved in it. Reduce final addition of butter to 2 tablespoons and add 2 tablespoons of freshly grated Parmesan cheese.

Rice Pilaff with Peas | Riso Pilaf con Piselli

6 Tbl butter
¾ pound Italian sweet sausage,
   peeled & minced
1 small onion, finely chopped
¼ cup Brown Sauce (page 269)
¼ cup water
4 cups water

1 tsp salt
2 cups rice
2 cups Chicken Broth
   (page 44), heated
⅓ cup grated Parmesan cheese
1½ cups shelled green peas
Salt & pepper

Heat the butter well in a saucepan and in it lightly brown the sausage and onion. Stir into them the brown sauce and the ¼ cup water, and let mixture heat through for just a moment. Set pan aside, off heat.

In a heavy casserole season the 4 cups water with the salt and bring liquid to a rolling boil. Stir in the rice and cook it, covered, over low heat for 10 minutes. Preheat oven to 375 degrees. Drain rice thoroughly and blend into it the heated chicken broth, the sausage mixture, and grated cheese. Cover casserole and transfer it to the preheated oven. Cook rice for 20 minutes. Uncover it, combine with it the peas, and add salt and pepper, if needed. Continue cooking for 10 minutes longer or until rice develops a nicely browned crust. Serves 6.

Home-Style Rice | Risotto Casalingo

2 Tbl olive oil
5 Tbl butter
2 small onions, finely chopped
1 cup rice
4 cups Chicken Broth (page 44),
   heated to boiling

1 bay leaf
1 pound mushrooms, sliced
6 links Italian sweet sausage
   (about 1 pound)
1 cup grated Parmesan cheese
1 Tbl finely chopped parsley

In a heavy casserole heat together the olive oil and 2 tablespoons of the butter and in it sauté the onions and rice over low heat, stirring them constantly until they begin to take on color. Stir into them the boiling hot broth, add the bay leaf, and continue cooking, with pan covered, for 25 minutes or until broth is completely absorbed and the grains of rice are tender. Preheat oven to 300 degrees.

In a skillet heat the remaining 3 tablespoons butter and in it cook the mushrooms until all rendered juice evaporates and the slices are lightly browned. Cut the sausage links into 1-inch pieces. Combine mushrooms, sausage, and ½ cup of the grated cheese with rice in the casserole. Correct the seasoning, adding salt if needed. Transfer casserole, partially covered, to the preheated oven and bake rice for 30 minutes. Remove casserole from oven. Sprinkle rice with the parsley and remaining grated cheese and serve it hot. Serves 6.

Rice Cakes with Cheese | Frittelle di Riso con Ricotta

¾ cup well-drained ricotta cheese
Salt & white pepper
6 cups Boiled Rice (page 114)
3 eggs, beaten
¼ cup finely chopped parsley
1½ cups fine dry bread crumbs
6 Tbl olive oil
6 Tbl butter

Season the cheese with salt and white pepper to taste. Shape 3 cups of the rice into 12 cakes, molding them each in a ¼-cup measure. Place 1 tablespoon of the seasoned cheese in the center of each cake. Cover each with another cake, similarly shaped, molded from the remaining rice. Press together in the palms of your hands to form a ball, enclosing cheese completely. Dip them into the beaten eggs and coat them well with the parsley and bread crumbs, combined.

In a skillet heat together enough of the olive oil and butter (about 2 tablespoons of each) to sauté 4 of the ricotta rice cakes at one time. Add more olive oil and butter as needed to complete the cooking. Brown rounds well on both sides. Drain them quickly and serve them at once. Serves 6.

Rice with Fennel, Parmesan Style |
Risotto con Finocchi alla Parmigiana

2 medium tomatoes
3 medium heads fennel
   (about 1 pound)
4 Tbl butter
1 medium onion, thinly sliced
2 cups rice

8–10 cups Beef Broth (page 44),
   heated to boiling
Salt & pepper
½ cup grated Parmesan cheese
2 Tbl finely chopped parsley

Peel, seed, and coarsely chop the tomatoes and set them aside. Wash and dry the fennel, and trim off any tough outside layers. Cut the globes into thin slices. In a heavy saucepan heat the butter and in it, over low heat, cook fennel until it is soft but not brown. Add the onion and rice and let them brown lightly. Stir into them the chopped tomatoes and 1 cup of the boiling hot broth. Increase heat slightly and cook ingredients until liquid is absorbed. Add another cup of broth. Continue replacing each cup of broth as it is absorbed until rice is tender. Season it with salt and pepper to taste and blend into it the grated cheese and chopped parsley. Serves 6.

Rice and Green Peas | Riso e Bisi

4 Tbl butter
1 Tbl olive oil
2 ounces salt pork, minced
1 pound shelled green peas
   (about 2 cups)

6½ cups Chicken Broth (page 44),
   heated to boiling
Salt & white pepper
2 cups rice
4 Tbl grated Parmesan cheese

In a heavy saucepan with a securely fitting lid heat 2 tablespoons of the butter and all of the olive oil and in them brown the bits of salt pork. Add the peas, stirring to coat them thoroughly with the fat, and pour over them ½ cup of heated broth. Add salt and white pepper to taste. Let broth bubble for a few seconds over medium heat, and add 2 more cups of it. When it boils, add the rice gradually a little at a time. Cover pan and cook over low heat for 5 minutes or until only about ⅓ cup of broth remains. Add another 2 cups and continue cooking until liquid is again reduced. Add 1 cup more of broth. By the time that broth has been almost entirely absorbed, the rice should be properly cooked, which for this preparation means *al dente* and moist. If further cooking is necessary, add remaining broth, or as much more as may be required, ½ cup at a time. Stir into the cooked rice the remaining 2 tablespoons of butter and the grated cheese. Serve rice with additional cheese, passed separately. Serves 6.

Green and White Fritters | Frittelle Bicolori

3 cups cooked spinach	**Salt & pepper**
2½ cups cooked rice	**½ cup olive oil**
1 cup grated Parmesan cheese	**¼ cup vegetable oil**
4 eggs, beaten	

Drain the spinach well and chop it finely. In a mixing bowl combine it with the rice, cheese, and eggs, and season with salt and pepper to taste. In a deep skillet heat together the olive and vegetable oils, and in it cook spoonfuls of the rice-and-spinach mixture, a few at a time, browning the fritters well on both sides. Drain them on paper toweling and transfer them to a warm serving platter. Serve them hot. Serves 6.

Rice and Zucchini | Risotto con Zucchini

6 medium zucchini, about 2 pounds	**4 cups Chicken Broth (page 44), heated**
3 Tbl butter	
1 Tbl olive oil	**Salt**
1 small onion, finely chopped	**½ cup grated Parmesan cheese**
2 cups rice	

Wash the zucchini and dry them well. Trim off the stem ends and cut the squash into slices about ½-inch thick.

Lightly brown the onion in the butter and olive oil, heated together in a heavy casserole. Add the zucchini and cook the slices until they are lightly browned and slightly softened. Combine the rice with them, stirring until grains are well coated with fat and heated through. Sprinkle combined ingredients with salt to taste and pour over them the chicken broth. Bring liquid to a boil. Cover pan, reduce heat, and cook rice and zucchini at simmer for 25 minutes, or until liquid is absorbed and rice is tender. Remove casserole from heat. Gently blend the grated cheese into rice and zucchini and serve them at once, accompanied by additional grated cheese, passed separately to be added as desired. Serves 6.

Molded Rice, Compagnale Style | Bombe di Riso alla Compagnola

4 Tbl butter

2 Tbl olive oil

1 large onion, finely chopped

¼ pound lean pork, finely ground

¼ pound lean beef, finely ground

4 cups canned, peeled
   plum tomatoes with juice

2 cups rice

3 cups Beef Broth (page 44),
   heated

1 cup grated Parmesan cheese

4 eggs, beaten

In the butter and olive oil, heated together in a saucepan, lightly brown the onion and the meats, mashing meats with a fork to break up lumps. Stir into them the tomatoes with their juice and cook them until liquid has been reduced somewhat. Add the rice and pour over it the hot broth. Stir rice to separate grains. Cover pan and cook mixture for 20 minutes or until liquid is almost entirely absorbed and rice is tender. Remove pan from heat and let mixture cool. Preheat oven to 250 degrees. Add to rice ½ cup of the grated cheese and thoroughly blend into it the beaten eggs. Pour mixture into a well buttered 8-cup mold and set mold in a pan of hot water in the preheated oven. Bake rice for 45 minutes, or until molded rice is firm. Unmold it onto a warm serving platter and sprinkle it with the remaining grated cheese. Serves 6.

Rice Croquettes | Crocchette di Riso

¼ cup olive oil

6 chicken livers

1 small onion

4 cups hot Boiled Rice (page 114)

6 Tbl butter

6 Tbl grated Parmesan cheese

1 large clove garlic
½ pound mushrooms
½ pound lean beef, finely ground
3 Tbl tomato paste
1 cup Chicken Broth (page 44)
Salt & pepper

3 egg yolks
3 egg whites
3 whole eggs
Fine dry bread crumbs
Bland cooking oil for deep frying
Sprigs of watercress

Heat the olive oil in a large skillet and in it cook the chicken livers until they begin to take on a little color and are firm. Remove them to a cutting board and chop them finely. Also finely chop the onion, garlic, and mushrooms.

In the hot oil remaining in skillet cook the onion and garlic until they are soft but not brown. Add the beef and cook it just until it loses its redness, mashing it with a wooden spoon to eliminate lumps. Add the mushrooms and, when they have been heated through, add the tomato paste and chicken broth, and salt and pepper to taste. Cover pan and continue cooking at simmer for 30 minutes or until liquid is completely absorbed. Return livers to pan and blend them into sauce.

In a mixing bowl combine the rice, butter, and grated cheese, and stir the meat sauce into them. Let mixture cool completely, and beat into it the 3 egg yolks. In another bowl beat together the 3 egg whites and the whole eggs.

Shape rice mixture into small balls. Dip them into the beaten eggs and coat them well with bread crumbs. Fry them, a few at a time, in deep hot cooking oil (370 degrees) until they are nicely browned. Drain them, arrange them on a warm serving platter, and decorate dish with sprigs of watercress. Serve the croquettes hot. Serves 6.

Rice, Fisherman's Style | Risotto del Pescatore

½ pound small shrimp
1 pound halibut
1 pound codfish
¼ cup olive oil
1 clove garlic, peeled & flattened

2 Tbl brandy
Salt & white pepper
2 cups rice
2 Tbl butter
½ cup grated Parmesan cheese

De-vein the shrimp through a slit cut into the shells with a scissors, but leave shells otherwise intact. Cook shrimp in their shells in a saucepan with 6 cups boiling water seasoned with 1 teaspoon salt for 3 minutes. Remove shrimp and shell them. Set shrimp aside. Return shells to liquid and cook them over medium heat for 15 minutes. Strain broth and reserve it. Discard shells. Bone the halibut and codfish and cut them into ¾-inch cubes.

Heat the olive oil in a heavy casserole and in it brown the garlic. Remove and discard it. Add the cubes of fish and cook them, stirring gently to brown them very lightly on all sides. Pour the brandy over them, set it ablaze, and shake the pan until the flame burns out. Remove fish to a warm side plate. Sprinkle them with salt and white pepper to taste and keep warm.

Pour into a pan the reserved shrimp broth and bring it to a boil. Add the rice and cook it, covered, over low heat for 25 minutes, or until liquid is completely absorbed and rice is tender. If more cooking is needed, add a little boiling hot water.

Stir into the cooked rice the butter and grated cheese and gently distribute through it the cubes of fish and the shrimp. Let rice and its accompaniments heat through for just a few minutes over low heat, then serve at once. Serves 6.

Rice in Squid Sauce | Risotto in Salsa di Calamari

3 large squid	3 medium tomatoes, peeled,
3 Tbl olive oil	seeded & coarsely chopped
2 small onions	Freshly ground black pepper
1 clove garlic, mashed	3 Tbl butter
1 cup red wine	1½ cups rice
1 bay leaf	3 cups Chicken Broth (page 44)

Clean the squid according to directions on page 130 and steam them (page 132). In a skillet heat the olive oil and in it cook 1 onion, sliced, and the garlic until they are soft. Cut the squid into small pieces and brown them lightly with the onion and garlic. Stir into them the wine and let it reduce almost completely. Add the tomatoes, bay leaf, and pepper to taste, and continue cooking for 15 minutes, adding a little chicken broth

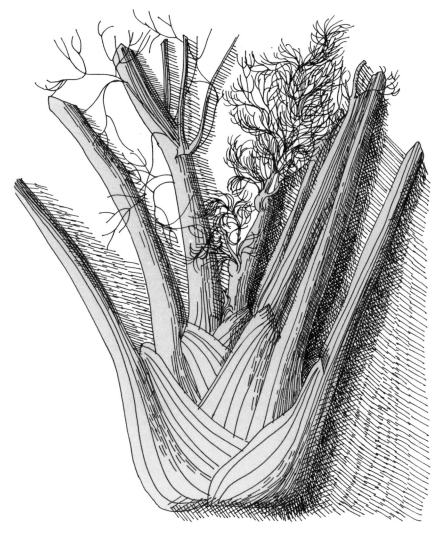

if sauce thickens excessively.

     Chop the remaining onion. Melt the butter in a heat-proof casse-role and in it lightly brown onion over low heat. Add the rice, stirring to coat grains uniformly with butter. Pour the chicken broth over rice and bring it to a boil. Cover casserole and cook rice for 20 minutes, or until liquid is completely absorbed and rice is tender. Combine squid and sauce with rice and let them heat through for a few minutes to blend the flavors. Serves 6.

Rice with Shrimp | Risotto ai Gamberi

2 pounds small shrimp
4 Tbl butter
1 small onion, thinly sliced
1 small carrot, finely chopped
4 medium tomatoes, peeled,
   seeded & coarsely chopped
¼ tsp dried thyme

1 bay leaf
1 Tbl finely chopped parsley
Salt & pepper
2 Tbl brandy
2 Tbl olive oil
2 cups rice

Cook the shrimp as directed for Boiled Shrimp (page 132), reserving the shrimp shells and the poaching broth. Cook shells in the poaching broth for 20 minutes. Remove and discard shells.

In a saucepan heat 2 tablespoons of the butter and in it lightly brown the onion and carrot together. Add the tomatoes, thyme, bay leaf, and parsley, and cook them with the onion and carrot, covered, until tomatoes are soft. Season the sauce with salt and pepper to taste and stir the brandy into it. Continue cooking until liquid evaporates somewhat. Add the shrimp and keep them warm in the sauce. Do not cook them further.

In another saucepan heat together the olive oil and remaining butter. Stir into them the rice, heating the grains until they are well coated. Reheat the prepared poaching broth and strain it into the rice. Cover pan and cook rice over low heat for 25 minutes, or until liquid is completely absorbed and rice is tender. Transfer it to a warm serving bowl and pour shrimp and sauce over it. Serve rice at once. Serves 6.

Rice with Meat | Risotto con Carne

½ cup dried Italian mushrooms
2 ounces salt pork, in small dice
1 small onion, finely chopped
6 ounces boned raw pork, veal,
   or chicken, minced
¼ cup dry white wine
¼ tsp oregano

3 cups canned,
   peeled plum tomatoes
Salt & pepper
6 cups hot Boiled Rice (page 114)
½ cup grated Parmesan cheese
3 Tbl butter

Soften the dried mushrooms in a little warm water and drain them. Set them aside. Over moderate heat try out the salt pork and when much of the fat has been rendered and it is lightly browned, add the onion and let it take on a little color. Add the meat and let it heat through. Stir the wine and oregano into it, and reduce liquid almost completely. Add the tomatoes and cook them at simmer for 10 minutes. Blend the mushrooms into them and continue cooking for 30 minutes. Season the sauce with salt and pepper to taste. Combine the rice with the sauce and stir the grated cheese and the butter into it. The flavor will improve if the dish is prepared a day in advance and reheated. Serves 6.

Rice with Sweetbreads | Risotto con Animelle

2 pairs sweetbreads	¼ pound prosciutto, minced
(about 2 pounds)	1¼ cups dry white wine
1 Tbl vinegar	3 cups Chicken Broth (page 44)
8 Tbl butter	1 bay leaf
1 medium onion, finely chopped	Salt & pepper
1½ cups rice	¼ cup grated Parmesan cheese

Soak the sweetbreads in ice-cold water for 1 hour. Drain, place in a saucepan with enough boiling water to cover, and stir into it the table-spoon of vinegar. Cook sweetbreads at simmer for 20 minutes. Drain again and cool in ice-cold water. Dry well. Remove the membranes and tissues and cut sweetbreads into medium dice. Set them aside in a warm side dish.

In another saucepan heat 3 tablespoons of the butter and in it lightly brown the onion. Add the rice and prosciutto, stirring until they are well coated with butter and heated through. Pour over them 1 cup of the wine and all of the chicken broth. Add the bay leaf and salt and pepper to taste, and bring liquid to a boil. Cover pan and cook rice over low heat for 25 minutes, or until liquid is completely absorbed and grains of rice are tender. Remove and discard bay leaf.

In a skillet heat 3 more tablespoons of the butter. Add prepared sweetbreads and brown them lightly. Season them lightly with salt and pepper. Blend the remaining wine into sweetbreads and browned bits in bottom of pan.

In a warm serving bowl combine sweetbreads and all remaining liquid with prepared rice. Stir into the mixture the remaining 2 tablespoons butter and sprinkle with the grated cheese. Serves 6.

Rice with Sausage | Risotto con Salsiccia

1 pound Italian sweet sausages
4 Tbl butter
1 small onion, thinly sliced
½ pound mushrooms, thinly sliced
4 medium tomatoes, peeled,
   seeded & chopped

Salt & pepper
4 cups Chicken Broth (page 44),
   heated to boiling
2 cups rice
1 bay leaf
¼ cup grated Romano cheese

Skin and mince the sausages. Then cook them in a saucepan with 2 tablespoons of the butter, well heated, until the bits of meat are crisp. Add the onion and cook the slices until they are soft. Combine the mushrooms with them and sauté them for a few minutes over high heat until they begin to render their liquid. Add the tomatoes and salt and pepper to taste and continue cooking, over reduced heat, for 15 minutes or until tomatoes are soft.

In a separate saucepan with the broth heated to boiling cook the rice with the bay leaf over low heat for 25 minutes or until rice is dry and tender. Remove and discard bay leaf. Transfer rice to a warm serving bowl and blend into it the remaining butter. Pour over it the prepared sauce and sprinkle with the grated Romano cheese. Serves 6.

Cornmeal Mush | Polenta

8 cups water
2 Tbl salt

1½ cups cornmeal

In a large saucepan bring the water to a rolling boil and season it with the salt. Stir the cornmeal into it, a little at a time so that the boiling is not stopped. Reduce heat to low and continue cooking, stirring almost constantly, for 30 minutes, or until the cooked cornmeal leaves sides of pan easily. For thicker polenta, to be molded and sautéed or baked, continue cooking and stirring for 15 minutes longer. This recipe will provide 6 to 8 servings.

Cornmeal Mush, Parmesan Style | Polenta alla Parmigiana

Polenta (above)
1 cup dried Italian mushrooms
   (about 1 ounce)
3 links Italian sweet sausage
   (about 6 ounces)
⅓ cup olive oil
1 medium onion, finely chopped
1 small clove garlic, mashed

1 bay leaf
¼ tsp oregano
6 cups canned,
   peeled plum tomatoes
2 Tbl finely chopped parsley
Salt & pepper
1 cup grated Parmesan cheese

Prepare polenta following basic instructions, but use 10 cups water and 2 cups cornmeal, plus the indicated quantity of salt. Cook as required for molded polenta. Transfer cooked meal to a buttered bowl and let it remain for 10 minutes or until it is firm. Turn it out onto a flat plate, cut it into moderately thick slices, and keep it warm.

Soak the dried mushrooms in warm water for 30 minutes, drain them, and chop them coarsely. Set them aside. Peel and crumble the sausage links. Heat the olive oil in a large saucepan and lightly brown the onion in it. Add the sausage, garlic, bay leaf, and oregano and let them heat through. Stir into the mixture the tomatoes, chopped mushrooms, parsley, and salt and pepper to taste. Cook the sauce, covered, for 1 hour or until the tomatoes are well cooked but still in recognizable pieces. Correct the seasoning, adding more salt, if needed. Preheat oven to 250 degrees.

Spread ¼ of the sauce over the bottom of a deep serving platter and sprinkle it with ¼ cup of the cheese. Arrange over that ⅓ of the polenta slices, overlapping them slightly. Cover them with another ¼ of the sauce and ¼ cup of the cheese. Continue so with 2 more layers of polenta, interspersing the slices with proportionate quantities of sauce and cheese. Reserve enough to cover top also. Set platter in the preheated oven and let polenta heat through. Serve it at once. This recipe will provide 6 to 8 servings.

5 | entrées

In Italian cooking, the overtures to the repast and the grand finale of the meal are frequently so impressive that they almost overshadow the entrées. Almost, but not quite. For the main dishes, too, are truly distinguished: the hardy *bollito misto* with its lusty green sauce no less than the delicate veal scallop perfumed with white truffle.

Italian waters provide fish generously and in great variety, and the Italians have evolved particularly imaginative preparations of eel, mussels, octopus, and squid. Although these dishes may be departures from universal taste, they are well worth undertaking for those who can appreciate them.

Each region of Italy has its homely specialties, some of which are now world-famous. But there are others which one rarely comes upon except in their native provinces. Here we have assembled the gusto of perhaps a dozen of these regions. Many have international repute; of the rest, many will surely achieve it.

fish and seafood

To Clean Eel

Slit skin of the eel around the neck, taking care not to sever the head. Tie a stout cord securely around the slit and fasten the cord on a nail or hook driven into a board. Using pliers, grasp skin at the slit and pull it off, downward toward the tail. Trim off fins. Cut off head and discard it. Cut a gash in the eel's underside and flush out the innards. If fish is to be boned, cut an incision along its full length on each side of the backbone. Using a piece of clean cloth in each hand, grasp the bone and the flesh, at the head end, and pull them apart. The eel may be filleted by cutting directly through it along its full length on each side of the backbone.

To Clean Mussels

Use only mussels which are firmly closed. Wash them and scrub them with a stiff brush. Remove the "beards," the tuft of bristles protruding from one side of the shells. Using a small, sharp paring knife loosen one end of the "beard" and pull it off. Place cleaned mussels in a large basin and cover with barely lukewarm water. Leave them for several minutes during which time they should rid themselves of any sand they may contain. Rinse clams again in cold water.

To Clean Squid and Octopus

To clean squid, cut across its cylindrically shaped body and pull out the translucent supporting bone. Hold the cylinder under running water and thoroughly flush out the insides, or turn the body inside out and remove them. Remove and discard head unless its use is required in recipe, in which case remove only the eyes. If the squid is to be prepared in its own ink, take care not to puncture the ink sac below the head. If not, remove and discard it. Cut out the hard, little toothlike protrusion between tentacles and discard it also. Finally, rub off the outside skin. If it is difficult to remove (which may indicate that the squid is not as young as it should be), it can be released by immersing the fish in warm water for a moment or two. Thoroughly cleaned, the squid will be snowy white, as it is meant to be.

An octopus is cleaned in much the same way, but is without a supporting bone. In its place is a papery cartilage, which should be removed along with the ink sac.

Boiled Lobster Tails | Code d'Aragosta Bollite

Broth for Poaching Fish (page 45)   **12 frozen lobster tails**

Bring the poaching broth to a boil in a large saucepan. Add the lobster tails, unthawed, and cook them at simmer for 5 minutes, timing the cooking when broth returns to boil. Cool lobster tails in broth, if they are to be served cold. Remove shells before chilling them. Serves 6 when used as an entrée.

Boiled Shrimp | Gamberetti Bolliti

2 pounds shrimp   **Broth for Poaching Fish**
                                                       (page 45)

Shell and de-vein the shrimp before cooking or clean them after they
have been cooked, as you prefer. Shelled first they are likely to be more
delicate in flavor.

Heat the poaching broth. Add the shrimp and cook them at a gentle
boil for 3 minutes (2 minutes longer if shrimp are very large). If shrimp
are to be served cold, let them cool in broth. If they have been cooked
in the shells, peel and de-vein them before chilling. Serves 6 when used
as an entrée.

Steamed Squid | Calamari a Vapore

6 cups water   **12 squid (about 3 pounds)**
1 Tbl salt

Clean the squid as directed (page 130). In a large saucepan season the
water with the salt. Bring water to a boil and add squid. Steam them,
covered, for 1 hour or until they are tender, adding boiling hot water as
needed to maintain the steam. Drain squid and cool them. Prepare them
as required in specific recipes.

Fisherman's Plate | Piatto del Pescatore

6 cooked baby lobster tails,   **12 raw cherrystone clams on**
   split lengthwise   **half shells**
3 cooked squid, in ½-inch slices   **24 cooked jumbo shrimp**
36 cooked small shrimp,   **shelled and de-veined**
   shelled and de-veined   **2 Tbl Spring Sauce (page 281)**
12 steamed mussels   **2 Tbl Green Sauce (page 274)**
                                            2 cups Cocktail Sauce (page 281)

For directions on how to cook lobster tails, squid, and shrimp see pages
130–132, for directions on how to steam mussels see Mussels in Green
Sauce (page 15). Chill all the fish and apportion them among 6 individual serving plates as follows:

In the center of each plate set a split lobster tail. Between the halves arrange ⅙ of the slices of squid and over them distribute 6 of the small shrimp. Around the lobster tail arrange in a decorative pattern 2 mussels on half shells, 2 clams on half shells, and 4 jumbo shrimp. Dress 1 mussel with 1 teaspoon spring sauce and the other with an equal quantity of green sauce. At one end of the plate set a sauce glass filled with ⅓ cup of the cocktail sauce, to be used as desired. Serves 6.

Mussels in Tomato Sauce | Cozze al Pomodoro

2 cups canned, peeled plum tomatoes	60 mussels, beards removed & scrubbed clean
3 cloves garlic, very finely chopped	Salt
⅓ cup olive oil	⅛ tsp freshly ground pepper
1 cup white wine	2 Tbl chopped parsley

Drain the plum tomatoes and chop them coarsely. In a large saucepan over gentle heat cook the garlic in the oil until the bits just begin to take on color. Add the wine and reduce it over high heat to ½ cup. Lower heat, stir in the tomatoes, and heat them through. Add the mussels and steam them, covered, until the shells open. Discard immediately any that do not open.

Transfer mussels, in their shells, to a serving bowl. Season the sauce with salt, if needed, and with the pepper. Pour sauce over mussels and sprinkle them with the chopped parsley. Serves 6.

Shrimp Sailor Style | Gamberi alla Marinara

48 large raw shrimp (about 3 pounds)	4 cups canned, peeled plum tomatoes with juice
1 small onion, finely chopped	¼ tsp oregano
2 cloves garlic, minced	Salt & pepper
⅓ cup olive oil	1 Tbl finely chopped parsley
2 Tbl dry white wine	

Shell and de-vein the shrimp. Set them aside for the moment. In a large saucepan over moderate heat lightly brown the onion and garlic in the olive oil. Blend in the wine, stirring up the cooking glaze at the bottom of pan. Add the tomatoes with their juice, the oregano, and salt and pepper to taste, and continue cooking for 10 minutes. Add the shrimp and cook them in the sauce for 5 minutes. Serve over Rice Pilaff (page 115) sprinkled with the chopped parsley. Serves 6.

Skewered Shrimp | Spiedini di Gamberi

36 large shrimp	**1½ cups raw rice**
½ pound prosciutto, thinly sliced	**½ cup olive oil**
3 cups bouillon	**⅓ cup finely chopped onion**
1 clove garlic, peeled	**1 cup canned**
1 small bay leaf	**plum tomatoes with juice**
1 Tbl butter	**¼ cup butter, melted**
1 tsp salt	

Shell and de-vein the shrimp. Cut the prosciutto into strips about 2 by 3 inches. Roll each shrimp in a strip of prosciutto. Thread 6 wrapped shrimp, in pairs, seam to seam on each skewer.

In a large saucepan combine the bouillon, garlic, bay leaf, butter, and salt, and bring the liquid to a boil over high heat. Stir in the rice and,

Quail baked in a rich brown sauce and served in a molded ring of rice make a handsome entrée.

when liquid returns to boil, reduce heat, cover pan securely, and cook rice at simmer for 25 minutes, or until all the liquid is absorbed and the grains are tender. Remove and discard herbs. Preheat oven to 400 degrees.

In another saucepan heat the olive oil and in it lightly brown the onion. Add the tomatoes and their juice and cook mixture at simmer for 10 minutes, or until liquid is absorbed. Combine the onion and tomatoes with the cooked rice and keep warm.

Arrange skewered shrimp in a baking dish and brush them with the melted butter. Set pan in the preheated oven and bake shrimp for 10 minutes. Mold rice mixture on a warm serving platter and arrange skewered shrimp over it. Remove the skewers. Pour Sauce for Shrimp (see below) over the prosciutto-enclosed shrimp and garnish the platter with wedges of lemon and sprigs of parsley. Serves 6.

Sauce for Shrimp:

⅓ cup butter

2 cloves garlic, mashed

¼ cup dry white wine

¼ cup lemon juice

2 leaves fresh basil
  (or ¼ tsp dried basil), crushed

Salt & pepper

1 Tbl chopped parsley

In a saucepan over low heat lightly brown the garlic in the butter. Stir in the wine and lemon juice, add the basil, and cook the sauce at simmer for 15 minutes. Remove and discard garlic. Season sauce with salt and pepper to taste, and blend in the chopped parsley.

Red Snapper alla Zoni | Branzino alla Zoni

⅓ cup olive oil

6 fillets of red snapper
  (6–8 ounces each)

Salt & white pepper

Flour

2 cups sliced mushrooms

⅓ cup medium-dry white wine

⅓ cup lemon juice

6 Tbl butter, in small pieces

⅓ cup toasted pine nuts

Orange sections

3 Tbl finely chopped parsley

Wedges of lemon

Preheat oven to 350 degrees. Heat the oil in a large shallow pan. Season the fillets with salt and white pepper to taste, and dredge them lightly

Spiedini of Lamb: Strips of peppers, mushrooms, and cubes of lamb are marinated in a spicy sauce, then skewered, and baked in the Italian manner.

in flour. Arrange them, skin sides down, in the pan and sauté them for 3 minutes. Turn them carefully and surround them with the mushrooms. Set pan in the preheated oven and continue cooking for 5 minutes. Remove pan from oven and, taking care not to dislodge the fish and mushrooms, drain off all remaining oil. Return pan to top of stove over low heat. Combine the wine, lemon juice, and bits of butter, and pour the mixture over the fish and mushrooms. Distribute the pine nuts over the surface. Cook the fish and mushrooms for a final 3 to 4 minutes, basting them frequently with the liquid in pan. Arrange fish and mushrooms on a warm serving platter. Scatter orange sections over top and sprinkle with the chopped parsley. Decorate platter with wedges of lemon. Serves 6.

Trout with Pine Nuts and Mushrooms | Trota ai Pignoli e Funghi

6 trout (about 10 ounces each)
Salt & pepper
Flour
4 Tbl olive oil
½ cup butter
2 bunches scallions,
    white parts only, thinly sliced

½ pound mushrooms, thinly sliced
1 cup pine nuts
¼ cup dry white wine
¼ cup lemon juice
Salt & white pepper

Clean and bone the trout. Season them with salt and pepper to taste and dredge lightly with flour. In a skillet heat 2 tablespoons of the olive oil and in it sauté 3 of the trout over moderate heat for about 6 minutes in all, or until they are well browned on both sides and tender. Turn fish just once. Remove trout to a warm serving platter and keep them warm. Cook the other 3 trout in the same way in as much of the remaining olive oil as needed. Transfer these trout also to the serving platter. Drain off all the oil remaining in skillet. Heat the butter in that pan and in it gently sauté the scallions until they are soft but not brown. Add the mushrooms, increase heat to high, and cook mushrooms until they begin to brown. Stir the pine nuts into the scallions and mushrooms and let them heat through. Pour the wine and lemon juice into the mixture and season with salt and white pepper to taste. Pour mixture around fish in the serving platter and serve at once. Serves 6.

Fillets of Sole with Almonds | Filetti di Sogliole alle Mandorle

6 fillets of sole (about 2½ pounds)
Salt & pepper
Flour
½ cup butter
½ cup thinly sliced almonds

½ cup dry white wine,
   heated slightly
Juice of ½ lemon, strained
1 Tbl finely chopped Italian parsley
Wedges of lemon
Sprigs of parsley

Season the fillets of sole with salt and pepper to taste and dredge them lightly in flour. Heat 6 tablespoons of the butter in a large skillet and in it cook the fillets until they are tender, but still firm, browning them lightly on both sides. Stir in the almonds around the fish, browning them lightly also. Pour the heated wine around fish and cook at bare simmer for 2 minutes longer. Transfer fillets to a warm serving platter and keep them warm. Blend the lemon juice into the ingredients in pan. Increase heat and let mixture bubble for a few moments until liquid is reduced to about ⅓ cup. Blend into it the chopped parsley and the remaining butter. Pour sauce over fillets in the serving platter and garnish with the lemon wedges and sprigs of parsley. Serves 6.

Fillets of Sole, Marechiaro Style | Sogliole alla Marechiaro

6 fillets of sole (2½–3 pounds)	2 cloves garlic, finely chopped
Salt & pepper	¼ cup dry white wine
Flour	½ cup Marinara Sauce (page 277)
4 Tbl butter	1 Tbl finely chopped parsley
2 Tbl olive oil	Wedges of lemon

Season the fish lightly with salt and pepper and dredge them with flour. Heat the butter and olive oil together in a skillet. Add fillets of sole and cook them, turning them once, until they are lightly browned on both sides and flake easily when tested with a fork. Transfer fish to a warm serving platter and keep them warm. In the butter and oil remaining in the skillet sauté the garlic until the bits are soft but not browned. Stir in the wine and continue cooking, over moderate heat, until it is reduced almost to a glaze. Decrease heat, add the marinara sauce, and let it heat through. Pour sauce over fish and sprinkle with the parsley. Decorate platter with wedges of lemon. Serves 6.

Marinated Fillets of Sole Eva | Filetti di Sogliole alla Eva

6 fillets of sole (2½–3 pounds)	2 bay leaves
Flour	3 Tbl seedless white raisins
1⅓ cups olive oil	3 Tbl pine nuts
Salt	2 cloves
2 medium onions, thinly sliced	½-inch stick cinnamon, crushed
½ cup white vinegar	¼ tsp pepper
½ cup dry white wine	

Dredge the fish lightly in flour and sauté them in ⅓ cup of the olive oil, browning them on both sides, but turning them only once. Drain fish on paper toweling and sprinkle with salt.

Add another tablespoon of oil to that remaining in the skillet and heat it. Add the onions and brown them lightly. Stir into them the vinegar, wine, and bay leaves and continue cooking at simmer for a few minutes. Remove pan from heat and blend into the mixture the remaining olive oil. Arrange fish in a single layer in a glass baking dish and pour the oil and vinegar blend, with onions and bay leaves, over them. Sprinkle with the raisins, pine nuts, cloves, cinnamon, and pepper. Cover dish with plastic wrap and place in refrigerator. Let fish marinate so for 24 hours. Before serving, drain off the liquid only and remove bay leaves. Serves 6.

fowl and game

Breast of Chicken, Valle d'Aosta Style |
Petti di Pollo alla Valdostana

6 whole chicken breasts
    (about 1 pound each)
	3 white truffles (about ½ ounce),
	    sliced paper thin

Salt & white pepper	**12 thin slices Fontina cheese**
Flour	**¾ cup dry white wine**
7 Tbl butter	**¾ cup Chicken Broth (page 44)**
¼ cup brandy	

Split the chicken breasts into halves, bone them, remove skin, and flatten the meat slightly with a pounder. Sprinkle the breasts lightly with salt and white pepper and dredge them with flour. In a large skillet heat 3 tablespoons of the butter and in it gently sauté 6 of the breast halves for 10 to 12 minutes, turning them once midway during the cooking. Remove them to a side platter and keep them warm. Add as much more of the remaining butter as needed, but reserving 1 tablespoon, and cook the remaining 6 breast halves in the same way. Return the first 6 to the skillet and pour the brandy over all of them. Set the spirit ablaze and let flame burn out. Transfer breasts to a shallow broiler pan and distribute the truffle slices equally over them. Cover with the slices of cheese.

De-glaze the skillet by stirring the wine and broth into the brown glaze at the bottom. Add salt and white pepper to taste. Over moderate heat reduce liquid until it begins to thicken. Stir in the reserved tablespoon of butter. Keep sauce warm. Place the broiler pan with the chicken breasts under a medium-hot broiler and leave it just long enough to melt the cheese. Serve the breasts at once, 2 to a serving, with the sauce passed separately. Serves 6.

Broiled and Baked Chicken | Pollo ai Ferri

3 broiling chickens
   (about 2 pounds each), split
1½ cups olive oil
1½ cups white wine vinegar
½ tsp dried oregano

1 Tbl fresh basil
   (or ¼ tsp dried basil)
1 Tbl salt
⅓ cup dry white wine
Wedges of lemon
Sprigs of parsley

Place the halves of chicken in a flat pan in a single layer and pour over them a marinade composed of the olive oil, vinegar, oregano, basil, and salt thoroughly combined. Let chickens remain in the marinade for 2 hours, turning the halves from time to time to season them uniformly. Drain chickens and arrange the halves, skin sides up, in a broiler pan and brown them nicely, the skin sides only, under a hot broiler. Preheat oven to 400 degrees. Transfer the halves to a baking pan in the oven and continue cooking them for 30 minutes, turning them once midway during the cooking and basting them occasionally with a little of the marinade. Remove the halves to a warm serving platter and keep them warm. Stir the white wine into the residue in the baking pan and heat it through quickly on top of stove. Pour sauce over chicken and serve it at once, garnishing platter with wedges of lemon and sprigs of parsley. Serves 6.

Chicken Giacomo | Pollo alla Giacomo

1 tsp salt
¼ tsp white pepper
¼ tsp dried basil
¼ tsp dried oregano
¼ tsp cayenne pepper
½ tsp ground ginger
¼ tsp dried tarragon
¼ tsp chili powder
3 chickens (2½ pounds each),
   in serving pieces

½ cup olive oil
2 medium onions, thinly sliced
1 bay leaf
¾ pound fresh mushrooms,
   thinly sliced vertically
½ cup white rum
3 cups canned,
   peeled plum tomatoes
¼ cup chopped parsley

Prepare a seasoning mixture by thoroughly combining in a mixing bowl

all of the ingredients through the chili powder. Sprinkle the pieces of chicken with all of the mixture.

In a large skillet heat the olive oil and in it cook the chicken until the pieces begin to take on color. Add the onions and bay leaf and continue cooking until the onions are soft. Stir the sliced mushrooms into the seasoned chicken and onions, continuing to stir until the mushrooms have rendered their juice. Add the white rum and blend in the tomatoes. Cook the chicken so, uncovered, for 10 minutes, stirring ingredients from time to time to prevent their sticking to the pan. Add the parsley, cover pan, and cook chicken for 20 minutes longer, or until tender. Serves 6.

Breast of Chicken in Brandied Meat Sauce |
Petti di Pollo alla Fabrizio

3 whole chicken breasts	**6 Tbl brandy**
Salt & pepper	**½ cup Meat Sauce for Pasta**
Flour	**(page 279)**
6 Tbl butter	**¼ cup heavy cream**

Split the chicken breasts into halves, bone them, and remove skin. Flatten them slightly with a meat pounder or the flat of a cleaver, season with salt and pepper to taste, and dredge them in flour. Heat the butter in a skillet large enough to accommodate the 6 breast halves, add them, and brown them well over moderate heat. Pour the brandy over them and set the spirit ablaze. Let flame burn out and stir the meat sauce into the juices in pan. Cook chicken, covered, for 10 minutes or until it is tender. Remove the breasts to a warm serving platter and keep them warm. Stir the cream into the meat sauce and heat mixture through without letting it boil. Pour sauce over chicken in serving platter and serve it at once. Serves 6.

Chicken, Hunter's Style | Pollo alla Cacciatora

½ cup dried Italian mushrooms	**½ pound fresh mushrooms,**
¼ cup olive oil	**thinly sliced**
½ cup butter	**1 small stalk celery, thinly sliced**
2 broiling or frying chickens	**1 small carrot, slivered**
(3 pounds each), in pieces	**1½ pounds tomatoes, peeled,**
1 medium onion, finely chopped	**seeded & chopped**
4 large shallots, finely chopped	**2 Tbl chopped parsley**
1 bay leaf	**1 cup Chicken Broth (page 44)**
½ cup dry white wine	**or more as needed**
	Salt & pepper

Soak the dried mushrooms in warm water for 30 minutes, drain, and chop them. Heat the olive oil and ¼ cup of the butter in a skillet and in it brown the pieces of chicken, a few at a time, transferring them to a large heatproof casserole as they are cooked. In the fat remaining in the skillet

cook the onion and shallots until they are soft and add them to the
chicken in the casserole, along with the bay leaf. De-glaze the pan by
pouring into it the white wine and blending it with the browned bits. Pour
wine over chicken. Set casserole over low heat to keep chicken warm.

In another skillet sauté the fresh mushrooms in 3 tablespoons of the
remaining butter, browning them lightly, and add them to chicken. Heat
the remaining tablespoon of butter in the skillet and in it just heat together the slivers of celery and carrot. Stir them into ingredients in casserole along with the softened dried mushrooms, the tomatoes, 1 tablespoon of the parsley, and ½ cup of the broth. Cover casserole and cook
chickens over moderate heat for 30 minutes or until chickens are tender.
Season them with salt and pepper to taste and continue cooking for 2 or
3 minutes longer. Add more broth during the cooking if the liquid cooks
away. Remove the pieces of chicken to a warm serving platter and keep
them warm. Remove and discard bay leaf. If sauce is now too thin,
reduce it over high heat, stirring it constantly. Pour it over the chicken
pieces, sprinkle with the remaining parsley, and serve at once. Serves 6.

Roman-Style Chicken | Pollo alla Romana

2 3-pound chickens,
   in serving pieces
Flour
¼ cup olive oil
¼ cup butter
Salt & pepper

1½ cups dry white wine
2 tsp finely chopped fresh rosemary
   (or ¼ tsp dried rosemary)
2 Tbl finely chopped Italian parsley
1 cup heavy cream, heated

Dredge the chicken lightly in flour. Heat the olive oil and butter together
in a skillet and brown the chicken pieces in it. Transfer the pieces to a
heat-proof casserole and keep them warm. Sprinkle them with salt and
pepper to taste. Drain the fat from the skillet. De-glaze skillet by pouring
the white wine into it and stirring up the browned bits remaining at the
bottom. Add the herbs and pour the seasoned wine over chicken in
casserole. Cover casserole and cook chicken over low heat for 45 minutes, or until tender. Baste frequently. Blend the cream into the cooking
liquid during the last 10 minutes. Serve chicken with the sauce. Serves 6.

Chicken Tetrazzini | Pollo alla Tetrazzini

1 large carrot
1 medium onion
2 stalks celery
2 3-pound frying chickens, halved
1 small clove garlic, peeled
½ tsp peppercorns
Salt
4 Tbl butter
¾ pound fresh mushrooms,
   sliced (about 2½ cups)

¼ pound cooked ham,
   in julienne strips
½ cup dry sherry
3 cups heavy cream
1 white truffle, chopped
   (about 2 Tbl) (optional)
Salt & white pepper
4 cups cooked spaghetti
⅓ cup freshly grated
   Parmesan cheese
1 Tbl finely chopped parsley

Peel and coarsely chop the carrot and the onion. Scrape and coarsely chop the stalks of celery. In a large saucepan combine the vegetables, chicken, garlic, and peppercorns. Pour over them enough cold water to cover chicken halves completely and add 1 teaspoon salt to each 2 cups of water used. Bring water slowly to a boil and skim it. Cover pan and cook chicken for 45 minutes or until tender. Remove chicken and when cool enough to handle, skin the halves and remove the bones. Cut meat into bite-size cubes. Four cups are required for this recipe, reserve the remaining chicken under refrigeration for other uses. Strain and reserve the broth also for use as a base for soup or as required.

Heat the butter in a skillet and in it cook the mushrooms over high heat until the slices are lightly browned and their rendered liquid has evaporated. Add the ham and sauté the bits for a moment or two. Combine mushrooms, ham, and prepared chicken in a saucepan. De-glaze the skillet by blending the sherry into the brown bits remaining in the pan. Reduce wine over moderate heat to ¼ cup and pour it over chicken mixture in saucepan. In the skillet heat the cream and blend it also into chicken mixture. If truffle is used, add it at this point along with salt and white pepper to taste. Cook the mixture gently, without boiling, for 5 minutes to blend the flavors.

In a flame-proof serving platter make a nest of the cooked spaghetti and pour the prepared chicken into it. Sift the Parmesan cheese over chicken. Set platter under a hot broiler and let it remain until the cheese

is lightly browned. Sprinkle with the chopped parsley and serve at once.
Serves 6.

Chicken in White Wine | Pollo al Vino Bianco

**2 broiling or frying chickens
(3 pounds each), in pieces**
Flour
⅓ cup olive oil
6 Tbl butter
Salt & pepper
½ cup finely chopped shallots

¼ tsp dried rosemary
⅛ tsp dried sage
3 cups dry white wine
1 cup Chicken Broth (page 44)
⅓ cup heavy cream, lightly whipped
2 Tbl chopped Italian parsley

Dredge the chicken pieces in flour. In a large skillet heat together as
much of the olive oil and butter as may be needed to brown a few pieces
of the chicken at a time. After browning them, season with salt and pep-

per to taste, and transfer to a large heat-proof casserole. In the oil and butter remaining in the skillet cook the shallots over low heat until they are soft. Add the dried herbs and wine. Increase heat to high and continue cooking until the wine is reduced to about 1½ cups. Decrease the heat again and combine the broth with the reduced wine. Let mixture heat through and pour it over the chicken in casserole. Cover pan and cook chicken over moderate heat for 45 minutes or until tender. Transfer the pieces of chicken to a warm serving platter and keep them warm. Strain sauce and return it to the casserole. Blend into it the lightly whipped cream and reheat the sauce without letting it boil. Pour sauce over chicken and sprinkle with the chopped parsley. Serves 6.

Cornmeal Mush with Chicken Livers |
Polenta con Fegatini di Pollo

Soft Polenta (page 126)	½ tsp chopped fresh sage
6 slices lean bacon	(or ⅛ tsp dried sage, crushed)
2 Tbl butter	1½ cups Brown Sauce II
18 chicken livers,	(page 270), heated
sinews removed & halved	Salt & pepper
	1 Tbl chopped parsley

Prepare polenta as directed in recipe and keep it warm in a serving bowl.

Place the bacon in a cold skillet. Set pan over medium-low heat and cook the slices until they are crisp but not too brown. Remove slices and set them aside to drain on paper toweling. Add the butter to the bacon fat in skillet and heat it. Add the chicken livers and cook them briskly for 2 minutes, stirring them constantly but gently to brown them uniformly. Drain off fat. Sprinkle livers with the sage and pour over them the heated brown sauce. Add salt and pepper to taste. Cook livers, at simmer for 3 to 4 minutes longer. Pour them along with sauce over the polenta in serving dish and sprinkle with the crisp bacon, crumbled, and the chopped parsley. Serve the livers at once. Serves 6.
NOTE: Cooked as these are, the livers will be pink inside. For well-done chicken livers increase cooking time by 3 to 4 minutes. Do not overcook them or they will be rubbery and tough.

Chicken Livers, Torino Style | Fegatini di Pollo alla Torinese

8 shallots, finely chopped
¼ cup olive oil
2 Tbl butter
2 pounds chicken livers,
    sinews removed

1 tsp finely chopped fresh basil
    (or ¼ tsp dried basil, crushed)
½ cup dry vermouth, heated
Salt & pepper
Chopped parsley
Rice Pilaff (page 115)

Cook the shallots, in the olive oil and butter heated together in a skillet, until they are soft but not browned. Increase heat, and add the chicken livers, stirring to brown them evenly. After 2 minutes add the basil and vermouth and continue cooking for 3 minutes longer. Season livers with salt and pepper to taste and sprinkle with a little parsley. Serve with Rice Pilaff. Serves 6.

Turkey Pappagallo | Tacchino alla Pappagallo

2 pounds boned & skinned
    breast of turkey
Flour, lightly seasoned with salt
3 eggs, beaten
6 cooked artichoke hearts

½ cup butter
1½ cups dry white wine
2 cups heavy cream
Salt & pepper
Finely chopped parsley

With a meat pounder or the flat of a cleaver pound the turkey meat to a thickness of about ⅛ inch and cut it into 12 slices of equal size. Dredge slices lightly with the flour and coat them with the beaten eggs. Dredge and coat the artichoke hearts similarly.

Cook turkey in butter, heated in a large skillet, using 2 tablespoons for each 4 slices. Cook slices over moderate heat for 5 minutes, turning once to brown them lightly on each side. Transfer slices to a warm side dish as they are cooked, and keep them warm. Brown the artichokes also on both sides, in same pan, augmenting the butter remaining in skillet as needed. Keep them warm in a side dish also.

Drain off butter remaining in skillet and de-glaze the pan by stirring into it the white wine. Increase heat to high and let wine boil down to ½ cup. Decrease heat again, add the cream, and cook mixture at simmer

until it thickens somewhat. Return the slices of turkey to skillet and let them heat through in the sauce. Arrange slices on a warm serving platter. Season the sauce with salt and pepper to taste and pour it over turkey slices. Sprinkle it with a little parsley and garnish platter with the artichoke hearts. Serve the turkey hot with rice, if desired. Serves 6.
NOTE: You may use either fresh artichoke hearts or drained canned ones.

Quail with Molded Rice | Sformato di Risotto con Quaglie

Rice with Meat (page 124)	1 clove garlic, mashed
Vegetable shortening	⅓ cup dry white wine
Fine dry bread crumbs	¾ cup red wine
6 slices fat bacon	½ cup Chicken Broth (page 44)
12 quail	¼ tsp dried sage
2 Tbl olive oil	1 bay leaf
2 ounces salt pork,	Salt & pepper
cut into small dice	Sprigs of watercress or parsley
1 medium onion, finely chopped	

Prepare Rice with Meat as indicated in the recipe, but omit the salt pork and reduce the other meat to 1 cup. Preheat oven to 350 degrees. Grease an 8- to 9-cup ring mold heavily with vegetable shortening and coat it with bread crumbs. Fill mold with the rice preparation, pressing it down level with top of container. Set mold in the preheated oven and let rice heat for 30 minutes. Remove pan and unmold rice on a serving platter. Keep it warm.

Cook the bacon in a large skillet until the slices are crisp but not too brown. Drain bacon on paper toweling and reserve. Retain the fat in skillet and reheat it. Add the quail and sauté them, turning them frequently until they are lightly and evenly browned. Remove quail to a large oven-proof casserole and keep warm. Drain off the bacon fat and discard it. Heat the olive oil in the skillet and in it lightly brown the salt pork. Add the onion and garlic and, when they are lightly browned, stir into them the wines, broth, sage, and bay leaf. Bring liquid to a boil and let it cook at simmer for a few minutes to blend the flavors. Season it with salt and pepper to taste and pour it over quail in casserole. Set pan in oven, still at 350 degrees, and cook the birds, covered, for 20 minutes, or until they are tender. Baste them frequently. Remove quail and arrange them, each with a slice of the reserved bacon, around the rice ring in the platter. Fill center of ring with sprigs of watercress or parsley.

Strain the sauce into a pan and, if desired, thicken it slightly over low heat by blending into it ½ teaspoon kneaded butter, that is, ¼ teaspoon each of butter and flour kneaded together. Strain sauce into a warm sauce boat and pass separately. This recipe provides 12 modest servings or 6 generous ones.

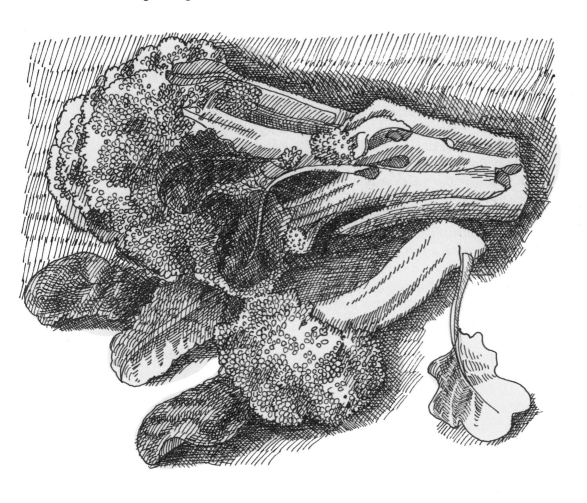

Stewed Rabbit with Polenta, Bergamo Style |
Coniglio con Polenta alla Bergamasca

½ cup dried Italian mushrooms
  (about ½ ounce)
2 young rabbits,
  (about 2½ pounds each)
⅓ cup olive oil
6 Tbl butter
½ cup chopped onion
1 large clove garlic,
  peeled & mashed
¼ cup chopped shallots

6 medium tomatoes, peeled,
  seeded & chopped
½ cup red wine, heated slightly
6 cups Chicken Broth (page 44)
⅔ cup chopped parsley
1 tsp chopped fresh sage leaves
  (or ¼ tsp dried sage, crumbled)
½ tsp rosemary
Salt & pepper
1 recipe thick Polenta (page 126)

Soften the dried mushrooms in warm water for 30 minutes, then squeeze them almost dry. Set them aside. Clean the rabbits and cut them into serving-size pieces. Wash the pieces well in cold water and dry them thoroughly. Put rabbit pieces in a large saucepan over moderate heat and stir them constantly with a spoon until they render most of their water content. Remove pieces and drain them in a colander. In another saucepan heat together the olive oil and butter. Add the onion and garlic, and cook over low heat until they take on a little color. Add the shallots and continue to cook until they are soft, but not browned. Stir in the tomatoes and cook mixture at a simmer for 5 minutes. Add the pieces of rabbit to tomato mixture and pour the warm wine over them. Continue cooking until wine is reduced to ½ its volume. Stir in the chicken broth along with ⅓ cup of the chopped parsley, the sage, rosemary, mushrooms, and salt and pepper to taste. Cover pan and cook rabbit, at simmer, for 1 hour or until tender.

Turn the thick polenta into a bowl and let it remain until it is firm. Keep it warm. Unmold polenta, cut it into thick slices and arrange them, overlapping somewhat, around the rim of a warm serving platter.

Remove the pieces of rabbit from saucepan and arrange them in the center of polenta. Reduce the cooking liquid over high heat until it thickens somewhat and pour it over rabbit and polenta in serving platter. Sprinkle the dish with the remaining chopped parsley and serve it immediately. Serves 6.

Red Snapper alla Zoni combines pine nuts,
mushrooms, and orange sections with red snapper fillets
for an unusual and welcome fish variation.

meat

Medallions of Beef in Wine Sauce |
Medaglioni di Manzo in Salsa di Vino

12 slices fillet of beef	1 tsp flour
(4 ounces each)	1 cup red wine
Salt & pepper	¼ cup Fresh-Tomato Purée
2 Tbl olive oil	(page 281)
2 Tbl butter	2 Tbl finely chopped parsley

Season the fillets lightly with salt and pepper. In a skillet large enough to accommodate 6 slices of the beef heat 1 tablespoon each of the olive oil and butter. When the fat is very hot add 6 slices of the fillet and cook over high heat for a total of 1½ minutes for rare meat, 2 minutes for medium done, and 3 minutes for well done, turning slices once midway during cooking. Transfer slices to a warm serving platter and keep them warm. Heat as much more of the remaining olive oil and butter as may be needed in the skillet. Add the remaining 6 slices of beef and cook them also to the desired degree of doneness. Transfer to the serving platter with others and keep them warm.

Drain off all but 2 teaspoons of the fat remaining in skillet. Blend in the flour and let it brown lightly over moderate heat. Add the wine and tomato purée gradually, stirring constantly to produce a smooth sauce. Correct the seasoning, adding salt and pepper if needed. Pour sauce over the slices of fillet and sprinkle with the chopped parsley. Serve at once. Serves 6.

Fillet of Beef Surprise | Filetto di Manzo a Sorpresa

6 slices fillet of beef	Salt & pepper
(6–8 ounces each)	Flour
6 thin slices prosciutto	3 eggs, beaten
6 thin slices mozzarella cheese	¼ cup olive oil
¼ pound fresh mushrooms,	1 cup red wine
very thinly sliced	1 Tbl minced parsley
3 Tbl butter	

Cut a deep pocket into each slice of beef, and trim the prosciutto and

Eva's Marinated Fillet of Beef, flavored with bay leaf, rosemary, sage, and onions, is excellent choice for a hot summer's evening because it can be made ahead and served cold.

cheese to fit the pockets. In a large skillet over moderate heat sauté the mushrooms in 2 tablespoons of the butter until they are lightly browned and have rendered some of their juices. Transfer mushrooms to a bowl. In same skillet, without additional fat, lightly sauté the prosciutto. Arrange the slices of prosciutto each on a slice of cheese and spread them equally with the cooked mushrooms. Season the slices of fillet inside the pockets with salt and pepper to taste, keeping in mind that the prosciutto will impart some if its salt also to the meat. Fit the 3-layered arrangements each into a pocket in the beef. Dredge fillets lightly in flour, place them in a single layer in a deep dish, and pour the beaten eggs over them. Let them remain so for 5 minutes. Turn and leave them for 5 minutes longer.

Heat the olive oil in the skillet. Drain fillets, arrange them in skillet, and cook them over moderate heat to degree of doneness desired: 2 minutes on each side for rare, 3 minutes for medium, and 5 minutes for well done. Remove cooked fillets to a warm serving platter and keep them warm. Drain off oil remaining in skillet and discard it. Over the heat de-glaze skillet by pouring the wine into it and stirring up the brown bits at the bottom. Reduce wine to about ½ cup and stir the remaining butter into it. Correct the seasoning, adding salt and pepper as needed. Cook sauce at simmer for 2 minutes or until it thickens slightly and pour it over the meat in the serving platter. Sprinkle fillets with the minced parsley and serve them at once. Serves 6.

Eva's Marinated Fillet of Beef | Filetto Marinato alla Eva

¼ **cup olive oil**
2 medium onions, finely sliced
2 cloves garlic, mashed
2 Tbl chopped Italian parsley
1 bay leaf, crumbled
¼ **tsp dried rosemary**
4 fresh sage leaves
   (or ⅛ tsp dried sage)

2 tsp sugar
1 tsp salt
¼ **tsp freshly ground pepper**
1 cup red wine vinegar
1 cup dry white wine
1 cup Beef Broth (page 44)
3 pounds rare roast fillet of beef,
   cooled

Heat the oil in a stainless steel or enamel-coated saucepan and in it

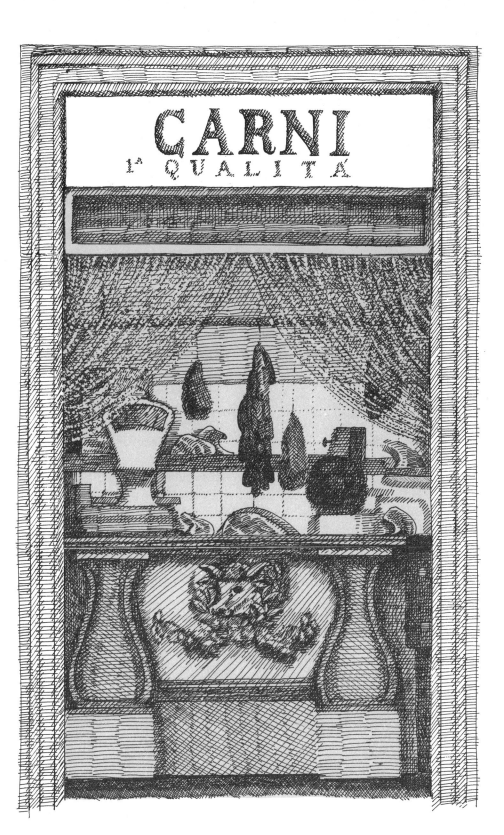

lightly brown the onions and garlic. Add the remaining seasonings and the vinegar, and cook the mixture over high heat for 5 minutes, or until the liquid has been almost entirely absorbed or has evaporated. Blend in the wine and beef broth and continue to cook for 10 minutes longer.

Cut the fillets into moderately thin slices. Arrange them, overlapping somewhat, in a glass or enamel-coated baking dish, and pour hot marinade over them. Chill beef in marinade for at least 12 hours. Serves 6.

Serve with accompaniments of freshly ground pepper, celery or fresh fennel, and crusty Italian bread, and all or some of the following: artichoke hearts in oil, pickles, olives, and pickled peppers.

Pot Roast with Barolo Wine | Stracotto al Barolo

4-pound piece top round of beef, trimmed of fat
Salt & pepper
Flour
⅔ cup olive oil
1 medium onion, coarsely chopped
1 stalk celery, coarsely chopped
1 large carrot, coarsely chopped
1 bay leaf
1 large clove garlic, peeled
2 cups Barolo (Italian red wine)
1 cup Beef Broth (page 44)
½ pound button mushrooms, washed & trimmed
1½ cups cooked tiny onions, or canned onions, drained
1 Tbl butter
½ cup cooked green peas

Season the meat with salt and pepper to taste and dredge it well with the flour. In a large skillet heat ⅓ cup of the olive oil and in it brown the meat well on all sides. Remove meat to a large, heavy heat-proof casserole and keep it warm over low heat. In the oil remaining in skillet brown all together the onion, celery, and carrot and add them, along with the bay leaf and garlic, to the beef in casserole. In a small saucepan heat together the Barolo wine and the beef broth, and pour it over the meat. There should not be more than an inch or so of liquid in casserole. Cover pan and cook meat at simmer for 3 hours or until it is tender, turning it several times during the cooking. If liquid cooks away add more wine and broth in the original proportions. Remove the cooked meat to a side platter and keep it warm. Strain the sauce and discard the solids. If sauce is in excess of 1 cup return it to casserole and reduce it over moderate heat to that quantity.

In a saucepan heat the remaining olive oil and in it, over high heat, sauté the mushrooms until they are lightly browned. Drain off oil and add the cooked onions and the strained sauce. Cook mixture at simmer for 5 minutes, and stir into it the tablespoon of butter. Continue cooking for a moment or two longer until the sauce thickens a bit more, stirring it constantly.

Cut the beef into thin slices. Arrange slices on a warm serving platter and pour the sauce and vegetables over them. Sprinkle with the cooked peas. This recipe provides 6 to 8 servings.

Beefsteak and Peppers | Bistecca alla Peperonata

2 large green peppers	1½ cups Marinara Sauce (page 277)
3 Tbl olive oil	6 porterhouse steaks, boned
3 Tbl butter	(about 8 ounces each)
1 medium onion, thinly sliced	Salt & pepper
2 medium mushrooms, thinly sliced	¼ cup red wine
1 bay leaf	

Core and seed the peppers, and cut them into short, thin strips. In a skillet heat 1 tablespoon each of the oil and butter and cook the green peppers and onion in it until they are soft but not brown. Add the mushrooms and bay leaf, stirring them into the peppers and onion, and cook for 2 minutes. Blend into them the marinara sauce and let mixture heat through.

In another skillet, with as much of the remaining oil and butter as may be needed, cook the steaks quickly, as many at a time as the pan can accommodate, to the degree of doneness desired. Turn them just once, and season to taste with salt and pepper immediately after they have been turned. Transfer the cooked steaks to a warm serving platter and keep them warm.

Drain off any remaining fat and de-glaze the skillet by stirring the red wine into the browned bits at the bottom of the pan. Blend the de-glazing liquid into the sauce mixture and let it all bubble for just a few seconds. Pour it over the steaks in the platter and serve at once. Serves 6.

Pizzaiola Steak | Bistecca alla Pizzaiola

6 shell steaks,
   (about 8 ounces each)
Salt & pepper
3 Tbl olive oil
¼ cup red wine

6 anchovy fillets
½ tsp oregano
1 clove garlic
2 cups Marinara Sauce (page 277)
¼ cup capers

Use a skillet that can easily accommodate the steaks. If necessary use 2 skillets (steaks must not be crowded in pan). Sprinkle steaks with salt and pepper to taste and slash the surrounding fat in several places to prevent curling. Heat the olive oil in skillet until it sizzles. Add steaks and cook them medium rare, about 3 minutes on each side. Take care in turning steaks not to pierce the meat; turn them with kitchen tongs or by lifting them with a fork through the fat.

Drain off oil. In a small saucepan gently heat the wine and blend it into the juices in skillet, along with the anchovy fillets, oregano, and garlic, all very finely chopped. Continue cooking until wine is reduced to ½ its volume. Stir in the marinara sauce and capers, and heat them through. Transfer steaks to a warm serving platter and pour the sauce over them. Serves 6.

Tripe Stew | Trippa in Umido

2 pounds tripe
1 medium onion
2 stalks celery
Salt
2 Tbl butter
2 ounces pork fat, in small dice
1 large onion, thinly sliced
2 carrots, in thin strips
½ tsp dried sage

3 medium tomatoes, peeled,
   seeded & coarsely chopped
⅓ cup dry white wine
6 medium potatoes, peeled
½ cup boiling hot water
Salt & pepper
½ cup grated Parmesan cheese
2 Tbl finely chopped parsley

In a saucepan cover the tripe with cold water and bring water to a boil. Drain tripe and cut it into strips 3-inches long and ½-inch wide. Place the strips in a saucepan along with the whole onion and 1 stalk of celery.

Cover them with cold water, seasoning each 4 cups with 1 teaspoon salt. Bring liquid slowly to a boil. Cover pan and cook tripe at simmer for 4 hours or until tender.

Heat the butter and pork fat together in another saucepan and in it lightly brown the sliced onion, carrots, and the remaining stalk of celery, finely chopped. Add the sage, tomatoes, and white wine and let cook at simmer for a few minutes to blend the flavors. Add the prepared tripe, the potatoes, boiling hot water, and salt and pepper to taste, and cook them for 20 minutes or until the potatoes are tender. Transfer stew to a serving bowl and sprinkle it with the grated cheese and parsley combined. Serves 6.

Breaded Veal Chops | Costolette Panate di Vitello

6 loin veal chops
   (each about 6 ounces)
2 eggs, beaten
1 clove garlic, very finely chopped
1 cup fine dry bread crumbs
½ tsp salt
⅛ tsp pepper

¼ cup grated Parmesan or
   Romano cheese
¼ cup finely chopped parsley
3 Tbl olive oil
3 Tbl butter
Wedges of lime or lemon

Put the chops in a deep dish and pour the eggs over them. Let them remain so, at room temperature, for 1 hour, turning them from time to time to keep them coated evenly with the eggs.

Rub the garlic completely into the crumbs and combine them with the seasonings, cheese, and parsley. Drain chops slightly and dredge them in the crumb mixture, coating them well on both sides. Heat the oil and butter together in a skillet large enough to accommodate the chops. Cook chops in the fat over moderate heat for about 20 minutes, turning them once midway through the cooking. Serve each chop with a wedge of lime or lemon to be squeezed over the meat as desired. Serves 6.

Veal Scallops, Bolognese Style | Saltimbocca alla Bolognese

2 pounds boned leg of veal
18 thin slices prosciutto
18 fresh sage leaves
   (or 1 tsp dried sage)
White pepper

Flour
6 Tbl butter
1 cup dry white wine, heated
17 thin slices mozzarella cheese

Cut the leg of veal into 18 thin slices about 4 inches square. Trim the prosciutto so that the slices are slightly smaller than the veal slices. Place a leaf of fresh sage, or a few bits of dried sage, on each slice of veal and cover it with a slice of the prosciutto. With a meat pounder or the flat side of a cleaver flatten the 2 slices together to secure them, or secure the 2 slices by threading a toothpick through them. Sprinkle the slices with white pepper to taste and dredge them lightly with flour.

In a large skillet heat the butter and in it briskly sauté the double slices a few at a time, turning them to brown them lightly on both sides. Place all the slices in skillet and pour the heated wine over them. Reduce heat, cover pan, and continue cooking for 10 minutes or until meat is tender. Remove the slices and arrange them in a heat-proof baking pan, overlapping them slightly and interspersing them with the slices of mozzarella cheese. Pour the remaining wine in skillet over them. Set pan under a hot broiler to melt cheese. Serve at once. Serves 6.

Veal Scallops, Florentine Style | Scaloppine alla Fiorentina

2¼ pounds boned leg of veal	Flour
1 cup butter	½ cup dry Marsala wine
¼ pound mushrooms, sliced	1 cup Brown Sauce (page 269)
¼ cup olive oil	1 pound spinach, trimmed of stems
Salt & pepper	1 Tbl finely chopped parsley

Cut the leg of veal into 18 slices of uniform size and pound them thin with a cleaver. In a skillet heat ¼ cup of the butter and in it sauté the mushrooms over high heat until they are lightly browned. Remove them to a side dish.

Add ½ cup of the butter and the olive oil to butter remaining in skillet and heat. Sprinkle the slices of veal with salt and pepper to taste and dredge lightly in flour. Sauté them in the heated fat, a few at a time, browning them on both sides. Drain off all the fat, place veal slices in skillet, and pour the Marsala over them. Cover pan and cook meat until it is tender, about 10 minutes longer. Add the mushrooms and brown sauce and let them all heat through for a few moments to blend the flavors.

In a separate skillet heat the remaining ¼ cup butter and in it sauté the spinach leaves until they wilt, stirring to coat them well with the butter. Transfer the leaves to a warm serving platter and arrange the veal over them. Cover with the mushrooms and sauce and sprinkle with the chopped parsley. Serves 6.

Veal Scallops with Marsala Wine and Mushrooms |
Scaloppine al Marsala con Funghi

¼ **pound mushrooms,** **sliced (about 2 cups)**	**Salt** **Flour**
1 Tbl lemon juice	**⅔ cup dry Marsala wine**
⅔ cup olive oil	**1 Tbl butter**
2¼ pounds boned leg of veal	**Finely chopped parsley**

Sprinkle the mushrooms with the lemon juice and brown them lightly in ¼ cup of the olive oil, heated in a skillet. Drain them.

Cut the veal into small, thin slices. Sprinkle veal with salt to taste and dredge the slices very lightly with flour. In another skillet heat the remaining olive oil and in it cook veal over moderate heat, a few slices at a time, browning them lightly on both sides. Remove them to a warm side dish as they are cooked. When the last of the veal has been sautéed, drain oil from pan. Return all of the slices to skillet and the heat, and combine the sautéed mushrooms with them. Add the wine and when it is heated through blend in the butter. Correct the seasoning, adding salt if necessary. Place the scallops with the sauce in a serving dish and sprinkle with chopped parsley. Serves 6.

Veal Scallops with White Wine |
Scaloppine di Vitello al Vino Bianco

2¼ pounds boned leg of veal	**1 cup dry white wine**
Salt & white pepper	**1 Tbl chopped Italian parsley**
Flour	**1 Tbl butter**
6 Tbl butter	**Sprigs of Italian parsley**
3 Tbl olive oil	

Cut the veal into 18 slices of equal size. With a meat pounder or the flat of a cleaver pound the slices, without breaking them, to a thickness of ⅛ inch or less. Sprinkle them with salt and white pepper to taste and dredge them lightly with flour. In a skillet heat proportionate quantities of the butter and olive oil as needed to sauté the veal scallops a few at a time.

Sauté the slices over moderate heat, browning them nicely, about 1 minute on each side. Drain them and keep them warm on a serving platter.

Pour off fat remaining in skillet and pour in the wine, blending it into the remaining meat glaze. Reduce liquid slightly over moderate heat and stir into it the chopped parsley and the tablespoon of butter. Continue cooking for a moment or two until the sauce thickens somewhat, and pour it over the scallops in the serving dish. Decorate platter with sprigs of parsley and serve scallops at once. Serves 6.

Veal Scallops Stresa with Truffles | Scaloppine Stresa con Tartufi

2¼ pounds boned leg of veal	Fine, dry bread crumbs
6 thin slices prosciutto	⅓ cup olive oil
12 thin slices mozzarella cheese	⅓ cup dry sherry, warmed
Salt & white pepper	2 cups Brown Sauce (page 269)
Flour	1 small black truffle, chopped
2 eggs, beaten	(about 1 Tbl)

Cut the veal into 12 slices of equal size. Place a slice of prosciutto between each 2 slices of cheese and enclose each of the little sandwiches between 2 slices of veal. Salt veal sparingly (the prosciutto and cheese will also contribute salt), and sprinkle with white pepper to taste. Dredge them with flour and coat them with the beaten eggs and with bread crumbs. Press edges of the veal firmly together to secure the cheese and ham in place.

In a skillet heat the olive oil and in it cook the scallops over medium-low heat, browning them well on both sides. Turn them carefully so as not to dislodge the fillings. Drain off the olive oil remaining in pan and reduce heat to medium. Pour the sherry around the scallops, set it ablaze, and let flame burn out. Baste scallops a few times with the hot wine and transfer them to a warm serving platter. Keep them warm.

Stir the brown sauce into the pan, blending it with the sherry and the cooking glaze at the bottom. Add the chopped truffle. Let sauce simmer for a moment or two. Correct the seasoning, adding salt if needed, and pour sauce around scallops in the serving platter. Serves 6.

Veal Shanks, Milanese Style | Osso Buco alla Milanese

4 pounds veal shanks,	**1 cup dry white wine**
cut in 3-inch lengths	**3 large tomatoes (about 1½ pounds)**
Salt & white pepper	**1 cup Chicken Broth (page 44)**
Flour	**⅓ cup finely chopped Italian parsley**
¼ cup butter	**1 clove garlic, very finely chopped**
¼ cup olive oil	**Grated rind of 1 lemon**

Season the veal shanks with salt and white pepper to taste and dredge them lightly with flour. In a large skillet heat the butter and olive oil together and in them brown the veal shanks well on all sides. Drain shanks and arrange them upright, so as not to lose the marrow, in a large heavy casserole, and pour the wine over them. Cover casserole and cook veal shanks over moderate heat for 10 minutes or until wine is almost completely reduced. Meanwhile, peel, seed, and chop the tomatoes. Add tomatoes and chicken broth and continue cooking, covered, over low heat for 1½ hours. Add a little more broth, if needed, during the cooking. Correct the seasoning, adding salt and pepper, if needed. Transfer veal shanks to a warm serving bowl and pour the sauce around them. Combine the parsley, garlic, and grated peel. Sprinkle the mixture over the shanks and serve them at once with, if desired, Milanese Style Rice (page 115). Serves 6.

Stuffed Veal Rolls | Rollatine di Vitello

9 anchovy fillets	**½ cup butter**
18 thin slices mozzarella cheese	**1½ cups white wine**
18 thin slices veal, cut from leg	**2 Tbl chopped Italian parsley**
(about 2 ounces each)	**Salt**
Flour	**Sprigs of Italian parsley**

Cut the anchovy fillets in half lengthwise. Cut the slices of mozzarella cheese so that they are slightly smaller than the slices of veal. Place a length of anchovy on each slice of veal and cover it with a slice of cheese. Roll the slices, tucking in edges to enclose fillings, and secure them each with a toothpick. Dredge the rolls in flour, coating them

lightly but completely. Heat butter in a skillet and in it brown the veal rolls well on all sides. Pour the wine, heated slightly, over them and cook the rolls for 5 minutes, turning them occasionally, until the meat is well infused with the sauce and the rolls are tender. Transfer them to a warm serving platter and keep them warm. Over high heat reduce the sauce to about ¾ cup and stir in the chopped parsley. Season with salt (sparingly, the anchovies in the veal rolls may be very salty), and pour over the veal. Decorate platter with sprigs of parsley. Serves 6.

Sautéed Calf's Brains | Cervello di Vitello Soffritto

3 calf's brains	1 Tbl butter
Salt	1 Tbl flour
White wine vinegar or lemon juice	½ cup dry white wine
Flour	½ cup Chicken Broth (page 44)
3 eggs, well beaten	½ cup light cream
⅓ cup olive oil	Salt & white pepper
⅓ cup butter	Sprigs of watercress

Wash the brains thoroughly and place in a bowl with enough cold water to cover them. Let them soak for 2 hours. Drain and carefully trim off membranes and veins. Place the brains in a saucepan and cover with boiling water, seasoning each 4 cups with 1 teaspoon salt and 1 tablespoon white wine vinegar or lemon juice. Cook, at simmer, for 20 minutes or until tender. Let brains cool in the cooking liquid, drain, and dry well.

Cut the brains into thick slices. Dredge them with flour and coat with the beaten eggs. In a skillet heat together a part of each of the olive oil and butter, enough to sauté as many slices at a time as pan can accommodate. Cook slices for 10 minutes, browning well on both sides and turning them carefully just once. Transfer slices to a warm serving platter.

Drain off any oil and butter remaining in skillet. Add the single tablespoon of butter to skillet. Heat it and blend into it the tablespoon of flour. Add the wine, chicken broth, and cream gradually, stirring constantly to produce a smooth sauce. Season it with salt and white pepper to taste and, if desired, a few drops of lemon juice. Pass the sauce in a separate bowl to accompany the calf's brains. Decorate platter with sprigs of watercress. Serves 6.

Calf's Liver, Milanese Style | Fegato alla Milanese

2 pounds calf's liver	**¼ cup finely chopped Italian parsley**
Salt & pepper	**¾ cup butter**
Flour	**Wedges of lemon**
3 eggs, beaten	**Sprigs of Italian parsley**
2 cups fine dry bread crumbs	

Cut the calf's liver into 12 thin slices. Sprinkle liver with salt and pepper to taste and dredge the slices lightly with flour. Dip slices in the beaten eggs. Combine the bread crumbs and parsley, rubbing them together, and spread the mixture on a sheet of waxed paper. Press the egg-moistened slices of liver into the bread-crumb mixture, coating them well on both sides. Arrange slices in a single layer on a sheet of waxed paper and let them remain for about 15 minutes to absorb the seasoning.

Heat, in a skillet, as much of the butter as may be needed to sauté the slices a few at a time. Add more butter as required. Cook slices over medium heat for 3 minutes or until they are golden in color, turning just once midway during cooking. Transfer slices to a warm serving platter and keep them warm. Blend any remaining unused butter into butter in skillet and melt it. Pour the butter sauce over liver in serving platter and garnish dish with wedges of lemon and sprigs of parsley. Serve the liver immediately. Serves 6.

Calf's Liver, Venetian Style | Fegato alla Veneziana

2½ pounds calf's liver	**½ cup red wine vinegar**
6 Tbl butter	**Salt & pepper**
1 large onion, thinly sliced	**Chopped parsley**
Flour	

Cut the calf's liver into strips 1 inch by ½ inch. In a large skillet heat the butter and in it cook the onion over high heat until the slices are lightly browned. Dredge strips of liver lightly with flour. Add them to the onions and stir constantly to brown them lightly and evenly. In a small saucepan heat the vinegar and stir it into the liver and onions. Season mixture with salt and pepper to taste, and continue cooking for 2 to 3 minutes over lowered heat until liquid is reduced somewhat. Transfer liver and onions, along with reduced vinegar, to a warm serving platter and serve at once, sprinkled with a little parsley. Serves 6.

Veal Kidneys with Mushrooms | Rognoni di Vitello e Funghi

6 veal kidneys (about 2 pounds)	**3 Tbl red wine vinegar**
Milk	**2 small leaves fresh sage, chopped**
1 medium onion, finely chopped	**(or ¼ tsp dried sage, crushed)**
1½ cups sliced mushrooms	**⅓ cup olive oil**
(about ¼ pound)	**Salt & pepper**
4 Tbl butter	**1½ cups Brown Sauce (page 269)**
⅓ cup red wine	**¼ cup chopped parsley**

Trim the kidneys of all fat and membranes and cut into ½-inch cubes. Put them in a mixing bowl with enough milk to cover, and let them remain so, at room temperature, for 1 hour. Drain and dry completely in paper toweling.

In a skillet over moderate heat, cook the onion and mushrooms in the butter until they are lightly browned. Stir in the wine, vinegar, and sage, and continue cooking until liquid is almost totally absorbed.

In another skillet heat the olive oil until it sizzles. Add the drained kidneys and cook briskly for 2 minutes (no longer!), shaking pan to sear cubes evenly on all sides. Drain off the remaining fat, and season with salt and pepper to taste. Add the mushrooms and onion to them, and blend in the brown sauce. Let the mixture heat through gently for 2 to 3 minutes to blend the flavors, and transfer it to a warm serving dish. Sprinkle it with the chopped parsley and serve with Polenta (page 126) or Rice Pilaff (page 115). Serves 6.

Savory—but easy to prepare—dinner includes Chicken Giacomo, salad of lettuce, onion rings, and tomatoes, and a glass of wine.

Pork Chops Pizzaiola | Costolette di Maiale alla Pizzaiola

Olive oil
12 loin pork chops,
   rather thinly cut
2 cups Marinara Sauce (page 277)

6 anchovy fillets, in small pieces
¼ cup capers
Pepper & salt
2 Tbl chopped parsley

Preheat oven to 350 degrees. In a large skillet heat 3 tablespoons olive oil and in it cook the chops, as many at a time as skillet will accommodate, until they are well browned on both sides, adding additional heated oil as needed. Transfer chops to a roasting pan as they are cooked. When they are all cooked, pour over them any oil remaining in skillet. Set roaster in the preheated oven and cook chops, covered, for 20 minutes or until they are tender. Drain off fat and remove chops to a warm platter. Keep them warm.

Heat the marinara sauce in the roaster on top of stove, blending it into any browned bits at the bottom of pan. Stir into it the anchovies and capers and cook sauce at simmer for a few minutes to blend the flavors. Add chops and let them heat through. Season sauce with pepper to taste. The anchovies may have provided sufficient salt. Add more, if needed. Arrange chops on a warm serving platter and pour sauce over them. Sprinkle with the chopped parsley and serve at once. Serves 6.

Spiedini of Lamb | Spiedini d'Agnello

3 medium green peppers,
   cored & seeded
12 small mushrooms
2 pounds boned leg of lamb
1 medium onion, thickly sliced
1 large stalk celery, thickly sliced
½ tsp dried rosemary
2 tsp salt

¼ tsp white pepper
½ cup dry white wine
1 cup olive oil
3 medium-thick slices lean bacon
Rice Pilaff (page 115)
2 cups White Wine Sauce (page 284)
   using chicken broth
Paprika

Split the peppers lengthwise and cut each half in two. Trim the stems from the mushrooms (reserve stems for other uses). Gently wash and thoroughly dry the mushroom caps. Blanch the 12 pieces of green pep-

Ziti, tube-like pasta, enclosed in a thin
shell of eggplant slices give this Eggplant Timbale,
Bologna Style its unique appearance.

per for 1 minute. Drain and dry them. Cut the lamb into 30 cubes of uniform size. Place the cubes of lamb, mushrooms, and green peppers in a large bowl. In another bowl combine the onion, celery, seasonings, wine, and olive oil. Pour the mixture over lamb and vegetables, stirring them gently to coat them well. Cover bowl and let vegetables marinate under refrigeration for 12 hours, stirring them carefully from time to time. Remove bowl from refrigerator at least 1 hour before the ingredients are to be cooked and drain them. Cut each slice of bacon into 4 equal pieces and cook in simmering water for 15 minutes.

Preheat oven to 450 degrees. Thread 6 long skewers with the lamb, mushrooms, peppers, and bacon. Place the skewered pieces in a baking pan and sprinkle them with salt. Set pan in the preheated oven for 10 to 12 minutes for medium rare, 15 minutes for medium done, and 20 minutes for well done.

On a warm serving platter shape the rice into 6 long mounds and place a skewer of vegetables and meat along the length of each one. Remove the skewers. Drain off any oil remaining in roasting pan and stir in the prepared white wine sauce. Let it heat through on top of stove and pour it over the meat and vegetables on the rice pilaff. Sprinkle the sauce with paprika. Serves 6.

1½ pounds calf's tongue
1 medium onion
2 cloves
1 medium carrot
1 medium tomato, cored
1 small celery root, peeled
1 parsley root, peeled
1 clove garlic, peeled
1 bay leaf

1 Tbl salt
¼ tsp peppercorns
1½ pounds raw cotechino
   (see Glossary)
2 pounds boned beef
   (chuck, rump, or cross rib)
1 2½–3 pound chicken
3 cups Green Sauce (page 274)

Wash the tongue in tepid water and scrub it clean. Place it in a large saucepan or kettle along with the onion, stuck with the cloves, the remaining vegetables, herbs, salt, peppercorns, and sufficient boiling water to cover all completely. Cook tongue at simmer for 2 hours or until it is tender. Drain it, reserving the cooking liquid, strained. Skin tongue and trim out the roots. Set tongue aside. Let cooking liquid cool.

Prick the skin of the cotechino in several places (to allow the fat to drain off during cooking) and put the sausage in a deep skillet. Cover it with boiling hot water and cook it, uncovered, over low heat for 1 hour, or until it is tender. Drain and set aside. Place the beef in the cooled cooking liquid in the saucepan, adding cool water, if needed, to cover meat completely. Bring liquid to boil and skim it. Cook beef, covered, over low heat for 1 hour. Split the chicken and cook the halves with the beef for 45 minutes or until the beef and chicken are tender. Add the cooked tongue and cotechino and continue the cooking for 15 minutes or until they are heated through.

Remove the meats (reserving the cooking liquid for soups, sauces, or as required). Cut the beef and tongue into thin slices, the cotechino diagonally into thick ones, and the chicken into serving pieces. Arrange them attractively on a warm serving platter, and serve them, steaming hot, with the green sauce heated and poured over them. Serves 8 generously.

NOTE: Calf's head and calf's brains are traditional ingredients of the Italian Boiled Dinner, but since they are not often readily available, they have been omitted from this recipe.

Sausage with Lentils | Cotechino con Lenticchie

2 stalks celery, coarsely chopped
1 large carrot, coarsely chopped
1 medium onion, coarsely chopped
1 bay leaf
6–8 peppercorns
1 Tbl salt
3 quarts water
1 3-pound piece raw cotechino
(see Glossary)
2 Tbl olive oil

2 Tbl butter
2 medium onions, finely chopped
1 large clove garlic,
finely chopped
2½ cups lentils, soaked overnight in
cold water & drained
1½ cups red wine
6 cups Beef Broth (page 44)
Salt & pepper
2 Tbl finely chopped parsley

In a saucepan combine the coarsely chopped vegetables, bay leaf, peppercorns, and tablespoon of salt, and cook them in the water over moderate heat for 10 minutes. Add the cotechino and cook it gently for 1½ hours. Drain the sausage and keep it warm on a side platter.

In a large saucepan heat the olive oil and butter and in it lightly brown the onions and garlic over moderate heat. Add the lentils and stir, coating them well with the oil and butter. Stir into them the wine and when it is completely absorbed, after about 5 minutes, add the broth. Season mixture with salt and pepper to taste and cook it, covered, at simmer for 1 hour or until lentils are tender but still whole and the cooking liquid is thick. Transfer lentils to a warm serving platter. Cut the sausage into thick slices and arrange around the lentils. Sprinkle lentils with the chopped parsley. Serves 6.

Cabbage and Sausage | Cavolo e Salsicce

1 head cabbage (about 2 pounds)
¼ cup butter
¼ pound salt pork, minced
2 medium onions, thinly sliced

¼ cup red wine vinegar
Salt & white pepper
12 Italian sausages (about 2 pounds)

Trim the cabbage of any wilted or discolored outer leaves and core it. Shred cabbage coarsely and wash the shreds in a colander under running cold water. Drain them well. In a large saucepan heat the butter

and salt pork. Add the onions and cook them over low heat just until the slices wilt. Add cabbage. Increase heat and stir until cabbage is lightly browned. Stir in the vinegar and season with salt and white pepper to taste. Prick the sausages and arrange them over cabbage. Cover pan, reduce heat to low, and continue cooking for 1 hour. Shake pan occasionally to prevent sticking. Serves 6.

Stuffed Eggplant | Melanzane Ripiene

4 small eggplants	**¼ tsp dried oregano**
2 Tbl olive oil	**¾ cup Tomato Sauce (page 282)**
1 small onion, finely chopped	**Salt & pepper**
6 ounces lean beef, finely ground	**½ cup grated Parmesan cheese**
3 ounces lean pork, finely ground	**½ cup fine dry bread crumbs**
⅓ cup red wine	

Wash the eggplants. Set 1 aside. Dry 3 of them very well and trim off the stem ends, but do not peel them. Split them lengthwise. Arrange them cut sides down on a lightly oiled baking sheet in a 400-degree oven and bake for 10 minutes or until eggplants are semi-soft. Remove the baking sheet and let eggplants cool on it. Lower oven to 350 degrees.

In a skillet heat the olive oil and in it cook the onion until it is lightly browned. Add the ground meats and sauté them until they are well browned. Meanwhile, peel and finely chop the remaining eggplant. Blend the chopped eggplant and the wine into the meat and onion, and cook for 10 minutes, or until the liquid rendered by the vegetables evaporates and the wine is somewhat reduced. Blend the oregano and the tomato sauce into it, and season with salt and pepper to taste. Cook at simmer for 15 minutes longer, stirring frequently. Remove skillet from heat and stir into the mixture the grated cheese and the bread crumbs. If it is too moist to hold a shape, blend a few more bread crumbs into it. Let mixture cool and heap it in equal portions along tops of eggplant halves. Return baking sheet to oven with eggplants arranged filled sides up, and bake them at 350 degrees for 12 minutes. Serve the stuffed eggplants, hot, cooled, or chilled. Serves 6.

pies and timbales

Pie Florentine Style | Torta alla Fiorentina

½ cup fettuccine
2 cups well-drained cooked spinach
1 cup grated Parmesan cheese
7 eggs
2 cups light cream

Salt & pepper
½ recipe Pie Dough (page 72)
2 Tbl vegetable shortening, melted
¼ cup fine dry bread crumbs

Cook the fettuccine (see How to Cook Pasta). Chop the spinach coarsely. In a mixing bowl combine the noodles, spinach, and cheese. In another bowl beat together 6 of the eggs and cream and blend them into the spinach mixture. Season this filling with salt and pepper to taste. Preheat oven to 350 degrees.

Prepare bottom and top crusts of pie pastry following the basic instructions. Line a deep 9-inch pie pan with the bottom crust, brush it with the melted shortening, and sprinkle the bottom with the bread crumbs. Pour the filling into pie shell and spread it evenly. Brush edges of crust with the remaining egg, beaten, and fit top crust over it, sealing edges. Prick top with a fork in several places to allow steam to escape during the baking. Bake in the preheated oven for 55 minutes. Let it cool slightly, but serve it warm, cut into 6 wedges.

Pie Alberto | Torta Alberto

½ recipe Pie Dough (page 72)
2 Tbl vegetable shortening, melted
¼ cup fine dry bread crumbs
6 ounces Italian-style salami
9 eggs

2 cups light cream
2 cups cooked lasagnette
 (see Glossary)
2 Tbl finely chopped Italian parsley
Salt & white pepper

Prepare top and bottom crusts for a deep 9-inch pie pan and line a pan with the bottom crust. Brush it with the melted shortening and sprinkle with the bread crumbs. Preheat oven to 350 degrees.

Cut the salami into julienne strips. In a mixing bowl thoroughly beat together 8 of the eggs and cream and stir into them the salami, lasagnette, parsley, and salt and white pepper to taste. Pour mixture into prepared pie shell, spreading solids evenly. Brush edges of that crust with the remaining egg, beaten, and fit top crust over it. Press edges to seal them. Prick top in several places with a fork to allow steam to escape during the baking. Bake pie in the preheated oven for 1 hour and 15 minutes, or until pastry is well browned and filling is set. Test by inserting a slender knife or a metal skewer through center of crust into filling. If it can be withdrawn clean, filling is set. Serves 6.

Fish Pie | Torta di Pesce

¼ **recipe Pie Dough (page 72)**	4 **eggs, beaten**
Vegetable shortening	½ **pound cooked crabmeat, flaked**
2 **squid (about ½ pound)**	1 **pound small raw shrimp,**
2 **cups Fish Broth (page 45)**	**shelled & de-veined**
½ **cup dry white wine**	1 **Tbl finely chopped chives**
36 **cherrystone clams, shucked**	1 **tsp salt**
1 **pound fillets of sole**	⅛ **tsp white pepper**
2 **Tbl butter**	¼ **cup fine dry bread crumbs**
1 **Tbl flour**	

Prepare a bottom crust only for a deep 9-inch pie. Preheat oven to 400 degrees. Line a pan with the dough. Lightly grease a 12-inch square of foil with vegetable shortening and fit it snugly into pie shell. Fill lining with dried beans to keep shell from cooking unevenly during preliminary baking. Set pie shell in the preheated oven and bake for 8 minutes. Remove beans (don't discard them, they are still usable) and foil, and return pan to oven for 2 minutes, or until pastry begins to take on color. Remove pan from oven and set it aside for the moment. Reduce oven temperature to 375 degrees.

Clean the squid (removing the heads) and steam them (see pages 130, 132). Cut squid into ¼-inch slices. In a saucepan heat together the fish broth and wine. Add the shucked clams and cook them for 2 minutes. Remove them to a warm plate and keep them warm. Add the fillets of sole to the cooking liquid and cook at simmer for 5 minutes or until they are almost tender. They should still be quite firm. Remove fillets and break or cut them into small pieces. Reduce liquid in pan over high heat to 1 cup.

In another saucepan heat the butter and blend the flour into it. Add the reduced cooking liquid gradually, stirring constantly until sauce thickens and is smooth. Cool sauce to lukewarm and blend the beaten eggs into it. In a bowl combine the squid, crabmeat, raw shrimp, the partially cooked clams and sole, the chives, and the indicated amounts of salt and white pepper or more to taste. Stir the cooled sauce into this.

Sprinkle the pie shell with the bread crumbs and spread the prepared mixture over them. Set pan in oven, now at 375 degrees, and bake pie for 30 minutes, or until filling is puffed and top is nicely browned. Cut pie into wedges for individual servings. Serves 6.

Salmon Pie | Torta di Salmone

1 stalk celery	1 very small onion, finely chopped
1 small onion	4 leaves fresh basil, finely chopped—
1 medium carrot	about 1 tsp (or ¼ tsp dried basil)
3 sprigs parsley	3 eggs
8 cups boiling hot water	1½ cups heavy cream
1 Tbl salt	¼ pound rotelle (see Glossary)
1 pound fresh salmon	Salt & white pepper
3 Tbl butter	½ recipe Pie Dough (page 72)

Scrape and thinly slice the celery. Peel and thinly slice the onion and carrot. In a saucepan large enough to hold the salmon make a poaching broth by cooking the celery, onion, carrot, and parsley in the water for 15 minutes over moderate heat. Season the broth with the salt.

Wrap the salmon in cheesecloth leaving the ends long to serve as handles, and tie it with kitchen twine. Lower the wrapped salmon into the broth and poach it at bare simmer for 10 minutes, or until it flakes easily when pierced with a fork through the cheesecloth. Remove salmon and unwrap it. Remove skin and bones and flake the fish.

In the butter, heated in a skillet, slowly cook the chopped onion until it is soft but not brown. Combine the flaked salmon and the basil with it and mash the mixture well with a fork. In a mixing bowl beat together

2 of the eggs and cream and combine them with the seasoned salmon, beating mixture until it is very smooth. Blend into it the pasta, cooked *al dente* (see How to Cook Pasta), and salt and pepper to taste.

Prepare pie pastry following the basic instructions for a bottom and top crust. Preheat oven to 400 degrees. Line a deep 9-inch pie pan to provide a bottom crust and pour the prepared salmon filling into it. Brush edges of crust with the remaining egg, beaten, and fit top crust over it, pressing edges to seal the 2 crusts together. Prick top in several places to allow steam to escape during baking. Bake pie in the preheated oven for 30 minutes or until pastry is golden brown. Serves 6.

Eggplant Pie, Country Style | Torta Rustica di Melanzane

1 medium eggplant (about 1 pound)	**1 cup small-diced**
½ tsp salt	**mozzarella cheese**
Bland cooking oil for deep frying	**3 anchovy fillets, in small bits**
½ recipe Pie Dough (page 72)	**2 Tbl capers**
2 Tbl vegetable shortening, melted	**6 Tbl grated Parmesan cheese**
¼ cup fine dry bread crumbs	**½ tsp dried oregano**
4 eggs	**Pepper & salt**
¾ cup cold Marinara Sauce (page 277)	

Cut the eggplant, unpeeled, into slices each ¼-inch thick. Spread the slices on a platter, sprinkle them with the ½ teaspoon salt, and let them remain so for 30 minutes to extract the liquid. Drain eggplant and dry slices between sheets of paper toweling. In a large saucepan or fryer, heat sufficient cooking oil to 375 degrees for deep frying and in it fry eggplant, a few slices at a time, until they just begin to brown. Remove slices, drain, and let cool. Preheat oven to 350 degrees.

Prepare bottom and top crusts for a deep 9-inch pie pan and line a pan with the bottom crust. Brush the crust with the melted shortening and sprinkle bottom with the bread crumbs. Arrange ⅓ of the fried eggplant in the prepared pie shell. Combine 3 of the eggs with the marinara sauce and pour ½ cup of this mixture over the eggplant in the pie shell. Cover the sauce with, in turn, ⅓ each of the mozzarella cheese, anchovy bits, capers, Parmesan cheese, oregano, and pepper to taste. Add salt, if desired, keeping in mind that the anchovies, capers, and cheese will contribute saltiness. Continue in that fashion with the remaining ingredients, to provide 2 more series of layers.

Brush edges of bottom crust with the remaining egg, beaten, and fit top crust over filling, pressing edges of 2 crusts to seal them. Prick top in several places with the tines of a fork to allow steam to escape during the baking. Bake the pie in the preheated oven for 45 minutes or until pastry is well browned. Serves 6.

Eggplant Timbale | Timballo di Melanzane

1 large eggplant	10 Tbl margarine
Flour	4 cups cooked ziti (see Glossary)
2 eggs, well beaten	½ cup grated Parmesan cheese
½ cup olive oil	3½ cups Meat Sauce for Timbales
Salt	(page 280), cooled

Peel the eggplant and cut it lengthwise into paper-thin slices. Dredge the slices lightly in flour and coat them with the beaten eggs. In a large skillet heat the oil, in small quantities as needed, and sauté the eggplant in it, a few slices at a time, browning them very lightly on both sides. Season them very lightly with salt. Preheat oven to 400 degrees. Grease an 8-inch tube pan (about 8-cup capacity) evenly with the margarine. The coating will be thick, as it should be. Line the pan, including tube, with the prepared eggplant slices, arranging them lengthwise down sides of pan and tube, overlapping them slightly and providing for an overhang of about 2 inches all around edge of pan and tube. Thoroughly combine the cooked ziti, the Parmesan cheese, and 2½ cups of the meat sauce. Fill the lined mold with the mixture, pressing it down gently. Fold the overhanging eggplant slices over filling, enclosing it completely, and brush top with a little olive oil.

Bake the timbale in the preheated oven for 25 minutes, or until eggplant shrinks somewhat away from the side of pan. Remove pan from oven and let timbale rest in a warm place for 15 minutes. To unmold it, run a sharp, narrow knife around sides of tube. Place a warm serving platter, topside down, over timbale and invert mold and platter together, thereby releasing timbale into position for serving. Heat the remaining meat sauce and pour it around timbale. Decorate platter with sprigs of parsley. This timbale will provide 6 generous wedge-shaped servings. It may be served hot or cold. If served cold, omit the additional sauce.

Vegetable Pie, Country Style | Torta Rustica di Verdura

½ recipe Pie Dough (page 72)
2 Tbl vegetable shortening
¼ cup fine dry bread crumbs
1 small eggplant
1 medium green pepper
2 leeks, white parts only
¼ pound fresh mushrooms
1 large onion
2 cooked medium carrots
⅔ cup olive oil (approximate)
½ cup cooked fresh peas
½ cup canned, roasted
   red peppers, sliced
7 eggs
1 cup light cream
1 cup grated Parmesan cheese
1 tsp salt
¼ tsp white pepper

Prepare pie dough and roll out enough of it to line a deep 9-inch heat-proof glass pie pan. Roll out sufficient dough to provide a rectangle 12 inches by 5 inches and ⅛-inch thick, and cut it lengthwise into 10 strips each ½-inch wide. On a lightly greased baking sheet arrange the strips in a diamond-patterned lattice, that is with 5 strips arranged diagonally ½-inch apart across the other 5 strips also set ½-inch apart. Line the pan with the prepared bottom crust. Brush it with the vegetable shortening and sprinkle the bread crumbs over it. Set the lattice in the refrigerator.

Peel, quarter, and thinly slice the eggplant (there should be about 1 cup). Core, seed, and thinly slice the green pepper. Also thinly slice the leeks, mushrooms, onion, and carrots. Heat a little of the olive oil at a time in a skillet and sauté separately, in turn, the eggplant, pepper, leeks, mushrooms, and onion, cooking them until they are soft but not brown. Drain the vegetables and combine them in a mixing bowl along with the cooked peas and carrots and the canned red pepper. In another bowl thoroughly combine 6 of the eggs, well beaten, the cream, grated cheese, salt and pepper, and blend the mixture into the combined vegetables. Spread the filling in the pie shell and press it down gently with a spatula to dispel any air bubbles. Preheat oven to 350 degrees.

Brush the edges of the bottom crust with some of the remaining egg, beaten. Place the lattice of dough carefully over it, securing the strips by pressing them onto the edge of the bottom crust. Trim off any overhanging strips. Brush the strips with beaten egg.

Bake the pie in the preheated oven for 1 hour or until the crusts are well browned. If the lattice browns too quickly, cover it lightly with greased foil. Cut the pie at the table into wedges to provide 6 servings.

6 | light meals

The Italian table characteristically does not stint either in quantity or imagination. Thus, when it comes to those informal meals that Americans call variously lunch, supper, late snack, or what have you, we find in the repertoire of Italy any number of dishes that are substantial, original, readily concocted, and remarkably satisfying. Certainly the omnipresent pizza satisfies on all these points (if you are wise enough to keep dough ready in the refrigerator). So does the *mozzarella in carrozza*—a fried cheese sandwich, and those overstuffed sandwiches called colloquially by such names as heroes, grinders, and submarines. (It is interesting to note the phenomenal acceptance of the pizza and the hero sandwich in the United States. They have helped considerably to civilize that American institution, the 45-minute lunch hour.)

Put together with the best ingredients and a light touch, the dishes in this section make sophisticated offerings on simple occasions.

The Classic Pizza | Pizza Classica

Dough for Pizza (page 72)
3 cups Marinara Sauce (page 277)
3 cups shredded mozzarella cheese

¾ tsp dried oregano
6 Tbl grated Parmesan cheese

Preheat oven to 450 degrees. Prepare pizza dough, following basic instructions, but use only 6 cups flour and about 3 cups water (and all remaining ingredients) to produce 6 balls of equal size. Line pans with the dough as indicated to provide pastry for 6 individual pizzas. Spread ½ cup of the marinara sauce over each dough-lined pan, leaving uncovered a rim of dough about 1-inch wide all around. Sprinkle each with ½ cup of the mozzarella cheese, ⅛ teaspoon of the oregano, and 1 tablespoon of the Parmesan cheese. Bake pizzas in the preheated oven for 15 minutes or until the crusts are well browned.

Cut pizzas into wedges and serve them hot in the pans in which they were baked. Serves 6.

Country-Style Pizza | Pizza Rustica

½ recipe Pie Dough (page 72)
1 pound ricotta cheese
2 Tbl grated Parmesan cheese
2 Tbl grated provolone cheese
2 Tbl grated Bel Paese cheese
2 eggs
1 egg yolk

½ tsp salt
Freshly ground black pepper
2 ounces prosciutto,
    cut into narrow, thin strips
2 ounces Italian-style salami,
    cut into narrow, thin strips

Prepare pie dough following basic instructions and line a deep 8-inch pie pan with ½ of it. Preheat oven to 375 degrees.

In a mixing bowl thoroughly combine the cheeses, 1 egg, the egg yolk, salt, and black pepper to taste. Spread the filling in the pie shell and sprinkle over it the strips of meat. Roll out the remaining dough into a top crust of proper size. Brush the rim of the bottom crust with the remaining egg, beaten. Fit the top crust over it and seal edges by pressing them firmly together. Prick the top in several places with the tines of a fork to allow steam to escape during baking.

Antipasto Sandwich—slices of cheese, salami, sausage, onions, peppers, and tomatoes in a round loaf of Italian bread— makes robust picnic fare.

Bake the pizza in the preheated oven for 45 minutes or until the crust is nicely browned. This pizza may be served hot, warm, or cold with an accompaniment, if desired, of additional prosciutto in paper-thin slices. Serves 6.

Trattoria-Style Pizza | Pizza Trattoria

¼ cup olive oil
1 medium onion, thinly sliced
3 medium mushrooms, thinly sliced
Dough for Pizza (page 72)
3 cups Marinara Sauce (page 277)
3 cups shredded mozzarella cheese
¾ tsp oregano

6 Tbl grated Parmesan cheese
6 small Italian sweet sausages,
   each cut into 7 slices
Green sweet peppers,
   sliced lengthwise,
   enough to provide 1½ cups

In a skillet heat 2 tablespoons of the olive oil and in it cook the onion slices until they are lightly browned. Transfer onion slices to a mixing bowl and set aside. Heat remaining oil in the skillet. Add sliced mushrooms and sauté them briskly until they begin to take on a little color. Transfer them to another mixing bowl and set aside for the moment also.

Prepare pizza dough following basic instructions, but use only 6 cups of flour and about 3 cups of water (and all of the remaining ingredients) to produce 6 balls of equal size. Line pans with the dough as indicated, to provide pastry for 6 individual servings. Preheat oven to 500 degrees.

Spread ½ cup of the marinara sauce over each dough-lined pan, leaving about 1 inch around the outside edge of the dough uncovered. Sprinkle each spread of sauce with ½ cup of the mozzarella cheese, ⅛ teaspoon of the oregano, and 1 tablespoon of the grated Parmesan cheese. Place a slice of the sausage in the center of each pan and 6 slices, equidistant from each other, around the edge of the sauce, but well removed from the uncovered dough. In each pan arrange equal portions of ¼ cup of the sliced green pepper in rows extending out from the center to the edge of the sauce between the slices of sausage. Flanking the rows of peppers arrange rows of onions and mushrooms, using ⅙ of each for each pizza.

Torta Primavera, "spring cake," is not a cake at all but an intriguing combination of thin pancakes, meats, cheeses, and vegetables coated with a smooth mayonnaise dressing.

Bake the pizzas in the preheated oven for 15 minutes. Serve them hot in the pans in which they were baked. Serves 6.

Fried Mozzarella Cheese | Mozzarella Fritta

1½ pounds mozzarella cheese	About 1½ cups fine,
Flour	dry bread crumbs
3 eggs	1½ cups light olive oil
½ tsp salt	Tomato Sauce (page 282), optional

Cut the cheese into 6 blocks of equal size, each about ¾-inch thick. Dredge the pieces with flour. In a mixing bowl beat the eggs with the salt and coat the cheese with the mixture. Roll the blocks in the bread crumbs. Coat the cheese again with, in turn, flour, eggs, and bread crumbs, and arrange the coated blocks on a cake rack. Let them remain so for 1 hour, or until coatings have dried somewhat.

In a skillet heat the oil. Add the coated blocks of cheese and fry them at 375 degrees until coatings are nicely browned. Drain blocks quickly and serve them at once with, if desired, the tomato sauce. Serves 6.

Antipasto Sandwich | Pane Imbottito con Antipasti

1 round loaf Italian white bread,	6 slices mortadella sausage
7 inches in diameter	11 slices coppa (see Glossary)
10 leaves romaine, shredded	12 slices tomato
1 cup roasted sweet red pepper	Green olives
10 thin slices onion	Black olives
9 thin slices provolone cheese	Peperoncini (see Glossary)
10 thin slices Italian-style salami	

Cut bread horizontally into 5 slices of equal thickness and set it on a serving platter. Lift off the top 4 slices and cover bottom slice with ½ the shredded romaine and all of the roasted pepper and onion. Replace the slice which was originally over it in exactly the same position and cover that one with the slices of provolone cheese and salami. Replace the next slice, again in its original position, and cover it with the remaining romaine and all of the mortadella. Replace the next slice, cover it with the slices of coppa and tomato, and fit the top crust neatly over it. Cut the sandwich into 6 wedge-shaped servings and decorate platter with green and black olives and peperoncini. Serves 6.

Trattoria Club Sandwich | Pane Imbottito alla Trattoria

Italian round white bread,
    cut horizontally into 12 slices
    ½-inch thick
	18 slices Italian-style salami
	12 slices capocollo (see Glossary)
	18 thin slices tomato

Softened butter	18 slices cooked turkey
6 hard-cooked eggs, peeled & sliced	12 peperoncini (see Glossary)
10 slices provolone cheese	12 large green olives
18 anchovy fillets	12 black olives

Coat the slices of bread lightly on one side only with the butter. On 6 of the buttered slices arrange equal amounts of all remaining ingredients, except the peperoncini and olives, in order indicated. Cover the fillings each with 1 of the remaining slices of bread, buttered side down. Cut the sandwiches in halves and serve them with a garniture of 2 each of the peppers and olives. Serves 6.

Mozzarella in the Carriage | Mozzarella in Carrozza

18 slices white bread,
    each about ¼-inch thick,
    trimmed of crust
	9 slices mozzarella cheese, each
	    about ⅛-inch thick & cut slightly
	    smaller than the slices of bread

Flour	6 Tbl butter
5 eggs	6 Tbl olive oil
⅓ cup milk	Anchovy Sauce (page 268)

Dredge both sides of the slices of bread lightly with the flour. In a mixing bowl beat together the eggs and milk. Coat 1 side of each slice of floured bread with the mixture. Sandwich a slice of cheese between the egg-coated sides of each 2 slices of bread. Cut sandwiches in halves, diagonally, and dredge cut edges with flour. Arrange the triangles in a shallow baking pan and pour the remaining egg-and-milk mixture over them. Let them remain so, turning from time to time, until they have uniformly absorbed all of the liquid.

In 2 skillets, large enough to accommodate all of the triangular sandwiches between them, heat together the butter and olive oil. Add the sandwiches and sauté them over moderate heat, browning them well on all sides. Drain the triangles quickly and serve them hot, 3 to a serving, as a light entrée, accompanied by anchovy sauce. Serves 6.

Country-Style Heroes | Pane Imbottito alla Paesana

6 individual loaves Italian bread
24 slices provolone cheese,
   folded in half
24 slices cooked ham, folded in half

6 hard-cooked eggs,
   peeled & halved lengthwise
12 peperoncini (see Glossary)
12 black olives
12 green olives

Cut the loaves of bread in half lengthwise. Remove some of the soft parts from bottom halves of the loaves and line hollows each with 4 of the folded slices of cheese. Cover them with 4 slices of the folded ham and reassemble loaves. Set each of the filled loaves on a serving plate. Garnish each with 2 halves of egg and 2 each of the peperoncini and black and green olives. Serves 6.

Small Heroes | Panini Imbottiti

⅔ cup olive oil
1 large onion, coarsely chopped
2 cloves garlic, mashed well
2 pounds lean veal, in small dice
12 medium mushrooms,
   thinly sliced (about 2 cups)
2 large green peppers,
   seeded & thinly sliced
⅓ cup dry white wine

1 bay leaf
¼ tsp dried oregano
⅛ tsp white pepper
Salt
2½ cups canned, peeled
   plum tomatoes with juice
6 individual long loaves Italian bread
2 Tbl finely chopped parsley

Heat the olive oil in a large saucepan and in it, over moderate heat, very

lightly brown the onion and garlic. Add the veal. When pieces begin to take on color, add the mushrooms and green peppers and continue cooking until mushrooms begin to render their juices and peppers are softened. Stir into the mixture the white wine and add the bay leaf, oregano, white pepper, and salt to taste. Let liquid reduce somewhat and blend in the tomatoes with their juice. Cover pan and cook this sandwich filling for 30 minutes or until the bits of meat are very tender and vegetables are thoroughly cooked. Stir mixture occasionally during cooking. Remove and discard bay leaf. If garlic has not completely disintegrated, remove any remaining pieces and discard them also.

Cut loaves of bread into halves lengthwise. Scoop out and discard the soft parts. Heat shells in a 300-degree oven for 15 minutes or until they are crisp. Arrange the loaves, crust sides down, each on a serving plate and fill halves equally with the prepared meat-and-vegetable mixture. Sprinkle each with 1 teaspoon of the chopped parsley and serve them hot. Serves 6.

Spring Torte | Torta Primavera

15 Thin Pancakes (see below)	4 thin slices cooked ham
1¼ cups Mayonnaise (page 286)	3 thin slices cooked veal
4 leaves romaine, trimmed	2 canned roasted red peppers,
of heavy ribs & flattened	split lengthwise & flattened
8 thin slices mortadella sausage	1 Tbl unflavored gelatine
8 thin slices provolone cheese	½ cup Chicken Broth (page 44),
½ cup cooked spinach leaves,	heated
well drained	1 Tbl dry white wine
4 thin slices cooked turkey breast	1 Tomato Rose (see below)
5 thin slices peeled tomato	Sprigs of parsley, without stems
6 thin slices salami	4 large stuffed green olives, sliced

Prepare the Spring Torte directly on the plate from which it is to be served, proceeding as follows:

Spread each pancake, on 1 side only, with about ½ teaspoon of the mayonnaise. Place 1 pancake, spread side up, on the plate and arrange on it evenly 2 of the lettuce leaves, overlapping them, if necessary. On top of this, stack 13 more of the pancakes, also spread sides up, interspersing them evenly with, in order, 4 slices of the mortadella, 4 slices of the cheese, ¼ cup of the spinach, the turkey, tomato slices, salami, the remaining spinach, ham, veal, roasted peppers, and the remaining slices of cheese, mortadella, and the lettuce. Place the remaining pancake on top, mayonnaise side down. Even up the stack, tucking in any loose ends if necessary.

Soften and dissolve the gelatine in the chicken broth and blend it into the remaining mayonnaise. Stir the white wine into the mixture. Coat the stack of filled pancakes with ½ of the mayonnaise-gelatine mixture. Secure the stack by inserting 4 skewers down through it at even intervals, and set the stack in the refrigerator until the glaze is set. Remove skewers and coat the pancakes again with the remaining gelatine-mayonnaise. When that is set place the tomato rose in the center of the top and surround it with a narrow ring of parsley. Decorate the rim of the top with the slices of olives. Arrange sprigs of parsley around base of the torte.

Chill the Spring Torte before cutting it in wedges to provide 6 to 12 servings.

Thin Pancakes:

1 cup flour	**1½ cups milk**
¼ tsp salt	**½ cup cold water**
2 eggs	**2 Tbl bland cooking oil**
1 egg yolk	**Butter**

In a mixing bowl combine all of the ingredients, except the butter, and beat them with a whisk to produce a smooth batter the consistency of medium-heavy cream. Chill the batter in the refrigerator for 1 hour. The batter will thicken somewhat as it chills. Thin it with equal quantities of milk and cold water to the original consistency.

Cook the pancakes in a 7-inch skillet. Heat the pan and grease it very lightly with butter. For each pancake, to be made separately, pour in ¼ cup of the batter and tilt and rotate the pan immediately, swirling the batter evenly over the bottom. Cook the pancake over moderate heat, browning it lightly on both sides. Proceed in the same way with the remaining batter, stacking the pancakes, as they are cooked, between sheets of waxed paper. This recipe will provide about 20 pancakes.

NOTE: If the pancakes are to be used as dessert, reduce the salt to ⅛ teaspoon and add ½ teaspoon sugar and 1 tablespoon brandy. The pancakes may be frozen.

Tomato Rose:

Using a small, very sharp knife, hold a small tomato upside down—that is, with the stem end at the bottom. With your right hand hold the knife blade firmly against the blossom end of the tomato (now at the top) and, with your left hand, turn the tomato counterclockwise against the blade, tilting the tomato as you turn it, thus peeling it in a continuous downward spiral. Peel the tomato as thinly as possible, taking great care not to break the peel. It must be continuous and unbroken. As the peeling procedure reaches the stem end, hold the peel in place and reverse the tomato. Hold it over a plate, free the last bit of peel, and let the spiral fall gently, blossom side down, onto the plate. Properly executed, the peel will fold itself into a rose and provide a decorative centerpiece for salads or as required.

Gourmet Omelette I | Frittata del Buongustaio I

4 Tbl butter
½ cup small-diced fat salt pork
1 medium onion, thinly sliced
¾ pound Fontina cheese, shredded

6 ounces provolone cheese,
  shredded
8 eggs, well beaten
Salt & pepper
1 Tbl chopped Italian parsley

In a large skillet heat the butter and in it lightly brown the salt pork. Add the onion slices and cook them until they are lightly browned, by which time the salt pork will be sufficiently cooked. Combine the cheeses, blend them into the pork-onion mixture, and continue the cooking until the cheese melts. Season the eggs with salt and pepper to taste and stir the parsley into them. Turn the cheese mixture and pour the eggs over it. Cook the combined ingredients until the eggs are set and the omelette is crisp around the edges. The 6 servings provided by this recipe may seem small, but they are ample, since this is a rich omelette.

Gourmet Omelette II | Frittata del Buongustaio II

Prepare each omelette separately with:
¼ pound young spinach
2 Tbl butter
1 Tbl olive oil
3 scallions, white parts only,
  finely chopped

2 ounces finely ground lean beef
3 eggs, beaten
Salt & pepper

Trim off any heavy stems of the spinach. Wash the leaves and shake off most of the water. In an uncovered saucepan over low heat cook the spinach only until it wilts, about 1 minute, in just the water that clings to the leaves. Drain the spinach thoroughly and chop it finely. Set it aside for the moment in a bowl.

Heat the butter and olive oil in a 7- or 8-inch skillet and in it cook the scallions until they are soft but not brown. Add the meat and cook it, over moderate heat, just until it begins to brown. Spread the meat and onions evenly in the pan and pour over them the beaten eggs. Immediately start to move the pan vigorously in a circle over the heat. Move it constantly, swirling the eggs up the sides of the pan and flipping them back again. Just before the eggs begin to set spread over them the reserved spinach, drained of any accumulated liquid, and continue the cooking, still keeping the pan in motion, until the eggs are lightly browned on the under side. Sprinkle the eggs with salt and pepper to taste. Carefully turn the omelette and brown the other side. Serve each omelette immediately as it is ready.

Minelli Omelette | Frittata alla Minelli

Prepare each omelette separately with:

3 Tbl butter	**¼ tsp salt**
¼ cup crumbled Italian sweet sausage meat	**⅓ cup cooked spaghetti cut into 1-inch pieces**
3 eggs	**2 Tbl finely chopped mozzarella cheese**
1 tsp cold water	

In a small skillet heat 1 tablespoon of the butter and in it brown the sausage meat well. Drain the meat and set it aside for the moment.

In a mixing bowl thoroughly blend the eggs, cold water, and salt, beating them with a whisk or fork. Stir into them the cooked spaghetti. In a 6- or 7-inch skillet heat the remaining 2 tablespoons butter. Into the pan, over low heat, pour ½ the egg mixture and let it cook for a few seconds until it begins to set. Sprinkle over it the chopped cheese and the sausage meat and cover them immediately with the remaining egg mixture. Increase the heat to moderate and move the pan in a circle vigorously and continuously over it until the under side of the omelette is lightly browned. Turn the omelette carefully, so as not to break it, and brown the other side. Serve the omelette at once.

Forester's Omelette | Frittata alla Guardia Forestale

For 6 omelettes:
4 Tbl butter
1 Tbl olive oil
3 cups thinly sliced
 fresh mushrooms

For each omelette:
3 eggs
1 tsp cold water
¼ tsp salt
1 Tbl butter
1 tsp olive oil
¼ tsp finely chopped chives

In a large skillet heat together the 4 tablespoons butter and the table-spoon of olive oil. Add the mushrooms and cook them briskly until the slices are lightly browned around the edges. Divide the cooked mush-rooms into 6 equal portions. Set them aside, but keep them warm.

Prepare each omelette separately, as follows:

In a mixing bowl combine the eggs, cold water, and salt, and beat them with a whisk or fork until the yolks and whites are well blended and the mixture flows evenly from the beater. (Do not use a rotary beater; it generates too much foam which may produce an uneven omelette.) In a 6- or 7-inch skillet heat together the single spoonfuls of butter and oil. Add 1 portion of the prepared mushrooms and when they are heated pour over them the beaten eggs. Immediately start to move the pan vigorously in a circle over the heat. Move the pan constantly, swirling the eggs up the sides of the pan and flipping them back again. Moving the pan in this way allows the omelette to cook in layers, making it light. Continue in that fashion until the eggs are lightly browned on the under side. Turn the omelette, taking care not to break it, and brown the other side. Slide the completed omelette out onto a warm serving plate. Sprinkle it with the chopped chives and serve it at once.

Variations of the Forester's Omelette follow.

Spinach Omelette | Frittata con Spinaci

3 cups chopped, cooked spinach
Thoroughly drain the cooked spinach and divide it into 6 portions. Then proceed with each serving as for Forester's Omelette, substituting the spinach for the mushrooms, but partially cooking the eggs in the butter

Pepper Omelette | Frittata di Peperoni

6 Tbl finely chopped green pepper   **2 Tbl finely chopped, canned roasted red pepper (drained)**

Proceed as for Spinach Omelette, substituting the green and red peppers for the spinach.

Onion Omelette | Frittata di Cipolle

3 Tbl butter   **2 cups firmly packed,**
3 Tbl olive oil   **finely chopped scallions**
    Salt & white pepper

Cook the onions in the butter and olive oil, heated together in a skillet, until the onions are soft but not browned. Drain them, season with salt and white pepper to taste, and divide into 6 portions of ⅓-cup each to provide the fillings for 6 omelettes, each to be prepared separately.

Make the omelettes as indicated for Spinach Omelette, substituting the onion preparation for the spinach.

Country-Style Omelette | Frittata Rurale

2 Tbl olive oil   **2 thin slices bacon, cooked**
1 Tbl butter   **fairly crisp & finely chopped**
1 cup diced, peeled, cooked potato   **2 tsp finely chopped parsley**
1 cup finely chopped onion   **⅛ tsp dried thyme**
¼ cup finely chopped cooked ham   **Salt & pepper**

In a skillet heat the olive oil and butter. Add the potato and brown the dice lightly. Add the onion and continue the cooking until it, too, is lightly browned, by which time the potatoes will be well browned, as they should be. Add the ham, bacon, parsley, thyme, and salt and pepper to taste, and let the meats heat through. Drain the mixture and divide it into 6 equal portions to be used as fillings for 6 omelettes.

Prepare the omelettes, following instructions for Forester's Omelette, substituting the above mixture for the mushrooms.

7 | vegetables

Italy holds vegetables in such great esteem that she accords them a place of honor as a separate course, often preceding the entrée. Throughout Italy a great variety of ingenious ways of preparing and serving vegetables has evolved.

Consider, for example, the zucchini. Merely simmered in lightly salted water, it might do as an accompaniment to the main course; but its solo presentation inspires other possibilities, perhaps sautéing it in garlic-flavored olive oil and adding a little cheese, or combining it with tomatoes and onions for added zest.

So also fresh spinach becomes tempting, even to reluctant juvenile palates, when the quickly cooked leaves are dressed with a few drops of olive oil and a spray of lemon juice.

For the initiate to the Italian manner with vegetables, the recipes that follow should be a revelation. These excellent natural foods come into their own, not as something dutifully included for the sake of good nutrition, but as grace notes in a delectable succession of courses.

Baked Assorted Vegetables | Verdure al Forno

2 large green peppers

1 large sweet red pepper,
    or 1 roasted red pepper

3 medium zucchini (about 1 pound)

1 medium eggplant

6 leeks, white parts only

2 medium onions, sliced

⅔ cup olive oil

Salt & pepper

Halve the green and red peppers lengthwise and remove the stems, seeds, and white pulp. Cut the halves, green and red separately, crosswise into thin slices. Slice the zucchini thinly. Thinly slice the eggplant and then quarter the slices. Slice the leeks thinly lengthwise.

Lightly oil a baking pan and in it arrange the vegetables in the order indicated. Pour the olive oil over them and sprinkle with salt and pepper to taste. Bake the vegetables at 450 degrees for 30 minutes, or until they are tender. Drain the vegetables and transfer them to a warm serving platter, arranging them in the same order in which they were baked. Serve them hot or cooled. Serves 6.

Molded Artichoke Bottoms | Sformato di Carciofi

12 large artichokes

2 quarts water

2 tsp salt

¼ cup lemon juice

2 Tbl flour

¼ cup olive oil

2 ounces prosciutto, finely chopped

1½ pounds plum tomatoes, peeled,
    seeded & coarsely chopped

1 medium onion, finely chopped

½ pound skinned
    & boned chicken breast

¾ pound chicken giblets,
    finely ground with breast meat

⅓ cup Brown Sauce (page 269)

1 bay leaf

Salt & pepper

3 eggs, beaten

⅓ cup grated Parmesan cheese

2 cups Béchamel Sauce (page 270)

Butter

Fine dry bread crumbs

Sprigs of parsley

Cut stems from artichokes, pull off all leaves except the few that cover the chokes, and trim bottoms neatly. In a large saucepan heat the water to boiling and stir into it the salt, lemon juice, and flour worked to a thin paste with a little of the water. Add artichoke bottoms and cook them at a gentle boil for 20 minutes, or until they are just tender. Do not overcook them. Test for doneness by piercing bottoms with a sharp, pointed knife. Drain artichokes. Remove remaining leaves and chokes and discard them. Cut bottoms into thick rounds and set them aside.

In a skillet heat 2 tablespoons of the olive oil and in it lightly brown the prosciutto. Add the plum tomatoes and cook them at simmer until they are reduced to a thick paste.

In another skillet gently heat the remaining 2 tablespoons olive oil and in it thoroughly brown all together the onion and the ground meats. Stir into the mixture the brown sauce, add the bay leaf, and continue cooking, at simmer, for 10 minutes. Remove and discard bay leaf. Season mixture with salt and pepper to taste. Preheat oven to 350 degrees.

In a mixing bowl combine the eggs and Parmesan cheese with the Béchamel sauce. Thickly butter a 2-quart oven-proof casserole and coat it well with the bread crumbs. Spread ⅓ of the Béchamel mixture over bottom. Cover it with the sliced artichoke bottoms and spread the plum tomato paste over them. Add ½ the meat mixture in an even layer and spread over it another ⅓ of the Béchamel. Cover that with remaining meat mixture and finish with remaining Béchamel.

Set the mold in the preheated oven and bake for 20 minutes, or until a knife inserted into the Béchamel custard can be withdrawn clean. Remove mold from oven and let it rest for 10 minutes. Unmold preparation carefully onto a warm serving platter, decorate with sprigs of parsley, and serve at once. Serves 6.

Stuffed Cabbage Rolls | Involtini di Foglie di Cavolo

1 large head cabbage	1 egg, lightly beaten
Salt	1 Tbl finely chopped parsley
1 Tbl butter	⅛ tsp dried sage, crumbled
4 cups ricotta cheese	Salt & pepper
1 cup grated Parmesan cheese	Olive oil
½ cup medium-dry bread crumbs	Heavy cream

Trim off the tough outer leaves of the cabbage and discard them. Cut out the core. Place cabbage in a deep saucepan and pour over it enough boiling hot water to cover head completely. Add 1 teaspoon salt to each 4 cups water used. Set pan over low heat and cook cabbage, uncovered, at simmer for 15 minutes. Drain head and cool it with cold water, running it into core opening, thereby also loosening leaves. Carefully remove and reserve 18 perfect large leaves and flatten them very gently between sheets of paper toweling. Finely chop enough of the remaining leaves to provide 1 cupful. Reserve the rest of cabbage, under refrigeration, for other uses.

Preheat oven to 400 degrees. Then in a skillet heat the butter and in it cook the chopped cabbage for a moment or two without letting it brown. Cool chopped cabbage and combine it in a mixing bowl with the ricotta and Parmesan cheeses, bread crumbs, egg, parsley, sage, and salt and pepper to taste.

Place about ⅓ cup of the cheese mixture near core end of each cabbage leaf. Roll up leaves, tucking in sides to enclose filling securely. Arrange rolls, seam sides down, in a lightly oiled baking pan, and brush with heavy cream. Set pan in the upper level of the preheated oven and bake rolls for 20 minutes, or until they are lightly browned. Serve them, 3 to a serving as a light entrée, or 2 to each as a first course. Serves 6 as an entrée, 9 as an appetizer.

Carrots and Peas Pie | Tortino di Carote e Piselli

½ cup olive oil	1 cup grated Parmesan cheese
5 cups shelled fresh peas	3 Tbl coarse bread crumbs
1 small onion, thinly sliced	5 Tbl milk
Salt & pepper	1½ cups coarsely chopped
8 eggs, beaten	cooked carrots

In a saucepan combine 6 tablespoons of the olive oil and enough cold water to fill pan to a depth of ½ inch. Heat liquid and in it cook the peas and onion slices for 15 minutes, or until peas are tender. Drain vegetables and season with salt and pepper to taste. Preheat oven to 325 degrees.

In a mixing bowl combine the eggs and Parmesan cheese. Soak the bread crumbs in the milk, squeeze them dry, and blend them into the egg

mixture. Combine that mixture with the cooked peas and onion and the carrots. Brush a deep 8-inch baking dish with the remaining 2 tablespoons of olive oil and spread prepared vegetables evenly in it. Set dish in the preheated oven and bake pie for 30 minutes or until eggs are set and top is nicely browned. Serves 6.

Cauliflower Messinese | Cavolfiore alla Messinese

2 small heads cauliflower	**1 large onion, finely chopped**
(about 2 pounds)	**White pepper**
12 jumbo-size green olives	**½ pound provolone cheese,**
6 anchovies	**thinly sliced**
½ cup olive oil	**1 cup dry white wine, heated**

Wash and trim the cauliflower and separate the heads into flowerets. Pit and thinly slice the olives. Drain the anchovies and cut them into small pieces. Preheat oven to 350 degrees.

Place 2 tablespoons of the olive oil in the bottom of a flame-proof casserole. In it spread ⅓ each of the onion, olives, and anchovies. Over them distribute ⅓ of the cauliflower pieces. Sprinkle them with white pepper to taste and cover with ½ of the cheese slices. Sprinkle that layer with 2 tablespoons of the olive oil and cover it with ½ each of the remaining onion, olives, and anchovies. Arrange a third layer of, in order, ½ of the remaining cauliflower pieces, a dash of pepper, 2 tablespoons olive oil, and the remaining onion, olives, and anchovies. Complete the preparation with the remaining cauliflower and olive oil. Pour the heated wine over and cover with the remaining cheese. Cover casserole, set it in the preheated oven, and cook for 20 minutes, or just until cauliflower is tender. Remove cover and set casserole under a hot broiler for a minute or two to brown top. Serve cauliflower from casserole. Serves 6.

Boiled Chestnuts | Castagne Bollite

2½ pounds chestnuts	Salt & white pepper
2 stalks celery, halved	¼ cup butter, melted
1½ cups dry white wine	Paprika
2½ cups Chicken Broth (page 44)	

Cut a cross in the flat side of the chestnut shells. Place chestnuts in a large saucepan with enough cold water to cover them. Set pan over moderate heat and bring water to a boil. Cook chestnuts for 5 minutes. Drain, peel, and rub off the skins. Return chestnuts to saucepan. Add the celery, wine, broth, and salt and white pepper to taste. Bring to a boil and cook chestnuts for 20 minutes, or until they are soft but still firm. Drain the nuts, discarding celery and liquid. Place chestnuts in a warm serving bowl. Pour the melted butter over them, sprinkle them with paprika, and serve hot. Serves 6.

Eggplant Parmesan Style | Melanzane alla Parmigiana

2 large eggplants	⅓ cup light cream
12 thin slices mozzarella cheese	Bland cooking oil for deep frying
Salt	3 cups Tomato Sauce (page 282)
Flour	6 Tbl grated Parmesan cheese
3 eggs, beaten	

Peel the eggplants and cut each lengthwise into 9 thin slices. Cut the cheese approximately the size of the eggplant slices. Set cheese slices aside. Arrange eggplant in a single layer on double thicknesses of paper toweling and sprinkle lightly with salt. Let them remain for 30 minutes. Cover them with a double layer of paper toweling and press slices to remove as much of the liquid as possible. Dredge slices in flour and coat them well with the eggs and cream, beaten together.

Cook eggplant, a few slices at a time, in deep oil at 370 degrees for 2 minutes, or until they are lightly browned. Remove slices and drain them. Preheat oven to 400 degrees.

Prepare individual servings in 6 gratin dishes, arranging ingredients in each in the following order: 2 tablespoons tomato sauce, a slice of eggplant, 2 more tablespoons of sauce, 1 teaspoon grated cheese, another slice of eggplant, 2 more tablespoons of sauce, a teaspoon of grated cheese, a slice of mozzarella, 2 more tablespoons of sauce, and a final slice of eggplant and teaspoon of grated cheese. Cut the remaining 6 slices of mozzarella into thin strips and arrange them over the top crisscrossed diagonally into a lattice pattern.

Set dishes in the preheated oven for a few minutes until sauce bubbles. Transfer them to a hot broiler until cheese melts and browns lightly. Serve eggplant in the gratin dishes. Serves 6.

Stuffed Eggplant | Melanzane Ripiene

1 large eggplant	1¼ cups grated Parmesan cheese
Flour	¼ cup fine dry bread crumbs
3 eggs	¼ tsp ground nutmeg
5 parts bland cooking oil	Salt & white pepper
to 1 part olive oil	4 cups Tomato Sauce (page 282)
1½ cups ricotta cheese	

Peel the eggplant and cut from the center, lengthwise, 18 paper-thin slices. Enclose remaining eggplant in plastic wrap and reserve it under refrigeration for other uses. Dredge the slices lightly in flour and coat them with 2 of the eggs, beaten. In a deep fryer heat the combined oils, poured to a proper depth, to 350 degrees. Add the slices of eggplant, a few at a time, and fry them briefly, just until they begin to take on a little color. Drain slices well on paper toweling.

    Preheat oven to 350 degrees. In a mixing bowl combine the ricotta, ¾ cup of the Parmesan, bread crumbs, the remaining egg, beaten, nutmeg, and salt and white pepper to taste. Place about 2 tablespoons of mixture near one end of each slice of eggplant, and roll slices to enclose fillings. Arrange rolls seam sides down in a buttered baking pan and pour 2 cups of the tomato sauce around them. Cover rolls with the remaining sauce and sprinkle them with the remaining Parmesan cheese. Bake them in the preheated oven for 15 minutes.

    Serve the rolls, 3 to a serving, with a quantity of the sauce. Serves 6.

Escarole Sicilian Style | Scarola alla Siciliana

1½ pounds escarole	**1 clove garlic, mashed**
Salt	**Salt & pepper**
6 Tbl butter	

Wash the escarole thoroughly under running cold water. Separate the leaves and put them in a saucepan. Cover them with boiling hot water and add ½ teaspoon salt to each 2 cups of water. Set pan over moderate heat and cook leaves for 12 minutes or until they are tender. Drain them well, dry them in paper toweling, and chop them coarsely. In a skillet heat the butter and in it brown the clove of garlic. Remove clove and discard it. Add escarole and cook it for 8 minutes, stirring frequently. Season leaves with salt and pepper to taste and transfer them to a warm bowl for immediate serving. Serves 6.

1¼ pounds tiny white onions, peeled	¾ cup Chicken Broth (page 44), heated
¼ cup olive oil	½ tsp salt
2 Tbl butter	½ cup dry white wine
2 small bay leaves	1 Tbl finely chopped parsley

In a mixing bowl steep the onions in boiling water for 3 minutes. Drain them well. In a skillet heat the olive oil and butter together. Add the onions, bay leaves, chicken broth, and ½ teaspoon salt or more to taste. Cook onions slowly over low heat until broth evaporates and onions begin to brown. Add the wine, cover pan, and steam onions until they are tender. Remove and discard bay leaves. Transfer onions to a serving bowl and sprinkle them with the chopped parsley. Serves 6.

Tomatoes Stuffed with Rice, Piedmontese Style |
Pomodori Ripieni alla Piemontese

6 large ripe tomatoes (about 6 ounces each)	1 Tbl dry white wine
⅓ cup unsalted butter	3 cups Chicken Broth (page 44), heated
1 small onion, finely chopped	¼ cup grated Parmesan cheese
4 shallots, finely chopped	1 small white truffle, grated
1 cup rice	Olive oil
2 medium mushrooms, finely chopped	

Cut a thin slice from the bottom (the blossom end) of each of the tomatoes and reserve them. Scoop out pulp, leaving a sturdy shell. Reserve pulp also. Drain shells upside down in a colander over a bowl.

In a saucepan combine the reserved tomato slices and pulp, any juice drained from shells, and 1 tablespoon of the butter, and cook them over low heat until they are reduced to a moderately thick paste. Force paste through a fine sieve to remove seeds and peel, and set paste aside in a bowl.

In a heavy heat-proof casserole heat 3 tablespoons of the remaining butter and in it lightly sauté the onion and shallots. Stir into them the rice, coating grains well with butter, and add the mushrooms. Cook them for 2 to 3 minutes or until rice grains begin to turn opaque. Blend the wine and chicken broth into the mixture and bring liquid to a boil. Let it bubble for a minute or two. Cover casserole securely and continue cooking over low heat for 25 minutes or until all of the liquid has been absorbed and rice is tender. Remove casserole from heat and stir the Parmesan cheese, truffle, and remaining butter into rice mixture. Fill tomato shells with the mixture. Coat tops with prepared tomato paste and sprinkle them each with a few drops of olive oil. Arrange tomatoes on an oiled baking sheet and bake them at 400 degrees for 20 minutes or until shells are tender. Do not overcook them or they will collapse. Serves 6.

Tomatoes Stuffed with Rice, Milanese Style |
Pomodori Ripieni alla Milanese

Prepare the tomatoes as for Piedmontese-Style Tomatoes Stuffed with Rice (above), omitting the mushrooms, but adding ¼ teaspoon saffron in strands dissolved in the chicken broth.

Baked Eggs in Tomatoes | Uova al Pomodoro al Forno

6 large ripe tomatoes
   (about 6 ounces each)
Salt & white pepper

6 large eggs
¼ cup grated Parmesan cheese

Trim off the tops of the tomatoes and scoop out just enough of the pulp to leave a shell about ¾-inch thick. Reserve pulp. Sprinkle insides of tomatoes with salt and white pepper to taste.

Preheat oven to 350 degrees. Cook tomato pulp in a saucepan, covered, over moderate heat until it is reduced to a moderately thick purée. Force purée through a fine sieve to remove seeds. Arrange tomatoes on a lightly buttered baking sheet and carefully break an egg into each of them. Pour purée in equal amounts over eggs and sprinkle them each with 2 teaspoons of the grated cheese.

Set pan in the preheated oven. For soft eggs, bake tomatoes 10 minutes. For medium-soft eggs, bake 12 minutes. Hard-cooked eggs require 15 minutes or more of baking time. Serves 6.

Potatoes Friuli Style | Patate alla Friulana

3 pounds potatoes,
  cooked in their jackets
3 Tbl butter
3 Tbl olive oil

¾ pound salt pork, finely chopped
1 large onion, finely chopped
Salt & white pepper
½ cup heavy cream

Peel and cut the potatoes into moderately thin slices. In a large skillet heat the butter and olive oil and in them sauté the bits of salt pork until they begin to take on a little color. Add the onion and continue cooking, over moderate heat, until it is lightly browned. Coarsely mash potatoes (they should not be smooth) and stir them into the onions and salt pork. Season them with salt and white pepper to taste and blend the heavy cream into them. Cook them until they are well browned on the under side. Fit a plate over the top of the potatoes and invert skillet and plate together, thereby unmolding the potato cake browned side up on the plate. Slide cake back into pan and brown other side. Serves 6.

Potatoes Family Style | Patate alla Casereccia

6 large potatoes (about 3 pounds)
½ cup olive oil
2 large cloves garlic, peeled
3 sprigs Italian parsley, with stems
1 bay leaf

¼ tsp rosemary
3 fresh sage leaves
  (or ⅛ tsp dried sage)
Salt & pepper

Peel the potatoes, wash them, and cut them each into 9 or 10 odd-size pieces. Do not slice them. Dry the pieces thoroughly on paper toweling. In a large skillet heat the olive oil and in it briskly sauté potatoes stirring them constantly to brown them lightly and evenly. Combine the garlic, parsley, bay leaf, rosemary, sage, and salt and pepper to taste with the potatoes. Reduce heat to medium low and continue cooking potatoes,

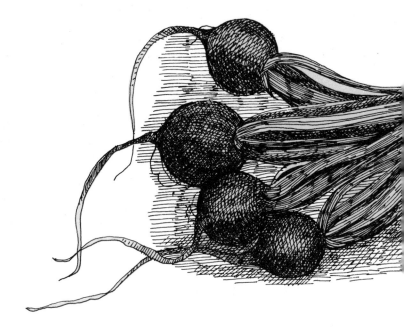

stirring them occasionally until they are tender, about 20 minutes longer. Remove garlic or not, as you prefer. Serves 6.

Spinach Parmesan Style | Spinaci alla Parmigiana

1½ pounds spinach   **Salt & pepper**
1 cup grated Parmesan cheese   **6 Tbl butter, melted**
⅛ tsp ground nutmeg

Trim off any tough stems of the spinach. Wash the leaves thoroughly and shake off most of the water. Place leaves in a large saucepan over moderate heat and cook them, uncovered, for 3 minutes in just the water that clings to leaves. Drain spinach well and chop it finely.

In a mixing bowl combine spinach with ½ cup of the grated cheese and season mixture with the nutmeg and salt and pepper to taste. Pour

3 tablespoons of the melted butter into an oven-proof casserole. Spread spinach-cheese mixture over it and flatten it gently with a wooden spoon or a spatula. Even top, pour over it the remaining melted butter, and sprinkle with the remaining grated cheese. Set casserole in a 450-degree oven and leave it for 8 minutes, or until top is lightly browned. Serves 6.

Zucchini with Cheese and Eggs |
Zucchini in Salsa di Uova e Formaggio

2 pounds medium zucchini
⅓ cup cold water
5 Tbl butter, melted & cooled
2 eggs

1½ cups heavy cream
1 cup grated Parmesan cheese
Salt & white pepper
2 Tbl firm butter, cut into bits

Cut the zucchini into slices ¼-inch thick. In a saucepan combine sliced zucchini, the water, and 1 tablespoon of the melted butter. Steam zucchini, covered, over moderate heat for 5 to 6 minutes, or until all water evaporates and slices are tender but still firm.

Preheat oven to 400 degrees. Transfer zucchini to a buttered heat-proof casserole. In a mixing bowl blend the eggs, cream, ½ cup of the grated cheese, and the remaining melted butter. Season mixture with salt and white pepper to taste and pour it over zucchini in the casserole. Sprinkle top with the remaining grated cheese and distribute over it the bits of butter. Bake zucchini in the preheated oven for 20 minutes, or until topping is lightly browned. Serves 6.

Grandmother's Zucchini | Zucchini della Nonna

6 medium zucchini
4 Tbl olive oil
1 clove garlic, finely chopped
½ tsp oregano
2 Tbl finely chopped parsley
Salt & pepper

Slice the zucchini into rounds about ¼-inch thick. In a skillet heat the oil and in it cook zucchini over high heat for 10 minutes, stirring rounds constantly so they do not burn. Blend in the garlic, oregano, parsley, and salt and pepper to taste, reduce heat to moderate, and continue cooking for 5 minutes longer. Serves 6.

Zucchini Stuffed with Farina | Zucchini Farciti con Semolino

3 medium zucchini
   (about 6 ounces each)
2 cups boiling hot water
2 cups milk
½ tsp salt
6 Tbl farina
1 egg yolk
¾ cup grated Parmesan cheese
1 Tbl butter, melted

Thoroughly wash the zucchini and trim off the stem ends. Split zucchini lengthwise and place in a saucepan with the boiling hot water. Cover pan and steam zucchini halves over medium heat for 3 minutes or until they begin to soften. Remove halves and scrape out of each a small quantity of the pulp. Reserve it. Cool halves.

In the top pan of a double-boiler season the milk with the salt and scald it over medium-low heat. Stir in the farina, a little at a time. Set pan over simmering water and cook farina, covered, for 10 minutes, stirring occasionally to keep it smooth. If it becomes too thick, thin it slightly with a little hot milk. It should, however, be quite thick. Remove pan from over water and beat the egg yolk, ½ cup of the grated cheese, and the reserved zucchini pulp, well mashed, into farina. Preheat oven to 350 degrees.

Arrange cooled zucchini halves on an oiled baking sheet. Using a pastry bag, fitted with a fluted tube, pipe farina mixture equally onto the scooped surfaces of the 6 zucchini halves. Brush them each with the melted butter and sprinkle them with the remaining grated cheese. Set baking sheet in the preheated oven and bake zucchini for 15 minutes or until tops are lightly browned. Serve stuffed zucchini hot. Serves 6.

Zucchini Parmesan Style | Zucchini alla Parmigiana

6 medium zucchini
   (about 2 pounds)
3 Tbl olive oil
3 Tbl butter
1½ cups canned,
   peeled plum tomatoes

⅓ cup juice reserved
   from plum tomatoes
Salt & pepper
⅔ cup grated Parmesan cheese

Thoroughly wash the zucchini and dry them well. Cut them into slices about ¼-inch thick. In a large skillet heat together the olive oil and butter and in them cook zucchini slices over high heat, browning them well on both sides. Turn them with a large metal spatula, taking care not to crush or break them. Gently stir into them the tomatoes and reserved juice, and season mixture with salt and pepper to taste. Reduce heat to medium and continue cooking for a few minutes to blend the flavors. Combine mixture in a heat-proof baking dish with ⅓ cup of the grated cheese. Sprinkle the remainder of the cheese over top. Set dish under a hot broiler to brown topping. Serve zucchini hot. Serves 6.

8 | salads

The beauty of the salad course is that it is many things to many people. It is a way of giving due appreciation to tender field greens as they come into season. It can use to advantage items from the meal of the day before, such as meat and rice. And it can be expanded to provide a cool and utterly satisfying main course.

In whatever way you enjoy salads, you will find here recipes to accommodate every approach. And don't overlook the recipes among the Antipasti that can be adapted for salad use: marinated mushrooms, for example, or broccoli with oil and lemon, or *caponata.*

One Italian green deserves special mention, since it has only recently come into favor here. This is arugola. If you are fortunate enough to be able to get it, you will find that a few pieces mixed with other greens will give your salad a pleasurable new flavor.

Here, with the salad, one has the opportunity to express that highly Italian characteristic of spontaneity—in using what is at hand, in making unusual combinations, in keeping the appetite very much alive.

Green Bean Salad | Insalata di Fagiolini Verdi

2 pounds young green beans	**1 clove garlic, peeled & mashed**
Boiling hot water	**1 Tbl finely chopped parsley**
Salt	**¼ cup red wine vinegar**
4 large scallions, white parts only,	**½ cup olive oil**
finely chopped	**Salt & pepper**

Trim the beans, put them in a large saucepan, and pour over them just enough salted boiling water to cover. Set over moderate heat and cook beans, uncovered, for 15 minutes, or until they are still rather crisp and *al dente.* Drain beans in a colander and cool them under running cold water. Dry them on paper toweling. Chill beans thoroughly.

Prepare salad dressing with the scallions, garlic, parsley, red wine vinegar, olive oil, and salt and pepper to taste, all combined in a mixing bowl. Cover bowl and let the dressing season at room temperature for at least 1 hour. Remove garlic and discard it.

Arrange beans in a chilled salad bowl and pour the dressing over them. Set bowl in refrigerator and let beans marinate in dressing until serving time. Serves 6.

Carnica-Style Salad | Insalata alla Carnica

¾ pound fresh mushrooms,	**4 radishes, thinly sliced**
thinly sliced	**1 small cucumber, peeled & sliced**
4 stalks celery, thinly sliced	**1 Tbl finely chopped parsley**
1 small head cauliflower,	**¼ cup red wine vinegar**
trimmed & broken into flowerets	**Salt & pepper**
1 large green pepper,	**½ cup olive oil**
seeded & thinly sliced	

Chill the prepared vegetables thoroughly and combine them in a large salad bowl. Sprinkle them with the chopped parsley.

In a mixing bowl dissolve salt to taste in the vinegar and add a good grinding of black pepper. With a whisk or fork beat the oil into the vinegar until an emulsion is formed. Dress the chilled vegetables with this vinaigrette and serve the salad at once. Serves 6.

Cheese and Pepper Salad | Insalata di Formaggio e Peperoni

8 sweet red peppers

¾ pound Swiss cheese, diced

⅓ cup pitted green olives

⅓ cup pitted black olives

2 tsp prepared Dijon mustard

1⅓ cups Salad Dressing (page 285)

Place the peppers on a baking sheet under a hot broiler and let them remain until the skins are well blistered. Turn peppers frequently to prevent their burning. Using a cloth, rub off skins. When they are cool enough to handle, core them and remove the white pulp. Cut peppers into moderately thin strips and chill them thoroughly.

In a chilled mixing bowl combine the peppers, cheese, and olives. Blend the mustard into the dressing and pour the mixture over the salad. Stir ingredients gently to coat them well. Serves 6.

NOTE: If sweet red peppers are not available, well-drained canned ones may be used.

Chef's Salad | Insalata del Cuoco

½ head escarole

½ head chicory

½ head romaine

1 clove garlic, cut

6 hard-cooked eggs,
    peeled & quartered

1 cup small-julienne
    provolone cheese

1 cup small-julienne
    mortadella sausage

8 slices Italian-style salami,
    cut in small julienne

3½-ounce can tuna fish,
    drained & flaked

1 small cucumber, peeled & cut
    into moderately thin slices

24 oil-cured Italian olives

Salad Dressing (page 285)

Wash, dry, and chill the escarole, chicory, and romaine. Rub 6 individual wood salad bowls well with the cut clove of garlic and discard it. Separate the leaves of greens and mix them. Distribute the assorted leaves equally among the 6 bowls. Place 2 halves of egg in the center of each bowl of greens and arrange around them, separately and attractively, equal quantities of the remaining ingredients. Dress the salads individually at the table. Serves 6.

Dandelion Salad | Insalata di Radicchio

2 pounds dandelion greens
12 slices bacon (about ½ pound)
2 cloves garlic, mashed

⅓ cup red wine vinegar
1 egg, beaten
Salt & pepper

Wash the dandelion greens thoroughly, floating them in a large quantity of water in a basin to remove all the soil. Drain greens and dry between sheets of paper toweling. Tear greens coarsely and arrange them lightly in a serving bowl.

Cut the bacon into ½-inch pieces and combine them in a skillet with the garlic. Set pan over moderate heat and cook bacon thoroughly without letting it become crisp. Remove and discard cloves of garlic. Slowly, to avoid splattering, stir the vinegar into the bacon and the rendered fat in skillet. Let mixture heat through to blend the flavors and remove pan from heat. Let dressing cool and pour it over greens in bowl. Blend in the beaten egg and season salad with salt and pepper to taste. Serves 6.

Fresh Fennel Salad | Insalata di Finocchi

6 medium heads fresh fennel	**¼ tsp dried oregano**
1 small onion, thinly sliced	**Salt & pepper**
6 red radishes, thinly sliced	**½ cup olive oil**
3 Tbl red wine vinegar	

Trim off the tops of the fennel and remove and discard any discolored leaves of the heads. Wash the heads under cool running water and drain and dry them well. Cut them crosswise into thin slices and combine them in a salad bowl with the onion and radishes. Prepare a dressing by combining the vinegar in a mixing bowl with the oregano and salt and pepper to taste, and beating into it the olive oil, a little at a time. Pour the dressing over the salad in the bowl. Chill salad before serving it as a separate luncheon course or, at dinner, as a first course. Serves 6.

Salad of Field Greens | Insalata di Rugola

¾ pound arugola (see Glossary)	**1 large clove garlic, peeled & cut**
4 scallions	**Pepper**
2 Tbl plus 1 tsp red wine vinegar	**6 Tbl olive oil**
½ tsp salt	**½ cucumber, peeled & sliced**

Trim off the stems of the arugola and remove any wilted or discolored leaves. Wash the greens, drain them, and dry them gently between sheets of paper toweling. Finely chop the scallions, including some of the darker green parts of the stalks.

Dampen a salad bowl with the teaspoon of red wine vinegar and sprinkle it with the salt. Rub the cut clove of garlic thoroughly into the salt. Discard remainder of clove. Stir the 2 tablespoons of vinegar into the seasoned salt and add a good grinding of black pepper. With a whisk or a fork beat the olive oil into the vinegar a little at a time. Stir the chopped scallions into the dressing and add the slices of cucumber and the arugola. Toss greens gently to coat them with dressing. Serves 6.

Green Salad with Truffle | Insalata Verde con Tartufi

1 large head romaine	**Salt & pepper**
1 small bunch celery hearts	**6 Tbl olive oil**
3 Tbl strained lemon juice	**1 medium white truffle**

Wash the romaine and drain it well. Wrap the leaves in paper toweling and chill them so in the refrigerator. Wash the celery and drain it. Wrap it in paper toweling and chill it also.

In a mixing bowl combine the lemon juice and seasonings and beat the olive oil, a tablespoon at a time, into the juice. Tear the chilled romaine leaves into serving pieces. Cut the celery hearts into slices about ⅛-inch thick. Brush the truffle and cut it in fine julienne. In a chilled mixing bowl combine the romaine and celery and pour the prepared dressing over them. Toss the salad, coating the greens and celery well with the dressing, and sprinkle the bits of truffle over them. Serves 6.

Salad of Italian Greens | Insalata Verde

1 medium head escarole	**⅔ cup Dressing for Antipasto**
1 medium head chicory	**(page 284)**
1 medium head romaine	**Salt & pepper**
	1 cup Garlic Croutons (page 75)

Separate the leaves from the heads of greens and wash them well. Shake them dry and wrap them lightly in several sheets of paper toweling. Chill wrapped greens thoroughly. At serving time break the leaves into medium-size pieces into a chilled salad bowl and pour the dressing over them. Toss greens lightly 2 or 3 times. Correct the seasoning with additions of salt and pepper to taste, if needed. Add the croutons and toss the salad again, gently, just enough to distribute croutons evenly and coat all the leaves with the dressing. This recipe will provide 6 to 8 servings.

Marisa's Salad | Insalata Marisa

½ pound arugola (see Glossary)	**2 Tbl chopped parsley**
1 head fennel	**½ cup olive oil**

2 cups cooked pea beans
6 ounces fresh mushrooms,
    sliced (about 2 cups)

2 Tbl red wine vinegar
Salt & pepper

Trim and wash the arugola and thoroughly drain it. Wash and thoroughly drain the fennel and slice it thinly. In a chilled salad bowl combine the beans, mushrooms, parsley, arugola, and fennel. Blend the olive oil slowly into the vinegar in a mixing bowl and season with salt and pepper to taste. Pour dressing over salad and stir ingredients gently. Serves 6.

Octopus Salad | Insalata di Polipi

4 octopuses,
    each weighing about 1½ pounds
1 carrot, peeled & coarsely chopped
3 stalks celery,
    scraped & coarsely chopped
1 lemon, quartered

1 large onion,
    peeled & coarsely chopped
½ tsp peppercorns
2 bay leaves
Boiling hot water
2 Tbl salt

Clean the octopuses (page 130) or have them cleaned at the fish market, but leave the skin intact. If you are using larger octopuses, they will probably need preliminary tenderizing, which is done by pounding cleaned octopuses with a wooden mallet until the muscle tissues are reduced almost to a pulp.

In a very large saucepan combine the octopuses and the vegetables and seasonings indicated for the cooking. Cover them deeply with boiling water and cook them, covered, for 1 hour or until octopuses are tender but still rather firm. Let octopuses cool in the broth. Remove them and rub off the skins.

Quarter octopuses and cut the quarters crosswise into thin slices. Put the slices in a bowl and coat them well with the dressing given below.

Dressing for Octopus Salad:

1 cup olive oil
⅓ cup lemon juice
½ tsp salt
2 cloves garlic,
    very finely chopped

8 large scallions, finely chopped
1 medium onion, thinly sliced
⅓ cup finely chopped parsley
Pepper

In a mixing bowl combine the olive oil, lemon juice, and salt, and beat the mixture with a whisk or a fork until an emulsion is formed. Thoroughly beat into it the garlic, scallions, onions, parsley, and a good grinding of black pepper. Cover bowl and let dressing season at room temperature for at least 1 hour before using it.

Chill the dressed slices of octopus for several hours or, better still, overnight. Remove bowl from refrigerator and leave salad at room temperature for 15 minutes. Stir slices again before serving salad. This recipe will provide 8 to 10 generous servings as a main course at luncheon or as antipasto at dinner.

Potato Salad | Insalata di Patate

2 pounds potatoes	1 Tbl finely chopped parsley
Salt	3 Tbl red wine vinegar
6 slices crisply cooked bacon, crumbled	½ cup olive oil
½ cup finely chopped scallions, white parts only	3 radishes, thinly sliced
	1 clove garlic, mashed
	Pepper & additional salt

Scrub the potatoes, put them in a large saucepan, and cover them with water. Add 1 teaspoon salt to each 4 cups water used. Cover pan and cook potatoes over moderate heat for 20 minutes, or until they are tender but still firm. Drain potatoes, cool them, peel them, and cut them into slices about ¼-inch thick. Combine them in a salad bowl with the bacon, scallions, and parsley, and pour over them a salad dressing made by combining in a mixing bowl the vinegar, oil, radishes, garlic, and salt and pepper to taste. Let the dressing season for about 1 hour. Remove garlic and discard it. Serves 6.

Rice Salad | Insalata di Riso

1½ cups raw rice	2 hard-cooked eggs, coarsely chopped
4 cups boiling hot water	1 Tbl finely chopped parsley
5 tsp salt	

1 cup shelled fresh peas
¼ cup capers
⅓ cup finely chopped, canned
   roasted sweet red peppers
⅓ cup olive oil
2 Tbl lemon juice
White pepper
Sprigs of parsley

Put the rice in a 2-quart saucepan and pour the boiling water, seasoned with 3 teaspoons of the salt, over it. Cook rice, covered, at a simmer for 20 minutes, or until grains are tender but firm. Drain rice in a colander and cool it under running water. Drain it again, thoroughly.

In a small saucepan with 1½ cups boiling water and 1 teaspoon of the salt, cook the peas, uncovered, over moderate heat for 5 minutes. Drain peas and combine them in a mixing bowl with rice. Add the capers, peppers, eggs, and parsley, and toss the mixture with a fork. Prepare a salad dressing by blending together in a small mixing bowl the olive oil, lemon juice, white pepper, and the remaining teaspoon of salt. Blend dressing into rice mixture. Mold salad in a bowl and chill it thoroughly. Unmold it onto a chilled platter and decorate platter with the parsley. Serves 6.

Peasant Salad | Insalata alla Contadina

2 cloves garlic,
   peeled & well mashed
½ tsp salt
¼ cup red wine vinegar
½ cup olive oil
⅛ tsp black pepper
5 large tomatoes,
   cored & thickly sliced
1 green pepper,
   seeded & thinly sliced
1 sweet red pepper,
   seeded & thinly sliced
3 scallions, thinly sliced
1 small cucumber,
   peeled & thickly sliced
1 Tbl whole Italian parsley leaves
3 anchovy fillets, cut in small pieces
¼ tsp oregano
6 black olives
6 green olives
3 hard-cooked eggs,
   peeled & thickly sliced

In a large salad bowl rub the garlic into the salt until the cloves are reduced to a smooth paste. Blend into it the vinegar and olive oil and add the black pepper. Distribute the remaining ingredients in layers in the

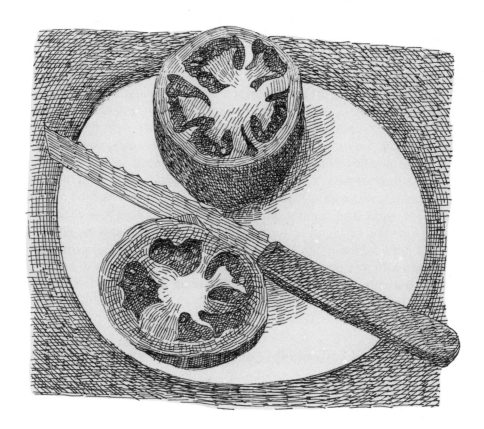

bowl in order listed and toss them together coating the vegetables well with the dressing. Set salad in a cool place for about 1 hour to meld the flavors. Correct the seasoning, adding more salt and pepper if needed. Toss salad again before serving. Serves 6.

Tomato Salad | Insalata di Pomodori

8 scallions, white parts only
6 medium tomatoes

¼ cup red wine vinegar
⅛ tsp white pepper

1 large clove garlic, peeled
½ tsp salt

6 Tbl olive oil

Slice the scallions very thinly. Peel the tomatoes and cut each tomato into 6 wedges. Set scallions and tomato wedges aside. In a mixing bowl thoroughly mash the garlic into the salt. Stir in the vinegar, dissolving the salt in it. Remove and discard garlic. Add the white pepper. With a whisk or a fork beat the oil, a little at a time, into the vinegar until an emulsion is formed. Stir the sliced scallions into the dressing.

Arrange the tomato wedges in a chilled salad bowl and pour the salad dressing over them. Stir tomatoes gently to coat them well. Serves 6.

A Salad of Tuna Fish and Beans | Insalata di Tonno e Fagioli

1 cup dried chick-peas (ceci beans)
1 cup dried navy beans
Cold water
1 medium onion
6 large scallions, white parts only
1 cup canned tuna fish

Salt & pepper
½ tsp salt
3 Tbl white wine vinegar
⅛ tsp pepper
6 Tbl olive oil

Place the chick-peas and navy beans in separate mixing bowls and cover them with cold water. Let them soak for 12 hours. Drain beans and transfer them to separate large saucepans, each with 6 cups fresh cold water. Bring water in each saucepan to boil over low heat. Cover pans and cook beans at simmer for 1½–2 hours, or until they are tender but still firm. Drain beans and cool them. Slice the onion very thinly and finely chop the scallions. Drain and flake the tuna fish. Combine beans in a mixing bowl with onion, scallions, and tuna fish. Season mixture with salt and pepper to taste.

In a small mixing bowl dissolve the ½ teaspoon salt in the vinegar and add the pepper. Beat into the vinegar the olive oil, a tablespoon at a time, until an emulsion is formed. Pour the dressing over salad in bowl, blending it in gently so as not to crush beans. Chill preparation before serving it as a main-course luncheon salad of 6 servings, or purée and serve it with crisp raw vegetables as a cocktail accompaniment.

9 | desserts

Haute cuisine may be the property of France, but *la dolce vita,* the sweet life, was born Italian. The people of Italy have always excelled as pastry cooks. History suggests that the French knew little of the art of fine baking until Catherine de Medici came to Paris for her marriage to the future king, Henry II, and brought her personal pastry chef along. The French, of course, have since added refinements of their own, but the ancestry of such marvels as fruit ices, pastry creams, and the tantalizing almond macaroons called *amaretti* is clearly traceable to Italy.

Italian pastries are unashamedly rich. There is no sparing of butter, cream, eggs, and pastes, the ingredients necessary to fine sweets. Frankly fattening though they may be, there must be—even in our diet-conscious life—an occasional joyful lapse from austerity to savor the extravagance of these delicious desserts.

Custard with Marsala | Zabaglione

8 egg yolks   **½ cup sweet Marsala wine**
¾ cup sugar

Combine the egg yolks and sugar in the top pan of a double boiler and beat them with a rotary beater until they are light and frothy. Blend in the Marsala and set pan over barely simmering water. Continue beating until custard is thick and has increased in volume. Apportion the 6 servings among sherbet glasses. Serve the custard warm or chilled.

Marsala Custard Parfait | Zabaglione con Gelato

Custard with Marsala (above)   **1 pint vanilla ice cream, softened**

Prepare the custard as directed in the recipe. Cool and chill it. Fold into it the softened ice cream and serve the mixture in chilled parfait glasses. Decorate each serving with a maraschino cherry. This recipe provides 8 to 10 servings.

Coffee Pudding | Budino al Caffè

¾ cup sugar   **1 Tbl instant espresso coffee**
1½ cups rich milk or light cream   **¼ cup cold water**
6 eggs   **1 Tbl unflavored gelatine**
⅛ tsp salt   **Coffee Sugar (see below)**
¼ tsp finely grated lemon peel

In the top pan of a double boiler directly over low heat dissolve ½ the sugar in the milk. Do not allow the milk to boil. In a heat-proof mixing bowl beat the eggs with the salt, lemon peel, and remaining sugar until the mixture is smooth and foamy. Add the heated milk gradually, beating constantly. Cook the mixture in the milk pan over simmering water, stirring constantly until it coats a spoon. Dissolve the instant coffee in the water and soften the gelatine in that liquid. Add it to the custard, stirring until the gelatine is dissolved. Pour the custard into a 3 to 4 cup decorative mold rinsed in cold water. Cool custard and chill it in refrigerator

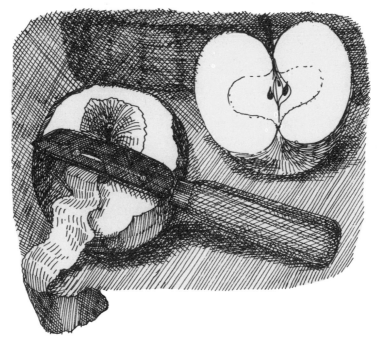

until it is set. Unmold pudding onto a chilled serving plate and sprinkle it with coffee sugar. If you like, decorate the base with rosettes of whipped cream, piped on with a pastry bag fitted with a star tube. This recipe will provide 6 to 8 servings.

NOTE: To make coffee sugar, combine ½ teaspoon instant espresso coffee with 1 tablespoon fine granulated sugar.

Ricotta Pudding | Budino di Ricotta

2½ cups ricotta cheese, sieved	Grated rind of 1 lemon
⅓ cup almond paste	½ cup flour
6 Tbl butter, melted	¾ cup powdered sugar
4 eggs, separated	¼ tsp ground cinnamon
2 Tbl rum	5 or 6 rings of canned pineapple,
½ cup finely chopped	drained & halved
mixed glazed fruit	

Preheat oven to 350 degrees. In a mixing bowl thoroughly combine the cheese, almond paste, melted butter, egg yolks, rum, glazed fruit, and grated lemon rind. Sift together and stir into the mixture the flour, ½ cup of the sugar, and the cinnamon. Beat the egg whites until they are stiff but not dry. Stir ¼ of them into the cheese mixture and thoroughly but gently fold in the remainder.

Pour the batter into a deep 6-cup capacity fluted mold and bake it in the preheated oven for 30 minutes or until a table knife inserted in the center can be withdrawn clean. Partially cool pudding in mold and turn it out onto a serving plate to cool completely. Sift the remaining powdered sugar over pudding and surround base with the halved pineapple rings, cut sides in. Serve with whipped cream flavored with vanilla. This recipe provides 6 to 8 servings.

Honey Pudding | Budino di Miele

½ cup honey	3 egg yolks
⅓ cup thinly sliced	⅓ cup sugar
blanched almonds	2½ cups light cream
3 eggs	½ tsp finely grated orange peel

Preheat oven to 350 degrees. Pour ¼ cup of the honey into an 8-inch cake pan and heat it gently until it turns a light caramel color. Remove pan from heat and rotate it to coat the bottom and sides evenly with the honey. Sprinkle the bottom with the sliced almonds. Set pan aside for the moment and let the coating cool.

In a mixing bowl combine the whole eggs and egg yolks and beat them with the sugar and the remaining honey. Blend in the cream and orange peel and pour mixture into the prepared pan. Set the pan in a pan of hot water in the preheated oven and bake for 1 hour or until a knife inserted in the center of the custard can be withdrawn clean. Cool the custard and chill it. Unmold it onto a chilled serving dish. This pudding will provide 6 servings.

Black and White Pudding | Budino Bianco e Nero

¾ cup sugar	1 Tbl unflavored gelatine
4 cups light cream	8 ounces semisweet chocolate,
4 eggs	melted & cooled

4 egg yolks	**36 ladyfingers**
4 Tbl cornstarch	**6 Tbl Strega liqueur**
6 Tbl water	**½ cup chopped pecans**

In the top pan of a double boiler directly over low heat dissolve ½ cup of the sugar in the cream. Do not let the cream boil. In a mixing bowl beat together the whole eggs, egg yolks, and remaining sugar. Slowly add the heated cream, beating constantly. Dissolve the cornstarch in 2 tablespoons of the water and stir it into the combined eggs and cream. Transfer the mixture to the double boiler pan and cook it over simmering water for 2 minutes, stirring constantly until the custard thickens. Soften the gelatine in 2 tablespoons of the water and dissolve it in the still hot custard. Cool the custard completely, stirring it frequently so that it does not set. Transfer ½ of the custard to a bowl and stir into it ½ the melted chocolate.

Lightly butter a mold 4-inches deep and 9 inches in diameter. Split the ladyfingers and line bottom and sides of mold with as many as are needed. Reserve the remainder. Combine the Strega and the remaining water and moisten the ladyfingers with the diluted liqueur. Pour in the chocolate custard. Chill custard in the mold until it is set. Pour the plain custard over it and continue the chilling until it, too, is set and firm. Cover the molded creams with the remaining halves of ladyfingers and chill again until serving time.

Unmold the pudding onto a chilled serving plate. Pour the remaining melted chocolate over it and sprinkle with the pecans. This recipe provides 6 servings.

Sponge Cake | Pan di Spagna

3 egg whites	**⅔ cup flour**
6 egg yolks	**⅔ cup cornstarch**
1⅓ cups sugar	**¼ tsp salt**
1 tsp vanilla extract	**2 Tbl butter, melted & cooled**

Preheat oven to 350 degrees. Butter and lightly flour 2 8-inch cake pans. In a mixing bowl combine the egg whites, egg yolks, sugar, and vanilla and beat the mixture until it is very thick. When it is properly thick, a

ribbon of the mixture, dripped from the beater into the mass, will remain visible for a few seconds.

Sift together the flour, cornstarch, and salt, and fold them gently into the eggs. Gently stir in the melted butter. Pour the batter into the prepared pans and bake it at the indicated temperature for 20 minutes or until a cake tester inserted in the centers can be withdrawn clean. Let the cakes cool in the pans for a few minutes until they shrink away from the sides. Turn out onto racks and let cool completely.

Chocolate Sponge Cake | Pan di Spagna al Cioccolato

Proceed as for plain sponge cake (page 235), reducing the flour and cornstarch to ⅓ cup each and adding ⅔ cup cocoa.

Coffee Sponge Cake | Pan di Spagna al Caffè

Proceed as for plain sponge cake (page 235), blending 1 tablespoon instant coffee into the batter.

Ricotta Cheese Cake | Cassata di Ricotta

1 layer Sponge Cake	**¼ cup finely chopped pistachio nuts**
(½ recipe, page 235)	**1 tsp vanilla extract**
18 glazed green cherries, halved	**½ tsp ground cinnamon**
18 glazed red cherries, halved	**2 Tbl unflavored gelatine**
3 pounds ricotta cheese, sieved	**⅓ cup hot water**
2 cups sugar	**Whipped cream**
6 ounces mixed glazed fruit,	**Grated semisweet chocolate**
finely chopped	

Split the single layer of sponge cake in half horizontally to provide 2 layers. Cut 1 of the layers into pieces the size of ladyfingers. Reserve the remaining layer whole. Butter the sides only of a mold 8 inches in diameter and 2 inches deep, and line sides with the pieces of sponge cake. Over bottom of pan arrange the green and red cherries in a decorative pattern.

In a mixing bowl combine the cheese, sugar, glazed fruit, pistachios, vanilla, and cinnamon. Dissolve the gelatine in the hot water and blend it into the cheese mixture. Pour the mixture carefully (so as not to dislodge the pieces of cake) into the prepared pan and set the remaining whole layer of cake on top. Chill cake in refrigerator for at least 2 hours. Unmold it onto a chilled serving plate and coat it lightly with whipped cream. Gently press grated chocolate into sides of cake and sprinkle some over top. Cut cake into wedges to provide 8 to 10 servings.

Gianduia Chocolate Cake | Torta Gianduia al Cioccolato

1 layer Chocolate Sponge Cake
  (½ recipe, page 237)
⅓ cup Chocolate Syrup (page 265)
3 Tbl rum
3 Tbl sugar
½ cup heavy cream, whipped

1 cup Pastry Cream (page 265)
3 ounces semisweet chocolate,
  melted & cooked
2 Tbl crème de cacao liqueur
Shaved unsweetened chocolate
Toasted blanched almonds, slivered

Split the single layer of chocolate sponge cake in thirds to provide 3 layers. Moisten the layers with the syrup, rum, and sugar combined. In a mixing bowl fold the whipped cream into the pastry cream and blend into them the melted chocolate and liqueur. Arrange the layers of moistened cake on a chilled serving plate interspersing them each with ⅓ of the cream mixture. Spread the top layer with the remaining chocolate cream. Sprinkle it with the shaved chocolate and the slivered almonds. Chill cake thoroughly before serving it in wedges to provide 6 to 8 servings.

Anise Cake | Biscotti all'Anice

1 recipe Sponge Cake batter
  (page 235)

3 Tbl anise liqueur
1 Tbl anise seeds

Stir the anise liqueur into the sponge cake batter and fold in the anise seeds. Bake as directed for the sponge cake. Cool cake on a rack. Cover it lightly and let it remain overnight. Cut it into slices ¾-inch thick and toast the slices under a broiler.

    Stored in a securely covered container the slices can be kept for a week or longer. Serve them with tea or coffee.

Anise Trifle | Zuppa all'Anice

Anise Cake (above)
3 cups heavy cream

⅓ cup sugar
¼ cup anise liqueur

Cut the toasted pieces of anise cake into halves and arrange ¼ of them in the bottom of a deep 8-inch round serving dish. Stiffly whip the cream sweetened with the sugar and stir into it the anise liqueur. Reserve ½

Elegant finale for a special dinner, this Cassata Gelata consists of layers of molded ice cream beautifully topped with whipped cream.

cup of the flavored whipped cream. Spread the layer of anise cake with ¼ of the remainder. Arrange the remaining ingredients in layers, alternating cake and cream and finishing with cake.

With a pastry bag, fitted with a decorative tube, pipe the reserved cream over the top in an attractive pattern. Chill the trifle thoroughly before serving it. Provides 6 to 8 servings.

Italian Trifle | Zuppa Inglese

1 layer sponge cake
   (½ recipe, page 235)
6 Tbl Rum Syrup (page 265)
1 cup Pastry Cream (page 265)
½ cup heavy cream, whipped
1 ounce semisweet chocolate,
   grated
1 Tbl finely chopped
   mixed glazed fruit

1 Tbl chestnut purée
2 slices Fruit Bread (page 252),
   cut horizontally about
   ½-inch thick
2 Tbl coarse macaroon crumbs
5 egg whites
½ cup sugar

Split the single layer of sponge cake in half to make 2 layers. Place 1 slice on a heat-proof dish and douse it with 2 tablespoons of the rum syrup. Combine the pastry cream and whipped cream and spread ½ of that over the layer of cake. Combine the grated chocolate, glazed fruit, and chestnut purée and distribute ½ of that over the cream. Cover with a slice of the fruit bread. Sprinkle it with 2 tablespoons of the syrup and spread it with the remaining combined creams. Sprinkle the macaroon crumbs over that and cover them with the remaining layer of cake. Dot with the remaining chocolate-fruit-chestnut combination. Place the remaining slice of fruit bread on top and brush it with the remaining syrup. Chill the filled layers thoroughly in the refrigerator.

Preheat oven to 550 degrees. In a mixing bowl beat the egg whites into soft peaks. Add the sugar gradually, continuing to beat until the whites are whipped to a stiff meringue. Spread it evenly over the chilled cake right down to the serving dish. Set in the preheated oven for 3 minutes or until the meringue is lightly browned. Let the trifle cool. Chill it briefly before serving it cut into wedges to provide 6 to 8 servings.

Assortment of desserts: Neapolitan Honey Balls
(center foreground and continuing clockwise), Chocolate
Truffle, Marsala Custard Parfait, Italian Trifle,
Volcano Cake, Zabaglione Cake (center), Latticed Apricot
Pie, and Sicilian-Style Cream Shells.

Strawberry Cream Cake | Torta alla Crema di Fragole

1½ pints fresh strawberries	1 layer Sponge Cake
1 6-ounce jar strawberry preserves	(½ recipe, page 235)
⅓ cup sweet sherry	2 cups heavy cream
	⅓ cup fine granulated sugar

Wash and hull the strawberries. In a mixing bowl mash 1 pint of the berries and combine them with ½ the strawberry preserves and all of the sherry. Let them steep for 30 minutes. Strain the mixture through a fine sieve and force the berries and jam through, discarding the residue. Split the single layer of sponge cake in thirds to provide 3 layers. Douse the layers with the strawberry syrup and place 1 of them on a serving platter.

Sweeten the cream with the sugar and whip it stiffly. Combine it with the remaining strawberry preserves. Spread ⅓ of the cream over the layer of cake on the platter. Cover it with a second layer of the syrup-moistened cake and spread it with another ⅓ of the cream. Fit over it the final layer of moistened cake and, using a pastry bag with a plain tube, pipe a lattice of the remaining cream over the top. Decorate it with the remaining whole strawberries. Chill the cake thoroughly before cutting it into wedges to provide 6 to 8 servings.

Zabaglione Cake | Torta allo Zabaglione

½ recipe Sweet Dough (page 264)	1 cup butter, softened
2 layers Sponge Cake (page 235)	1 Tbl rum
⅓ cup Rum Syrup (page 265)	2 ounces semisweet chocolate,
½ recipe Custard with Marsala	melted & cooled
(page 232)	

Roll the sweet dough ¼-inch thick and cut it into a round 8 inches in diameter. Bake the round at 350 degrees for 15 minutes or until it is lightly browned. (Cut 1½-inch rounds from any remaining dough and bake them as cookies.) Let the round cool completely. Split each sponge cake layer in ½ to provide 4 layers. Moisten the sweet dough round and the 4 sponge cake layers equally with the rum syrup.

In a mixing bowl with a rotary beater whip together the custard with Marsala, the butter, and rum into a smooth cream. In a mixing bowl combine ¼ of this cream with the melted chocolate and set aside.

On a serving plate spread 1 layer of the sponge cake with ⅓ of the remaining plain cream. Cover it with the pastry round spread with the chocolate cream. Fit over that 2 more of the sponge layers interspersed with ½ of the remaining plain cream and topped with the rest. Rub the remaining layer of sponge cake into fine crumbs. Sprinkle crumbs over top of the cake and press them gently into the sides. Chill cake for 1 hour. Dust with powdered sugar before serving. Cut cake to provide 6 to 8 servings.

Sofia Charlotte | Charlotte alla Sofia

½ recipe Sweet Dough (page 264)
1 layer Sponge Cake
   (½ recipe, page 235)
½ cup macaroon crumbs
2 ounces semisweet chocolate,
   grated
¼ cup finely chopped glazed fruit
2 slices canned pineapple,
   drained & chopped
¼ cup canned chestnut purée
3 cups light cream
4 eggs
4 egg yolks
1 cup sugar
1 tsp vanilla extract
2 Tbl shredded coconut
1 Tbl sweet cocoa powder

Preheat oven to 350 degrees. Butter a pan 1½ inches deep and 9 inches in diameter and line it with the dough rolled ⅛-inch thick. Cut the sponge cake into ladyfinger-size pieces. Distribute the pieces in the pan. Sprinkle them with the macaroon crumbs, grated chocolate, glazed fruit, and chopped pineapple and dot them with the chestnut purée. In a mixing bowl thoroughly combine cream, eggs, egg yolks, sugar, and vanilla, and pour about ¾ cup of the mixture over the cake. Set pan in preheated oven and bake for 15 minutes. If the fruit rises to the top, press it down gently with a spatula. Pour in the remaining cream mixture and continue the baking for 20 minutes longer or until filling is set. Cool the charlotte in pan and sprinkle top with the coconut and cocoa powder. This recipe provides 6 servings.

Italian Cheese Cake | Torta di Ricotta all'Italiana

½ recipe Sweet Dough (page 264)
Fine dry bread crumbs
1½ pounds (3 cups) ricotta cheese, sieved
1 cup sugar
1 tsp vanilla extract

1 Tbl orange-flower water
½ tsp finely grated orange rind
⅛ tsp ground cinnamon
4 eggs
¼ cup finely chopped mixed glazed fruit

Preheat oven to 400 degrees. Butter an 8-inch cake pan and line it with the dough rolled ⅛-inch thick. Sprinkle it lightly with bread crumbs.

In a mixing bowl thoroughly combine the cheese, sugar, vanilla, orange-flower water, orange rind, and cinnamon. Beat in the eggs, 1 at a time, and blend in the glazed fruit. Pour the mixture into the prepared pan and bake in the preheated oven for 20 minutes. Remove pan from oven for 20 minutes. Return it to oven for 20 minutes longer. Turn off the heat and continue to cook cake in oven with the door open. Cut cake in wedges to provide 6 to 8 servings.

Como-Style Cream Tart | Crostata di Como alla Crema

1 recipe Sweet Dough (page 264)
¾ cup seedless raisins
1 cup finely chopped mixed glazed fruit
1 cup thinly sliced blanched almonds

1 Tbl orange-flower water
1 recipe Pastry Cream (page 265)
1 egg, beaten

Preheat oven to 375 degrees. Butter a 9-inch cake pan 1½ inches deep and line it with some of the prepared dough rolled to a thickness of ⅛ inch and of a size to fit the pan with an overhang of about ½ inch all around. Reserve the remaining dough.

In a mixing bowl thoroughly combine the raisins, glazed fruit, almonds, and orange-flower water with the pastry cream and pour the mixture into the prepared pan. Roll the reserved dough to a thickness of ⅛ inch and cut it into strips ¼-inch wide. Weave a lattice of the strips over the tart and press ends of strips into the overhang of the bottom crust.

Trim off excess. Brush top with the beaten egg. Bake in the preheated oven for 25 minutes or until the pastry is well browned. This recipe provides 6 servings.

Volcano Cake | Torta Vulcano

Double recipe Sweet Dough (page 264)
1 cup Pastry Cream (page 265)
1 cup heavy cream, whipped
1 pint strawberries, hulled & coarsely chopped

2 6-ounce jars strawberry preserves
2 tsp unflavored gelatine
¼ cup milk, heated

Preheat oven to 350 degrees. Roll the prepared dough to a thickness of ¼ inch and cut from it 4 rounds, each 8 inches in diameter. Place the rounds on lightly buttered baking sheets, 2 to a sheet, and bake them in

the preheated oven for 15 minutes or until they are lightly browned. Transfer the rounds to racks and let cool completely.

Combine the pastry cream with the whipped cream. Combine the fresh strawberries and 1 jar of the strawberry preserves and fold the mixture into the combined creams. Reserve ¾ cup of the mixture and set it aside in a bowl in the refrigerator.

The following directions apply only to the remaining cream. Spread 1 of the baked rounds with ¼ of the cream and place it on a chilled serving plate. Fit a second round over it. Spread that one with ⅓ of the remaining cream. Cover that with the third round spread with ½ of the remaining cream. Cover that with the fourth round and with the remainder of the cream. Chill cake in refrigerator for 1 hour.

In a bowl dissolve the gelatine in the heated milk. Let the mixture cool completely. While it is still liquid stir it into the reserved ¾ cup strawberry cream. Fit a cork into the cone end of a 2-cup capacity funnel. Set funnel in a tall glass to keep it upright. Pour in the gelatine cream and set the filled funnel, upright in the glass, in refrigerator until cream is set. Unmold the cream onto top of cake. Make a hole in top of unmolded cream. Pour the remaining strawberry preserves into it, letting them flow down the sides of the mold to simulate flowing lava. Refrigerate cake until serving time. Cut it into wedges to provide 8 to 10 servings.

Apple Cake, Mantua Style | Torta di Mele alla Mantovana

4 medium-size tart cooking apples	**1 Tbl seedless raisins**
½ tsp ground cinnamon	**2 Tbl thinly sliced almonds**
6 Tbl butter	**½ tsp grated orange rind**
4 eggs	**¼ cup flour**
½ cup sugar	**1 tsp baking powder**
⅓ cup orange juice	**⅛ tsp salt**
4 tsp rum	**Powdered sugar**

Preheat oven to 350 degrees. Peel, core, and slice the apples and sprinkle them with the cinnamon. In a skillet heat the butter. Add the apples and cook them gently, stirring them occasionally, until they are tender but still firm. Do not let them brown. Cool them.

In a mixing bowl beat the eggs with the sugar until the mixture is smooth and creamy. Stir the orange juice and rum into it and add the raisins, almonds, orange rind, and cooled apples. Sift the flour with the baking powder and salt and fold it into the egg mixture.

Thoroughly butter a deep round 9-inch baking dish. Pour in the batter and bake it in the preheated oven for 30 minutes or until it is well browned and set. Turn this pudding-cake out onto a warm serving platter and sprinkle it with powdered sugar. Serve it warm with, if desired, vanilla ice cream or sweetened whipped cream. This recipe provides 6 servings.

Apple Cake | Torta di Mele

4 medium apples	1 layer Chocolate Sponge Cake
½ tsp cinnamon	(½ recipe, page 237)
1¾ cups sugar	½ recipe Pastry Cream (page 265)
¼ cup butter	¼ cup heavy cream, whipped
½ cup apple juice	5 egg whites
¼ cup apple brandy	

Preheat oven to 550 degrees. Peel, core, and dice the apples and sprinkle them with the cinnamon and ¾ cup of the sugar. Heat the butter in a skillet. Add the apples and cook over low heat until they are soft but not brown. Remove pan from heat and let apples cool.

In a mixing bowl dissolve 2 tablespoons sugar in the apple juice and stir in the apple brandy. Split the single layer of chocolate sponge cake in thirds to provide 3 layers. Douse the cake layers equally with the apple-juice mixture. Place 1 layer on a heat-proof serving dish and spread over it ½ of the cooked apples. Combine the pastry cream and whipped cream and cover the apples with ½ of it. Cover with a layer of the remaining apples and a layer of the combined creams. Fit the third layer on top.

Stiffly beat together the egg whites and remaining sugar and spread the meringue over the prepared cake, coating it completely. Set dish in the preheated oven and let the meringue brown lightly. Cool cake before cutting it into wedges to provide 6 to 8 servings.

Cherry Cake | Torta di Ciliege

1½ cups canned sour cherries,
    drained
⅓ cup sugar
¼ tsp cinnamon
1 recipe Sweet Dough (page 264)
1 6-ounce jar cherry preserves

1 layer Sponge Cake, split
    (½ recipe, page 235)
1 egg, beaten
½ cup thinly sliced
    blanched almonds

In a saucepan sprinkle the cherries with the sugar and cinnamon and heat them until the sugar dissolves. Remove pan from heat and let cherries cool.

Preheat oven to 350 degrees. Butter a deep 9-inch pie pan. Roll out the prepared sweet dough to a thickness of ¼ inch and use enough of it to line the pan with an overhang of ½ inch all around. Spread the cherry preserves in the lined pan and cover them with a layer of the sponge cake. Spread it with ½ the cherries and cover them with another layer of cake. Spread it with the remaining cherries. Brush the edges of bottom crust with the beaten egg and fit the remaining rolled dough over it. Press edges to seal the 2 crusts together. Brush top with beaten egg and sprinkle it with the almonds, and, if desired, a little sugar. Bake the cake in the preheated oven for 30 minutes. Cool cake in pan. Transfer it to a serving dish and cut it into wedges to provide 6 to 8 servings.

Almond Cake | Torta di Mandorle

½ recipe Sweet Dough (page 264)
1 cup butter, softened
1 cup almond paste
1 tsp vanilla extract
1 cup sugar
5 eggs

2⅔ cups cake flour
1 tsp baking powder
¼ tsp salt
½ cup thinly sliced
    toasted almonds

Preheat oven to 325 degrees. Butter a 9-inch cake pan and line it with the sweet dough rolled ⅛-inch thick.

In a mixing bowl work together the butter, almond paste, vanilla, and

all but 2 tablespoons of the sugar until smoothly combined. Beat in the eggs, 1 at a time. Sift together the flour, baking powder, and the salt and stir it into the almond mixture. When mixture is smooth pour it into the lined pan and sprinkle it with the almonds and the reserved 2 tablespoons sugar. Bake cake in the preheated oven for 30 minutes or until a cake tester inserted in the center of the cake can be withdrawn clean. Cool cake before cutting in into wedges to provide 6 to 8 servings.

Latticed Apricot Pie | Crostata di Albicocche

1 recipe Sweet Dough (page 264)
1 8-ounce can apricots
1 8-ounce jar apricot preserves

Butter a 9-inch pie pan and line it with some of the prepared sweet dough, rolled to a thickness of ¼ inch and of a size to fit the pan with an overhang of ½ inch all around. Reserve the remaining dough. Preheat oven to 350 degrees.

Drain, peel, pit, and chop the apricots. Combine the chopped apricots and the apricot preserves and spread them in the prepared pan. Roll the reserved dough to a thickness of ⅛ inch and cut it into strips ¼-inch wide. Weave a lattice of the strips over top of pie and press strips into the overhanging bottom crust. Trim off excess.

Bake the pie in the preheated oven for 25 minutes or until the pastry is nicely browned.

Milanese Coffee Cake | Ciambella Milanese al Caffè

6 Tbl butter	3 tsp baking powder
1 cup plus 2 Tbl sugar	¼ tsp salt
2 eggs	⅓ cup chopped glazed fruit
1 egg yolk	⅓ cup seedless raisins
⅓ cup milk	⅓ cup chopped walnuts
2 tsp grated lemon rind	½ tsp cinnamon
1 tsp vanilla extract	1½ cups ricotta cheese
3¾ cups cake flour	(¾ pound), sieved

Preheat oven to 350 degrees. In a mixing bowl cream together the butter and ⅔ cup of the sugar. Add 1 egg, the egg yolk, and milk and beat the mixture until it is smooth and creamy. Stir into it the lemon rind and vanilla. Sift the flour with the baking powder and salt and stir it thoroughly but gently into the butter mixture. Fold in the chopped fruit, raisins, and nuts. Spread the batter in a buttered and floured deep (about 2 inches) 9-inch pan. Brush top with a little of the remaining egg beaten (reserve the rest) and dust it with ¼ teaspoon of the cinnamon and 2 tablespoons sugar, combined. Bake cake in the preheated oven for 40 minutes or until a cake tester inserted in the center can be withdrawn clean. Remove cake from pan and cool it on a rack.

Split cake into 2 layers. In a mixing bowl beat together the sieved ricotta cheese, the reserved beaten egg, and the remaining cinnamon and sugar. Spread this mixture over the bottom layer of the cake and fit the top layer over it. This coffee cake provides 8 to 10 servings.

4 cups sifted cake flour

¼ tsp salt

2 Tbl lard or vegetable shortening

2 eggs

1¾ cups sugar

2 Tbl water

1 Tbl white wine vinegar

Bland cooking oil

6 cups ricotta cheese, sieved

1 tsp vanilla extract

½ tsp ground cinnamon

1 cup finely chopped glazed fruit

¼ cup finely chopped
  pistachio nuts

Powdered sugar

Sift the flour with the salt, and blend the lard or shortening and the eggs into it. Dissolve ¼ cup of the sugar in the water and vinegar and work the liquid into the flour mixture to produce a stiff dough. Knead it for several minutes until it is smooth and slightly elastic. Let it rest for 30 minutes. Roll it out thinly and cut it into rounds 5 inches in diameter. Roll them around wooden sticks or metal cylinders of ¾-inch diameter.

In a deep saucepan or fryer heat cooking oil for deep frying to 370 degrees. In it fry the dough (on the cylinders) for about 1 minute or until pastry is well browned. Remove them and cool slightly. Slip them off the retainers and let them cool completely before filling them with a mixture prepared as follows:

Combine the sieved ricotta cheese, the remaining sugar, the vanilla, cinnamon, glazed fruit, and chopped nuts. Pipe the mixture into the shells with a pastry bag fitted with a large plain tube. Sprinkle shells with powdered sugar. This recipe provides about 2 dozen filled shells.

Little Cream Tarts | Tartine alla Crema

1 recipe Sweet Dough (page 264)
1 recipe Pastry Cream (page 265)

1 egg, beaten

Roll out enough of the prepared sweet dough ¼-inch thick to line 12 little tart tins, each about 1½ inches in diameter and 1 inch deep. Reserve the remaining dough. Fit the rolled dough into the tins flush with the tops. Preheat oven to 400 degrees.

Fill each lined tin with 2 generous tablespoons of the prepared pastry cream. Brush edges of dough with the beaten egg. Cover tarts with the remaining dough rolled to a thickness of ⅛ inch and cut to fit. Press edges of the 2 crusts together to seal them. Brush tops with the beaten egg. Bake tarts in the preheated oven for 10 minutes or until pastry is lightly browned. Serve the tarts warm with tea or coffee.

Fruit Bread | Panettone

2 envelopes dry yeast	**⅔ cup sugar**
⅓ cup lukewarm water	**½ tsp salt**
5 cups flour	**1 tsp vanilla**
1 cup butter, melted &	**1 Tbl honey**
cooled to lukewarm	**¾ cup seedless raisins**
9 egg yolks	**¾ cup chopped mixed glazed fruit**
⅔ cup orange-flower water,	**1 Tbl butter**
heated to lukewarm	**1 egg, beaten**

Soften the yeast in the lukewarm water. Blend it, with the water, into 1¼ cups of the flour. Shape the dough into a ball and set it in a lightly buttered bowl. Cover bowl lightly and let dough rise in a warm place, free of drafts, for 30 minutes. Deflate the dough and work into it the remaining flour, the melted butter, egg yolks, warmed orange-flower water, sugar, salt, vanilla, and honey. Knead dough until it is very smooth, about 15 minutes, steadily. Spread dough into a square and sprinkle over it the raisins and glazed fruit. Fold dough in half over them and in half again. Knead it for 5 minutes to distribute the fruit evenly throughout. Shape dough into a ball, return it to the buttered bowl, and let it rise again, lightly covered, for 30 minutes. Deflate the dough. Divide it into 3 equal-size pieces and form each into a ball. Place each in a lightly buttered round baking pan, 8 inches in diameter and 3 inches deep. Cover pans lightly with cloths and let the pieces of dough rise until they double in bulk, about 1½ hours.

Preheat oven to 375 degrees. Cut a cross in the top of each piece of risen dough and place 1 teaspoon of the butter in each. Brush the tops with the beaten egg. Set pans, staggered (on 2 shelves, if necessary, but not directly over each other), in the preheated oven and bake for 45 min-

utes or until a cake tester inserted into center of loaves can be withdrawn clean. Remove loaves from pans and set them on racks to cool.

Neapolitan Honey Balls | Strufoli alla Napoletana

4 egg whites
¼ cup butter
½ cup sugar
3¼ cups flour
Bland cooking oil
¼ cup honey

½ tsp grated orange peel
½ tsp vanilla extract
½ tsp anise liqueur
Finely chopped glazed fruit or
    confetti sprinkles

Beat together the egg whites, butter, and sugar. Work in the flour, more
or less than the indicated amount, to make a dough that is soft but work-
able. Roll it out into cylindrical pieces about the size of a pencil and cut
the cylinders into 1-inch lengths. Roll the lengths between the palms of
your hands into balls.

Heat cooking oil for deep frying in a deep saucepan or fryer. Fry the balls of dough at 375 degrees for 2 to 3 minutes or until they are lightly browned. Drain them and mound them on a serving platter. Combine the honey and the grated orange peel and heat gently until it thins out slightly. Off the heat, add the vanilla extract and the anise liqueur, and pour it over the mound of balls. Sprinkle with chopped glazed fruit or confetti sprinkles. Cool, but do not chill. These are traditional Christmas cookies.

Cookies | Biscotti

1 recipe Sweet Dough (page 264)   **1 egg, beaten**

Preheat oven to 350 degrees. Roll the dough to a thickness of ¼ inch and cut rounds about 2½ inches in diameter from it. Brush them with beaten egg, decorate them (see suggestions below), and arrange them on a baking sheet. Bake the cookies in the preheated oven for 12 minutes or until they are lightly browned. Remove them to a rack to cool.

Chocolate cookies may be made with the same dough by blending into it 1½ ounces (1½ squares) semisweet chocolate, melted and cooled.

NOTE: Here are some suggestions for decorating cookies: maraschino cherries, pine nuts, cinnamon sugar (1 teaspoon ground cinnamon combined with ¼ cup granulated sugar), ginger sugar (ground ginger and granulated sugar), plain coarse sugar, chopped mixed glazed fruit, sliced glazed pineapple, or almonds, cashews, pecans, pistachios, or walnuts, sliced or chopped.

Fried Custard | Fritelle di Crema

Pastry Cream (page 265)   **1 cup butter**
Flour   **Cinnamon sugar or coarse sugar**
2 eggs, beaten   ** (see below)**

Prepare pastry cream as directed, but continue to cook it until it is very thick. Pour cream into a heat-proof baking dish to a depth of 1 inch. Cool and chill until it is very firm. Cut it into 1-inch squares. Dredge them with flour and coat with the beaten eggs. In a deep skillet heat the butter, without letting it brown, and in it fry the squares of cream, a few at a time, until they are lightly browned on all sides. Drain them on absorbent paper and sprinkle with cinnamon sugar or coarse sugar. Serve them warm with, if desired, vanilla ice cream.

NOTE: To make cinnamon sugar, combine 1 teaspoon ground cinnamon to each ¼ cup granulated sugar.

Sweet Rice Fritters | Fritelle Dolci di Riso

½ cup rice	¼ cup sweet Marsala wine
2 cups milk	½ tsp grated lemon rind
1 Tbl butter	½ tsp vanilla extract
⅓ cup sugar	Bland cooking oil
½ cup chestnut flour	Granulated sugar
1 tsp baking powder	

Cook the rice in the milk and butter, covered, over low heat for 25 minutes or until milk evaporates completely and grains of rice are tender. Cool rice completely and blend into it the sugar, chestnut flour, baking powder, Marsala, lemon rind, and vanilla. With a tablespoon shape the mixture into ovals and fry them in deep hot cooking oil (370 degrees) until they are lightly browned. Drain and roll them in granulated sugar. Serve the fritters with a sauce of melted vanilla ice cream flavored with brandy. Serves 6.

Soufflé Galliano | Sufflè Galliano

5 Tbl butter	⅓ cup Galliano liqueur
5 Tbl flour	8 egg whites
1½ cups milk	3 fresh peaches, peeled,
6 egg yolks	pitted & chopped
½ cup sugar	

Preheat oven to 375 degrees. In a saucepan melt the butter and blend

the flour into it. Cook this roux over low heat for 3 minutes without letting it brown. Slowly add the milk, stirring constantly until the mixture thickens. Remove pan from heat and vigorously stir in the egg yolks beaten with 6 tablespoons of the sugar and the Galliano liqueur. Let the mixture cool somewhat. Beat the 8 egg whites until they are stiff but not dry. Stir ¼ of them into the yolk mixture. Carefully fold in the remainder. Butter a 2-quart soufflé dish and coat it with the remaining 2 tablespoons sugar. Cover the bottom with the prepared peaches and pour over them the soufflé mixture. Bake it in the preheated oven for 30 minutes or until the soufflé is well puffed and browned. Serve it at once. This recipe provides 6 to 8 servings.

Vanilla Ice Cream | Gelato di Vaniglia

8 egg yolks	Thin peel of ½ lemon
¼ tsp salt	2 Tbl vanilla extract
1 cup sugar	3 cups heavy cream, whipped
3 cups light cream	

In a heat-proof mixing bowl beat the egg yolks with the sugar and salt until they are well combined. In the top pan of a double boiler scald the light cream with the lemon peel. Do not let the cream boil. Remove peel and discard it. Very slowly beat the heated cream into the blended yolks. Pour mixture into the double boiler pan. Set pan over simmering water and cook mixture, stirring it constantly, until it thickly coats a metal spoon. Remove pan from over water and stir in the vanilla extract. Let mixture cool completely and fold the whipped cream into it. Transfer mixture to deep refrigerator trays (you will need 2 deep 1-quart capacity trays, or you may use metal bowls). Cover trays and set in freezer compartment of refrigerator with temperature control set at its coldest point. Freeze the cream until it is firm, about 1½ hours, stirring it once only at the midway point. This provides about 2 quarts of ice cream.

Chocolate Ice Cream | Gelato di Cioccolato

Follow directions for Vanilla Ice Cream, but reduce vanilla to 2 teaspoons and blend 2 ounces unsweetened chocolate, melted, into the custard.

Mocha Ice Cream | Gelato Moka

Follow directions for Vanilla Ice Cream, but reduce vanilla to 2 teaspoons and stir 1 tablespoon instant espresso coffee into hot custard.

Strawberry Ice Cream | Gelato di Fragola

Follow directions for Vanilla Ice Cream, but reduce vanilla to 2 teaspoons and blend into the custard the contents of 2 packages frozen strawberry halves, defrosted.

Pistachio Ice Cream | Gelato di Pistacchio

Follow directions for Vanilla Ice Cream (page 257), but reduce vanilla to 1 teaspoon and blend into the custard 1½ cups pistachio nuts, pulverized, 1 cup whole pistachio nuts, and a drop or two of green vegetable coloring.

Peach Ice Cream | Gelato di Pesche

Follow directions for Vanilla Ice Cream (page 257), but omit vanilla and blend into the custard 1 tablespoon maraschino liqueur and 1 pound very ripe peaches, peeled, pitted, and puréed.

Nougat Ice Cream | Gelato al Torrone

Follow directions for Vanilla Ice Cream (page 257), but reduce the sugar content to ½ cup and the vanilla flavoring to 2 teaspoons, and add to the custard ingredients 6 ounces nougat, chopped. Cook the custard as directed until the nougat is melted.

Hazelnut Ice Cream | Gelato di Nocciole

Follow directions for Vanilla Ice Cream (page 257), but reduce the sugar content to ½ cup and the vanilla flavoring to 1 teaspoon. Add to the custard ingredients ½ cup Praline Powder (page 264), cooking the custard, as directed, until the powder is completely incorporated.

Pignolata Ice Cream | Gelato di Pignoli e Amaretti

Follow directions for Vanilla Ice Cream (page 257), but reduce the vanilla flavoring to 2 teaspoons. Pulverize enough dry macaroons and pine nuts to provide ½ cup of each. Blend the powder into the custard and continue cooking as directed.

Molded Ice Cream | Cassata Gelata

2 cups chocolate ice cream
2 cups vanilla ice cream
2 cups pistachio ice cream
2½ cups heavy cream

¼ cup sugar
½ cup finely chopped
   toasted hazelnuts

Coat the inside of a 2-quart bowl evenly with the chocolate ice cream and freeze until it is very firm. Cover it with an even layer of vanilla ice cream and freeze it in place. Spread the pistachio ice cream over that and freeze it.

Sweeten 1 cup of the heavy cream with 2 tablespoons of the sugar and whip it stiffly. Fold the chopped nuts into it and fill center of the ice cream with it. Cover bowl with waxed paper or plastic wrap and freeze for 2 hours. Unmold onto a chilled serving platter. Stiffly whip the remaining cream with the remaining sugar and spread it evenly over the mold. Freeze for 2 hours longer. Serve Molded Ice Cream cut into wedges to provide 8 to 10 servings.

Chocolate Truffles | Tartufi di Cioccolato

6 balls of hard-frozen
   chocolate ice cream
6 maraschino cherries

6 ounces unsweetened chocolate,
   cut into shavings

With a baller scoop out a small hole in each of the balls of ice cream. Place a maraschino cherry in each and replace the scooped-out ice cream. Roll ice cream balls in the shaved chocolate, coating them well. Freeze the prepared truffles. Remove them from the freezer 30 minutes before serving. Serves 6.

Italian Tortoni | Tortoni

6 Tbl powdered sugar
2 eggs, separated
1 cup heavy cream

1½ cups macaroon crumbs
2 Tbl rum

In separate bowls, each with 2 tablespoons of the sugar, beat the egg whites until stiff, the yolks until thick, and the cream until it holds a shape. Sprinkle 1 cup of the macaroon crumbs with the rum and beat them into the yolks. Fold in the cream and the egg whites. Pour mixture into 3-ounce paper baking cups and sprinkle tops with the remaining crumbs. Freeze for 3 hours or until mixture is firm. This recipe provides 10 to 12 servings.

Ice Cream Cake | Torta Gelata

1 layer Sponge Cake
   (½ recipe page 235)
2 cups soft coffee ice cream
2 cups soft vanilla ice cream

10 maraschino cherries, halved
1 cup heavy cream
1 tsp instant espresso coffee
2 tsp sugar

Split the single layer of sponge cake in thirds to provide 3 layers. Place 1 of the layers of cake in the pan in which cake was baked and spread it with the coffee ice cream. Cover it with a second layer of cake. Spread it with the vanilla ice cream combined with the cherries. Fit the remaining layer of cake over that ice cream and cover pan with waxed paper or plastic wrap. Freeze the ice cream cake for 2 hours.

With a knife free cake from sides of pan and turn it out onto a chilled serving plate. Flavor the heavy cream with the instant coffee and sugar and whip it stiffly. Pipe the cream onto cake, using a pastry bag fitted with a star tube, coating cake evenly. Freeze the cake again briefly before serving it cut in wedges to provide 6 to 8 servings.

Lemon Ice | Granita di Limone

2 cups fresh lemon juice
2 cups water
1 cup sugar
1 egg white, frothily beaten

2 tsp white corn syrup
¼ cup dry white wine
Finely grated rind of 2 lemons

In a stainless steel bowl thoroughly combine all of the ingredients. Set bowl in freezing compartment of refrigerator with temperature control at its coldest point and leave it for 45 minutes or until the edges of the liquid are almost frozen solid. Scrape them into center of bowl and beat mixture with rotary beater until it is smooth. Stir it again 30 minutes later. Continue the freezing without stirring until the ice is of the proper consistency. This recipe provides a little more than 1 quart.

Orange Ice | Granita d'Arancia

3 cups orange juice
¼ cup lemon juice
2 cups water
½ cup sugar

1 egg white
2 tsp white corn syrup
¼ cup dry white wine
Grated rind of ½ orange

Follow the directions for making Lemon Ice.

Minted Lime Ice | Granita di Cedro

Follow directions for making Lemon Ice but substitute lime juice for the lemon juice and add ¼ cup green crème de menthe.

Raspberry Ice | Granita di Lamponi

Follow directions for making Lemon Ice but omit the egg white and reduce the lemon juice to ¼ cup. Force the defrosted contents of 3 packages frozen raspberries through a fine sieve and add. Freeze as directed.

Grapefruit Ice | Granita di Pompelmo

Follow directions for making Lemon Ice, but use only ¼ cup of lemon juice and add 2 cups grapefruit juice and 1 or 2 drops of red vegetable coloring.

Coffee Ice | Granita di Caffè

2 Tbl sugar	**1 Tbl orange-flavored liqueur**
2 Tbl instant espresso coffee	**2 Tbl white corn syrup**
4 cups boiling hot water	**1 Tbl rum**

Dissolve the sugar and the instant coffee in the hot water and stir into it the liqueur, corn syrup, and rum. Cool mixture and freeze it in refrigerator trays until it is partially frozen. Beat it with a rotary beater until it is smooth. Let it partially freeze again and beat it once more. Continue the freezing without further stirring. This provides about 1 quart of ice.

Pear Ice | Granita di Pere

2 16-ounce cans pears with syrup	**2 Tbl white corn syrup**
⅔ cup sugar	**2 Tbl pear brandy**
½ cup lemon juice	**1 egg white**

Drain the pears, reserving the syrup, and force them through a fine sieve or reduce them to a purée in an electric blender.

In a saucepan over moderate heat bring the pear syrup to a boil. Stir in the sugar and cook the syrup for 5 minutes. Cool it and combine with it the lemon juice, corn syrup, pear purée, and pear brandy. Beat the egg white to a froth and blend it into the pear mixture. Pour the mixture into a metal bowl, cover it with plastic wrap, and set it in freezer compartment of refrigerator with the temperature control set at the coldest point. Freeze for 30 minutes or until it begins to frost around the edges. Beat it with a rotary beater until it is smooth. Continue the freezing for 30 minutes longer. Beat again and freeze the mixture until it is of the proper consistency. This recipe provides 6 servings.

Apricot Sherbet | Sorbetto di Albicocche

1 30-ounce can apricots with syrup **2 cups milk**
¼ cup lemon juice **1 tsp maraschino liqueur**

Strain the apricots through a fine sieve and force the pulp through, or purée them with the syrup in an electric blender. In a mixing bowl thoroughly combine the purée, lemon juice, milk, and liqueur. Pour the mixture into refrigerator trays and set them in the freezer compartment of refrigerator with the temperature control set at its coldest point. When the mixture is partially frozen, after about 45 minutes, beat it with a rotary beater until it is smooth. Cover trays and continue the freezing until the sherbet is set. This recipe provides about 3 pints of sherbet.

Sweet Dough | Pasta Frolla

2¼ cups flour **¼ tsp grated orange rind**
¾ cup sugar **2 egg yolks**
¼ tsp salt **½ tsp vanilla extract**
1 cup butter

Sift the flour, sugar, and salt together onto a pastry board or into a bowl. Make a well in the center of the mound and place in it the butter, orange rind, and the egg yolks and vanilla combined. With your fingers work those ingredients quickly into the flour mixture to produce a thick smooth paste. Shape it into a ball, wrap in waxed paper, and chill for 30 minutes. Use the paste as required in specific recipes. This recipe provides sufficient dough for bottom and top crusts for a deep 8- or 9-inch pie pan or for about 4 dozen small cookies.

Praline Powder | Farina di Mandorle Caramellate

½ cup sugar **½ cup unblanched almonds**

In a skillet over low heat cook the sugar and almonds until the sugar melts and becomes amber colored. Pour the mixture onto an oiled or buttered baking sheet. Let this praline cool and harden completely. Roll it into a powder or pulverize it in an electric blender. Store the powder in an airtight container to be used as required.

Pastry Cream | Crema Pasticcera

¼ cup sugar	2 tsp cornstarch
1⅓ cups light cream	⅛ tsp salt
2 egg yolks	¼ tsp vanilla extract
2 whole eggs	¼ tsp finely grated lemon rind

In a saucepan over low heat dissolve 2 tablespoons of the sugar in the cream. In a mixing bowl beat together the egg yolks, whole eggs, cornstarch, salt, and remaining sugar. Vigorously beat in the scalded cream and cook it, without boiling, for a few minutes until the cream thickens. Remove pan from heat and stir in the vanilla extract and grated rind. Let the mixture cool and chill it. This recipe provides about 2 cups of pastry cream. It may be kept under refrigeration for 2 or 3 days only. Do not freeze it.

Rum Syrup | Sciroppo al Rum

1 cup water	½ cup rum
½ cup sugar	

In a saucepan over low heat reduce the water and sugar to about ⅔ cup. Remove pan from heat and let syrup cool. Stir the rum into it. Use the syrup as required.

Chocolate Syrup | Sciroppo al Cioccolato

1 cup sugar	4 ounces unsweetened chocolate, grated
1 cup water	
⅛ tsp salt	1 tsp vanilla extract

Place the top pan of a double boiler over direct moderate heat and in it dissolve the sugar in the water. Add the salt and grated chocolate. Set the pan over simmering water and heat mixture until chocolate melts. Stir gently to blend it. When syrup is smooth, remove pan from over the water and stir in the vanilla extract. Cool the syrup and store it in a tightly covered container under refrigeration.

10 | sauces and dressings

When thinking of Italian sauces, it is natural that tomato sauce, which we all know as a wonderful partner for pasta, should first come to mind. Yet this sauce has some formidable rivals that should be better known to American cooks. There is, for example, *pesto,* which is mentioned in the Introduction as a glory of Genoese cuisine. Indeed it has such a rare-fied taste that one should look forward to the season of fresh basil in order to be able to serve spaghetti with this marvelous green sauce. (*Pesto* made with dried basil is unthinkable.)

The Italians tend to regard a sauce as a major element in a dish. Their sauces are likely to be assertive in character, with garlic, wine, and herbs making their presence felt, with bits of meat or fish retained to give consistency—as in clam sauce, chicken-liver sauce, and *carbonara.* In such ways the Italians both embellish pasta and make it more nutritious.

As for the familiar tomato sauce, it is not to be considered common or uninteresting. It admits of endless variation, and when made with fresh, vine-ripened tomatoes, it is a great delight.

Anchovy Sauce | Salsa d'Acciughe

1 large clove garlic, finely chopped
2 Tbl olive oil
½ tsp anchovy paste
10 anchovy fillets, finely chopped
1½ cups dry white wine

2 cups Brown Sauce (page 269)
½ cup Fresh-Tomato Purée
  (page 281)
1 Tbl finely chopped parsley

In a saucepan over low heat cook the garlic in the oil until the bits are soft but not browned. Blend into them the anchovy paste, add the chopped anchovies, and heat through gently. Pour in the wine and reduce it slowly to 1 cup. Combine with it the brown sauce, tomato purée, and parsley, and continue cooking, still at simmer, but with pan covered, for 30 minutes. Stir mixture occasionally. This recipe will provide about 3 cups sauce, sufficient to accompany the Mozzarella in Carrozza, as suggested, or 6 servings of pasta.

Bolognese Sauce | Salsa alla Bolognese

6 Tbl butter
1 cup finely chopped onion
1 cup finely chopped carrots
1 cup finely chopped celery
⅛ pound prosciutto, finely chopped
1 large clove garlic, finely chopped
2 pounds lean beef, finely ground
⅛ tsp dried basil
⅛ tsp dried sage
⅛ tsp dried oregano
¼ tsp white pepper

1/16 tsp ground nutmeg
1 cup dry white wine
1½ cups Fresh-Tomato Purée
  (page 281)
2 Tbl tomato paste
1½ cups Beef Broth (page 44)
1 Tbl butter
4 chicken livers
Salt & pepper
1 cup heavy cream

In a skillet with 3 tablespoons of the butter melted and heated, lightly brown all together the onion, carrots, celery, prosciutto, and garlic. In a mixing bowl thoroughly combine the ground beef, basil, sage, oregano, white pepper, and nutmeg. Heat the remaining 3 tablespoons of butter in a large saucepan. Add the beef mixture and brown it well, cutting through it frequently with a wooden spoon to separate it into small bits.

Combine vegetable mixture with beef mixture in saucepan and blend into them the wine, tomato purée, tomato paste, and broth. Cover pan, reduce heat to low, and cook for 1 hour or until it is quite smooth and somewhat thickened. Stir it occasionally. If the sauce thickens excessively, add a little more broth during the cooking.

In a small skillet heat the single tablespoon of butter and in it sauté the chicken livers until they are well browned and firm. Mash the livers well, stir them into the sauce, and continue cooking for 15 minutes longer. Season sauce with salt and pepper to taste. Stir in the heavy cream at the last moment and let it just heat through.

This recipe will provide about 8 cups of sauce. Without the cream, the sauce can be refrigerated for about 1 week. Frozen, it can be kept for about a month. Add cream in proportion to amount of sauce used at each time, 2 tablespoons cream to each approximate cup of sauce.

Brown Sauce I | Salsa Bruna I

1 pound veal bones	2 cups chopped celery
1 pound beef bones	2 cups chopped onion
1 pound pork bones	⅔ cup flour
½ tsp rosemary	2 cups red wine
½ tsp thyme	4 cups Fresh-Tomato Purée
3 bay leaves	(page 281)
4 cloves garlic, crushed	5 quarts water
1 tsp whole peppercorns, crushed	5 tsp salt
1 cup chopped carrot	

Spread the bones over the bottom of a large roasting pan and cook in the oven at 475 degrees for 30 minutes or until they are well browned. Cover bones with all the herbs, spices, and vegetables, and sprinkle them with the flour. Continue roasting for 15 minutes longer. Transfer ingredients to a large saucepan over moderate heat on top of stove, and stir the wine and tomato purée into them. Set roasting pan also on top of stove and de-glaze it, over moderate heat, by pouring the water into it and stirring up the brown bits at bottom of pan. Add the salt and let liquid boil for a moment or two. Pour the de-glazing liquid over the ingredients in saucepan. Reduce heat and cook sauce at simmer for 3 hours, stirring it from time to time and skimming it when necessary. Cool completed sauce and strain it. This recipe will provide about 3 quarts of brown sauce.

NOTE: Use of Brown Sauce I or II in recipes is at cook's discretion.

Brown Sauce II | Salsa Bruna II

6 Tbl butter
¼ cup lean veal, finely chopped
¼ cup cooked ham, finely chopped
¼ cup finely chopped carrot
¼ cup finely chopped celery
¼ cup finely chopped onion
¼ cup flour
4 cups Beef Broth
  (page 44), heated

1¼ cups red wine, heated
¼ cup red wine vinegar
¼ cup Fresh-Tomato Purée
  (page 281)
2 sprigs parsley
1 bay leaf
¼ tsp thyme
½ tsp salt
⅛ tsp pepper

In a large saucepan heat the butter and in it brown all together, over moderate heat, the veal, ham, carrot, celery, and onion. Blend into them the flour and brown it, also. Whisk in the heated beef broth, and red wine, beating constantly until the mixture thickens and is smooth. Stir into it the vinegar and tomato purée and add the remaining ingredients. Reduce heat to very low and continue cooking at bare simmer, with pan partially covered, for 2 hours. When done, the sauce should be the consistency of heavy cream. If it becomes too thick, add a little more beef broth during the cooking. Skim off the fat and strain sauce before using it. This recipe will provide about 4 cups. Brown sauce may be kept refrigerated for about a week, or frozen for about a month.

Béchamel Sauce | Salsa Besciamella

2 Tbl butter
2 Tbl flour

2 cups rich milk (or 1 cup milk,
  1 cup light cream), scalded
Salt

In a saucepan over moderate heat melt the butter and blend the flour into it. Cook mixture, stirring it constantly, for 1 minute, taking great care that it does not take on any color. Remove pan from heat and, using a whisk, vigorously beat in the hot milk, adding it gradually. Return pan to heat and stir sauce constantly until it has thickened and is smooth. Season it with salt to taste. This recipe will provide about 2 cups of a relatively thin sauce.

For a Medium Béchamel, increase the butter and flour to 3 tablespoons of each. The quantity of milk remains the same.

For a Thick Béchamel, use 4 tablespoons (¼ cup) each of butter and flour. The quantity of milk remains the same.

Sauce of Chicken Livers | Salsa di Fegatini

½ cup olive oil	8 cups canned,
2 medium onions, coarsely chopped	peeled Italian plum tomatoes
2 cloves garlic, mashed	1 bay leaf
1½ pounds chicken livers,	½ tsp basil
coarsely chopped	Salt & pepper
	Chicken Broth (page 44)

In a large, deep skillet heat the olive oil and in it cook the onions and garlic until they are lightly browned. Drain off the remaining olive oil into another skillet, reheat it, and in it cook the chicken livers, browning them well. Combine chicken livers and remaining oil with the onions and garlic in the large skillet and add to them the tomatoes, bay leaf, basil, and salt and pepper to taste. Cook mixture, covered, at simmer for 2 hours. If the sauce thickens excessively during the cooking, add chicken broth as needed. Remove and discard bay leaf. Correct the seasoning. This recipe will provide about 8 cups of sauce for pasta.

Garlic Sauce for Chilled Poached Fish | Salsa d'Aglio

2 cloves garlic, peeled & mashed	Mayonnaise (page 286)
½ tsp salt	Strained lemon juice

Work the garlic and salt to a paste in a mortar with a pestle or in a bowl with a wooden spoon. Prepare the quantity of mayonnaise sauce as directed in recipe and blend garlic paste into it. Add lemon juice to taste.

Country-Style Sauce | Salsa Paesana

1 cup Italian dried mushrooms (1 ounce)	⅓ cup red wine
3 Italian sweet sausages (about ¾ pound)	2 small bay leaves
	½ tsp dried oregano, crushed
⅔ cup olive oil	7 cups canned, peeled plum tomatoes
⅓ cup butter	2 Tbl parsley
1 cup finely chopped onions	Salt & pepper
2 cloves garlic, mashed	

Soak the mushrooms in warm water for 30 minutes, drain, and chop them coarsely. Set them aside for the moment. Peel and crumble the sausages. In a large deep skillet heat together the olive oil and butter, and in the hot fat lightly brown the onions and garlic. Add the crumbled sausages and heat them through. Stir in the wine, add the bay leaves and oregano, and cook over moderate heat until the wine has been reduced somewhat. Add the tomatoes, parsley, and mushrooms, and continue cooking at simmer, with pan covered, for 45 minutes, stirring occasionally. Season with salt and pepper to taste, and cook for 15 minutes longer. This recipe provides about 8 cups of sauce. It is a fine accompaniment to pasta.

White Clam Sauce | Salsa Bianca di Vongole

3 Tbl olive oil	¼ tsp dried oregano
1 Tbl butter	½ cup dry white wine
1 medium onion, finely chopped	4 dozen cherrystone clams
1 large clove garlic, mashed	White pepper
2 sprigs Italian parsley	Salt

Heat the olive oil and butter together in a large deep saucepan. Add the onion and garlic and cook them over moderate heat until they are soft

but not browned. Add the parsley and oregano, and stir in the wine. Cook combined ingredients for 2 minutes to blend the flavors. Add the clams and steam them, covered, over high heat until the shells open. Discard immediately any that do not open. Remove open clams, shuck them, and chop them coarsely. Put them in a bowl and set them aside for the moment. Remove and discard garlic and parsley.

If the amount of liquid in saucepan is greater than 2 cups, return pan to high heat and reduce liquid to that amount. Stir the chopped clams into the reduced broth and gently heat them through. Do not cook sauce further or clams will toughen. Season sauce with white pepper to taste and with salt, if needed.

NOTE: Cheese is not usually served with spaghetti dressed with clam sauce.

Red Clam Sauce | Salsa Rossa di Vongole

Proceed as for white clam sauce, but reduce the liquid to 1 cup. Add 1 cup Fresh-Tomato Purée (page 281) and finally the clams and seasoning.

Green Clam Sauce | Salsa Verde di Vongole

Proceed as for red clam sauce, but use 1 cup cooked spinach, very finely chopped and drained, instead of the tomato purée. One-half pound of spinach, trimmed of all heavy stems, will, when cooked, provide the required quantity.

Green Sauce | Salsa Verde

4 pickled peperoncini (see Glossary)	3 anchovy fillets, chopped
	½ cup white wine vinegar
1 cup chopped parsley	1 cup olive oil
2 capers, chopped	⅛ tsp white pepper
1 large clove garlic, chopped	1 tsp salt

Remove the stems and seeds from the peperoncini and chop the pep-

pers. Combine the peperoncini, parsley, capers, garlic, and anchovies and chop them again, all together, reducing mixture almost to a paste. Transfer it to a mixing bowl and blend the vinegar into it. Add the oil, a tablespoon at a time, beating in each addition vigorously until an emulsion is achieved. Season the sauce with the indicated quantities of pepper and salt, or more, to taste. This recipe will provide about 2 cups of sauce to serve as an accompaniment to fish or cold meats.

Green Sauce, Genoa Style | Pesto

4 cloves garlic, peeled & mashed	**½ cup grated Parmesan cheese**
4 cups fresh basil leaves	**2 cups olive oil**
¼ cup toasted pine nuts	

In a mortar work the garlic, basil, pine nuts, and cheese to a smooth paste with a pestle. Transfer the paste to a mixing bowl and beat into it the olive oil, a very little at a time, to produce a sauce about the consistency of mayonnaise. Pesto may be made also in an electric blender as follows:

     In a blender container combine the herbs, nuts, cheese, and ½ cup of the oil. Purée the ingredients at low speed. When they are reduced, begin adding the remainder of the oil. Pour it in a thin, steady stream until it has all been incorporated, by which time the sauce should be of the proper consistency. If it is not, continue blending for a few seconds longer until sauce thickens. Take care not to overblend or ingredients will liquefy. Add salt, if necessary. This recipe makes about 3 cups. Covered securely and stored in the refrigerator, the sauce can be kept for about 6 weeks.

Sauce with Sweetbreads | Salsa con Animelle

1 pound Italian sweet sausages
¼ cup cold water
½ sweetbread (about ½ pound)
⅓ cup olive oil
2 medium onions, finely chopped

½ cup dry white wine
6 medium tomatoes, peeled,
  seeded & coarsely chopped
2 Tbl chopped parsley
Salt & pepper

Prick the sausages in several places with the tines of a fork and place them in a saucepan with the cold water. Cover pan, set it over low heat, and let sausages steam until water evaporates completely and sausages begin to render some of their fat. Remove them and, when they are cool enough to handle, peel off the casings and discard them. Crumble the sausage meat.

Wash the sweetbread in cold water, place in a saucepan, and cover it with boiling water. Add ½ teaspoon salt and 2 teaspoons vinegar. Set pan over low heat and cook sweetbread at simmer for 15 minutes. Drain it, and when it is cool enough to handle, remove and discard membrane and tubes. Chop sweetbread finely.

In a skillet heat the olive oil and in it lightly brown the onions. Add the crumbled sausage meat and the chopped sweetbread and cook over moderate heat until sweetbread is delicately browned. Stir in the wine and continue cooking until liquid is reduced to ¼ cup. Add the tomatoes and parsley and cook combined ingredients at simmer for 20 minutes, stirring them occasionally. Season sauce with salt and pepper to taste, and cook it for 10 minutes longer. Makes about 3 cups.

Hunter's Style Sauce | Salsa alla Cacciatora

½ ounce dried Italian mushrooms
   (about ½ cup)
5 Tbl butter
2 carrots, finely chopped
2 stalks celery, finely chopped
½ pound fresh mushrooms,
   sliced (about 2 cups)
2 Tbl olive oil
1 medium onion, finely chopped

1 clove garlic, mashed
4 cups canned,
   peeled plum tomatoes
½ cup dry white wine
2 Tbl chopped parsley
2 bay leaves
½ tsp dried rosemary
Salt & pepper

Soak the dried mushrooms in warm water for 30 minutes, drain, and coarsely chop them. Set them aside for the moment. In a large skillet heat 4 tablespoons of the butter and in it slowly cook the carrots and celery until they are soft but not browned. Drain them, reserving butter remaining in skillet, and set them aside in a mixing bowl. Reheat the butter and in it cook the fresh mushrooms over moderately high heat, stirring until they have rendered most of their juice. Transfer mushrooms to the mixing bowl with the vegetables.

In a large saucepan heat together the olive oil and the remaining butter. Add the onion and garlic and cook over low heat until they are lightly browned. Add the prepared dried mushrooms, carrots, celery, and fresh mushrooms, the tomatoes, wine, parsley, bay leaves, and rosemary. Season mixture with salt and pepper to taste. Cover pan and continue cooking at simmer for 45 minutes. This recipe will provide about 6 cups of sauce, enough for 12 servings of pasta.

Marinara Sauce | Salsa alla Marinara

⅔ cup olive oil
8 cloves garlic, sliced paper thin
8 cups canned,
   peeled plum tomatoes

½ tsp oregano
Salt & pepper

In a saucepan over high heat cook the garlic in the oil until garlic is lightly browned. Reduce heat to low and add the tomatoes and oregano.

Take care; the tomato liquid may cause the fat to spatter. Cover pan and let sauce cook for 30 minutes or until it thickens. Crush tomatoes slightly during the cooking, but do not mash them. They should still be in recognizable pieces. Season sauce with salt and pepper to taste. This recipe provides about 6 cups of marinara sauce.

Mariner's Sauce | Salsa del Marinaio

1½ **cups olive oil**
3 **cloves garlic,**
    peeled & slightly mashed

3 **Tbl drained capers**
⅓ **cup finely chopped**
    pitted black olives

12 anchovy fillets, chopped
¼ tsp dried basil
2 Tbl finely chopped parsley
⅓ cup finely chopped
   pitted green olives
Salt & pepper

Heat the oil in a saucepan and in it over low heat brown the garlic well. Remove and discard garlic. Add the anchovy fillets and stir them until they are reduced to a paste. Blend into the oil and anchovies the basil, parsley, capers, and olives. Season sauce with pepper to taste and judiciously with salt, keeping in mind that the anchovies, capers, and olives will all contribute their own saltiness. Serve the sauce with spaghetti. Makes about 2½ cups.

Meat Sauce for Pasta | Ragù

½ cup Italian dried mushrooms
   (about ½ ounce)
⅓ cup olive oil
1 pound lean beef
1 pound lean pork,
   finely ground with beef
2 Tbl butter
1 cup finely chopped onion
2 cloves garlic, mashed

½ cup red wine
2 cups canned purée of
   plum tomatoes
1 tsp dried oregano, crushed
2 Tbl chopped parsley
1 bay leaf
3 cups Chicken Broth (page 44)
Salt & pepper

Soak the mushrooms for 30 minutes in warm water, drain, and chop them finely. Set them aside. In a large skillet heat 2 tablespoons of the olive oil and in it thoroughly brown the ground meats. In a separate skillet heat the butter with the remaining oil, and in the mixture lightly brown the onions and garlic. Blend in the wine and reduce it slightly. Stir in the tomato purée, add the herbs, and cook at simmer for 10 minutes. Combine onion mixture with meat mixture in the large skillet. Add the broth, chopped mushrooms, and salt and pepper to taste. Cover skillet and cook sauce at simmer for 1 hour. If sauce thickens excessively (it should be thick, but still "pourable"), add a little more broth during the cooking. When cooked to the proper consistency these ingredients will provide about 8 cups of sauce. It may be kept under normal refrigeration for a week to 10 days, or in a freezer for a month to 6 weeks.

Meat Sauce for Timbales | Sugo di Carne per Timballi

½ cup Italian dried mushrooms
   (about ½ ounce)
½ cup olive oil
½ cup finely chopped onion
2 cloves garlic, peeled & mashed
1 cup finely ground veal
1 cup finely ground pork

1 cup red wine
2 cups Fresh-Tomato Purée
   (page 281)
1½ cups Chicken Broth (page 44)
¼ tsp oregano
1 bay leaf
Salt & pepper

Soak the mushrooms in warm water for 30 minutes, squeeze them dry, and chop them. Set them aside for the moment. Heat the oil in a large skillet and in it lightly brown the onion and garlic. Add the veal and pork and brown them well.

In a saucepan over high heat reduce the wine to ½ cup. Add to it the tomato purée, chicken broth, oregano, and bay leaf, and heat through. Blend it into the meat along with the chopped mushrooms. Season with salt and pepper to taste. Cover pan and cook sauce at simmer until it thickens, 45 minutes or longer. This recipe makes about 6 cups of sauce.

Mushroom Sauce | Salsa di Funghi

½ cup olive oil
⅓ cup finely chopped shallots
½ cup finely chopped onions
3 cups thinly sliced
   fresh mushrooms
1 bay leaf, crumbled

1 tsp fresh oregano leaves
   (or ¼ tsp dried oregano),
   crushed
½ cup red wine
4 cups Brown Sauce (page 269)
Salt & pepper
2 Tbl butter
1 Tbl finely chopped parsley

Heat the oil in a large skillet and in it cook the onions and shallots over moderate heat until they are soft but not browned. Add the mushrooms and cook them, stirring occasionally, until they have rendered some of their juices. Add the bay leaf and oregano. Blend in the wine and continue cooking until most of the liquid has been absorbed or evaporated.

Stir the brown sauce into the mixture. Reduce heat to low, cover skillet, and continue cooking for 1 hour. Season sauce with salt and pepper to taste and stir into it the butter and parsley. Serve the sauce as required (there will be about 6 cups) with broiled or sautéed meats or with pasta.

Sauce for Seafood Cocktails | Salsa per Frutti di Mare

4 large tomatoes	1 Tbl finely grated fresh horseradish
1 very small dried hot red pepper	⅓ cup olive oil
1 large green pepper	2 Tbl lemon juice
1 medium onion, finely chopped	½ tsp salt

Peel, seed, and finely chop the tomatoes. Drain them well. Remove the seeds from the hot red pepper and pulverize it (there should be about ⅛ teaspoon). In a mixing bowl thoroughly combine the tomatoes and pepper with all of the other ingredients, adding more salt, if desired. Chill sauce for 1 hour or longer to blend the flavors.

Spring Sauce | Salsa Primavera

4 scallions, finely chopped	⅓ cup finely chopped
1 medium green pepper,	sour dill pickle
finely chopped	2 cups Mayonnaise (page 286)
⅓ cup finely chopped parsley	2 Tbl white wine vinegar
	Salt

In a glass mixing bowl combine all the ingredients, including salt to taste. Let the sauce season in the refrigerator for 2 hours before serving it with sautéed or fried fish. This recipe will provide about 3 cups of sauce.

Fresh-Tomato Purée | Purea di Pomodoro Fresco

2½ pounds ripe tomatoes, washed	½ cup water

Core the tomatoes, cut them into eighths, place in a saucepan over moderate heat, and pour the water over them. Cover pan and cook tomatoes for 15 minutes, or until the skins begin to separate from the pulp. Reduce heat and continue cooking, at simmer, until tomatoes are very soft. Force them through a fine sieve into a bowl. Discard residue of skins and seeds. Return sieved tomatoes to pan and the heat, and cook until they are reduced to a quite thick paste. Cool the purée and use it as required. This recipe will provide about 2 cups of purée.

NOTE: Fresh-tomato purée is very perishable. Even refrigerated, as it must be, it can be kept for only a short time. Make only as much as you may be able to use within 3 or 4 days. Thereafter the flavor begins to deteriorate.

Tomato Sauce | Salsa di Pomodoro

2 Tbl olive oil	1 cup Chicken Broth (page 44)
1 medium onion, finely chopped	¼ cup dry vermouth
¼ cup very finely chopped carrot	4 cups Fresh-Tomato Purée
2 Tbl finely chopped prosciutto	(page 281)
1 large clove garlic, finely chopped	2 Tbl tomato paste
½ tsp finely chopped celery leaves	Salt & white pepper

In a saucepan heat the olive oil and in it over moderate heat cook the onion, carrot, prosciutto, garlic, and celery leaves for 1 minute. Add the chicken broth and vermouth and cook mixture until liquid is reduced by ½. Stir into it the tomato purée and tomato paste and continue cooking, with pan partially covered, for 30 minutes. Strain sauce, season it with salt and white pepper to taste, and reheat it briefly. If sauce thickens excessively, add a little chicken broth during the cooking. This recipe will provide about 4 cups of sauce to be used as required.

Plum Tomato Sauce, Neapolitan Style |
Salsa di Pomodoro alla Napoletana

12 plum tomatoes	½ tsp dried basil, crushed
(about 2 pounds)	2 Tbl finely chopped parsley
⅓ cup olive oil	Salt & pepper
2 large onions, finely chopped	

Peel the plum tomatoes and slice them crosswise. Heat the olive oil in a skillet. Cook the onions in it over moderate heat until they are very soft and lightly browned. Add the basil and the tomatoes and cook for 10 minutes, or until tomatoes are moderately soft but not cooked apart. Add the parsley and salt and pepper to taste and conclude cooking after 1 more minute. This recipe will provide about 6 cups of sauce for spaghetti or fettuccine.

Tasty Sauce | Salsa alla Buongustaia

⅓ cup olive oil
1 large onion, coarsely chopped
1 large clove garlic, mashed
2 cans peeled plum tomatoes
   (30 ounces each)
1 bay leaf
½ tsp dried basil

½ pound lean pork
¼ pound lean veal
6 ounces lean beef,
   finely ground with pork & veal
Salt & pepper
Beef Broth (page 44)

In a large saucepan heat 2 tablespoons of the olive oil and in it lightly brown the onion. Add the garlic and sauté them together until onion is well browned and garlic is light golden in color. Add the tomatoes, with their juice, and the dried herbs, and cook mixture at simmer for 10 minutes.

In a skillet heat the remaining olive oil and in it sauté the ground meats, stirring constantly until they lose their red color. Immediately combine them with the onions and tomatoes in the saucepan. Add salt and pepper to taste. Cover pan, and continue cooking, still at simmer, for 2 hours. If sauce thickens excessively, thin it during cooking with a little beef broth. This recipe will provide 4 to 5 cups of sauce, enough for 10 servings with spaghetti or dumplings. It also may be used as a dressing for meatballs or meat loaves.

Red Wine Sauce | Salsa al Vino Rosso

2 Tbl olive oil
1 Tbl butter
4 shallots, finely chopped

1½ cups red wine
6 cups Brown Sauce (page 269)
Salt & pepper

In a deep skillet heat the olive oil and butter over moderate heat. Cook the shallots in the fat until they are soft but not browned. Stir into them the red wine and continue cooking until it is reduced to 1 cup. Add the brown sauce and cook, covered, at a simmer for 30 minutes longer. Season sauce with salt, if needed, and pepper to taste. Strain sauce through a fine sieve and force shallots through. Reheat sauce before using it as required. This recipe will provide about 6 cups.

White Wine Sauce | Salsa al Vino Bianco

4 Tbl butter
1 small onion, finely chopped
1 cup Broth, Fish (page 45)
   or Chicken (page 44)
1 cup dry white wine

2 cups thick Béchamel Sauce
   (page 270)
1 cup heavy cream
Salt & white pepper
½ tsp strained lemon juice

In a stainless steel or enamel-coated saucepan gently heat 2 tablespoons of the butter. Add the onion and cook it until it is soft, taking great care not to let it take on any color. Carefully, to avoid spattering, pour the broth and the wine over onion and reduce the liquid over high heat to ⅔ cup. Reduce heat to low and stir into the reduced liquid the Béchamel sauce and cream. Bring mixture just to boil, but do not let it actually bubble. Season sauce with salt and white pepper to taste and stir into it the lemon juice and the remaining butter. Serve the approximately 3 cups of sauce provided by this recipe as required.
NOTE: Bottled clam juice may be substituted for fish broth in this recipe.

Antipasto Dressing | Condimento per Antipasto

1 tsp chopped parsley
¼ tsp dried oregano, crushed
½ tsp salt

⅛ tsp white pepper
¼ cup red wine vinegar
½ cup olive oil

In a mixing bowl combine the parsley, oregano, salt, pepper, and vinegar. With a fork beat the olive oil into the mixture a little at a time. Correct the seasoning, adding more salt as needed. This recipe provides for about ¾ cup of dressing, enough for 4 servings of antipasto.

Salad Dressing | Condimento per Insalata

⅓ cup Mayonnaise (page 286)
1 egg
3 Tbl lemon juice
1½ cups olive oil
¼ cup red wine vinegar

3 tsp white wine vinegar
1 tsp salt
⅛ tsp white pepper
½ tsp dried oregano, crushed

In a mixing bowl combine the mayonnaise, egg, and lemon juice. Vigorously beat into the mixture ½ cup of the olive oil, a drop at a time. The mixture will thicken considerably. Slowly whisk in the red and white wine vinegars and add the salt, pepper, and oregano. Beat in gradually the remaining olive oil. The approximately 2½ cups of dressing provided by this recipe may be used with chilled vegetables or fish salads.

Oil and Vinegar Dressing for Green Salad |
Condimento all'Olio e Aceto per Insalata

¼ tsp salt	2 Tbl wine vinegar
⅛ tsp pepper	6 Tbl olive oil
1 clove garlic, mashed	

Make the dressing either in the bowl in which the salad is to be served or in a small mixing bowl. Combine the salt, pepper, garlic, and vinegar. Add gradually the olive oil, beating it in with a whisk until an emulsion is formed. Remove garlic before combining the dressing with the greens. This quantity of dressing, about ½ cup, is ample for 6 servings of salad.

Mayonnaise | Salsa Maionese

3 egg yolks	1¼ cups olive oil
1 tsp salt	1 tsp lemon juice

In a mixing bowl stir the egg yolks gently to combine them, and blend the salt into them. With a whisk, vigorously stir into the yolks 1 teaspoon of the oil. Beat in the remaining oil, literally drop by drop, until it is the consistency of very lightly whipped cream. You may need slightly more or somewhat less than the indicated amount of olive oil, depending upon size of yolks. The yolks will have absorbed sufficient oil when mixture begins to lose its shininess. Strain the lemon juice and blend it into the mayonnaise. Makes about 1½ cups.

Mayonnaise may also be made in an electric blender. Use 2 yolks and combine them in the blender container with the salt, ½ cup of the oil, and the lemon juice. Cover container and blend ingredients for 3 seconds, or until they are smooth. Continuing the blending, pour in the remaining olive oil in a thin but steady stream. As soon as all the oil has been added and the mixture is thick, stop the blending.

glossary

Agnolotti	Ravioli in half-moon shapes.
Al dente	A degree of doneness for pasta and rice: not too soft, not too hard, just gently resistant to the bite.
Antipasto	"Before the pasta": in other words, a first course.
Arugola	A field green: actually a pot herb, served as salad.
Barolo	One of the great full-bodied red wines of Italy, from the Piedmont.
Bel Paese	A delicate, semisoft cheese, native to an area not far from Milan, popular at table and in cooking. An excellent American copy is made in Wisconsin.
Bucatini	Hollow spaghetti.
Cannellini	White kidney beans.
Cannelloni	Large tubular pasta, or squares of dough rolled around filling.
Cannoli	Large cylinders of pastry, fried and usually filled with sweetened cheese.
Capocollo	Sausage similar to *coppa* (which see).
Cappelletti	Tiny meat- or chicken-filled pasta coronets.
Cavatelli	A pasta shape resembling tiny cradles.
Coppa	A highly spiced pork product which, depending upon the Italian province in which it is made, may be headcheese, pork loaf, sausage, or a kind of bacon.
Cotechino	Large raw pork sausage, a specialty of Modena and occasionally so called.
Ditalini	Very short pasta tubes, literally "little thimbles."
Espresso	"Specially made," most frequently referring to coffee (*Caffè espresso*) made in a special machine with steam forced through finely ground dark roasted coffee.
Farfalle	Pasta in bow or butterfly shapes.
Fettuccine	Narrow egg noodles.
Fontina	A fine creamy yet quite firm cheese with a somewhat nutty flavor and of excellent "meltability." Native to the Aosta Valley.
Fusilli	Spiral-shaped spaghetti.
Galliano	An Italian liqueur.
Lasagna	Heroic-size noodles, 1-inch or wider, usually baked with a meat sauce and cheese. *Lasagna riccie*, "curly" lasagna, is rippled along one or both edges.
Lasagnette	Smaller lasagna.
Linguine	Narrow (¼ inch or less) noodles.
Maccheroncelli	Small macaroni.
Maccheroni	Designation for all types and shapes of macaroni.
Manicotti	Pasta rolls resembling little muffs.
Maraschino	Italian liqueur made from a special type of cherry.
Marsala	Sweet or moderately sweet fortified wine for drinking and for cooking.
Maruzzelle	Little pasta shells.
Mortadella	Bologna-type sausage of cooked pork or pork and other meats seasoned with coriander and white wine and studded with bits of fat.

Mozzarella	Soft, delicate cheese, widely used in Italian cookery. Originally made in Italy only from buffalo's milk, now almost entirely from cow's milk.
Parmesan	A hard grainy cheese which has been a mainstay of Italian cookery for some 800 years.
Parsley, Italian	Plain-leaved parsley, called Italian probably because of its preference in Italian cookery.
Pasta	Generic designation for all types of macaroni, spaghetti, and noodles.
Peperoncini	Small hot peppers.
Peperone	Green or red sweet pepper.
Pignolata	Flavored with pine nuts, or a preparation so flavored.
Pizzaiola	Prepared with tomato sauce, oregano, and garlic.
Prosciutto	Italian-style cooked ham.
Provolone	Large characteristically pear-shaped cheese, somewhat salty and slightly smoky in flavor, yet mild and mellow. For table use and in cookery.
Ravioli	Squares of pasta to be filled with cheese, meat, or spinach preparations.
Ricotta	Creamy white, bland, vaguely sweet cheese somewhat similar in appearance to cottage cheese, but of considerably smoother texture.
Rigatoni	Large, ribbed macaroni.
Romano	Grainy-textured cheese similar to Parmesan but sharper and stronger.
Rotelle	Pasta shaped in series of small "wheels."
Salami, Genoa style	Misnomer for Italian-style salami (which see).
Salami, Italian style	Fine-grained cooked sausage of pork and other meats, salted, spiced, and herbed (predominantly with garlic).
Sausage, Modena	Cotechino (which see).
Semolina	Flour finely milled from durum (hard grain) wheat.
Spaghettini	Very thin spaghetti.
Tagliatelle	Long strips of noodles, somewhat less than ¼-inch wide.
Tagliatini	Noodles even narrower than tagliatelle.
Tomatoes, plum	Popularly called Italian tomatoes because of their wide use in Italian cookery. Actually pear-shaped, they are somewhat sweeter than the globe variety.
Tomato paste	Not to be confused with tomato sauce or purée, this is a highly concentrated plum tomato essence, the tomatoes reduced to less than ⅛ their volume. Tomato paste is packed in tins usually with a leaf of basil.
Tortellini	"Twisted" pasta shapes similar to cappelletti (which see).
Truffle, white	Native to Italy, this tuber is considerably less white than beige. In season, white truffles come to market in Italy frequently as large as baseballs.
Vermicelli	A very thin spaghetti, usually designated as Number 10.
Ziti	Large tubular pasta.

index

Caption references in italics

a

Agnolotti, 288
Almond cake, 248
Anchovy sauce, 268
Anise
   cake, 238
   trifle, 238
Antipasti
   artichokes, Roman style, 28
   artichokes, stuffed, *16,* 27
   broccoli in oil and lemon, 29
   clams with oregano filling, 14
   eels in marinade, 14
   eggplant, marinated, 30
   eggplant relish, 31
   eggplant, Sicilian style, 29
   escarole, stuffed, 32
   hot dipping sauce, 26
   Italian ham and melon, *16,* 26
   meat pie, country style, *18, 19,* 22
   mushrooms, marinated, 33
   mushrooms, pickled, 33
   mushrooms, stuffed, 34
   mussels in green sauce, 15
   onions, pearl, in saffron, *10,* 36
   onions, stuffed, 35
   peppers, green, stuffed, 37
   peppers, red, stuffed, 36
   pickled vegetable salad, *16,* 38
   squid with Genoa-style green sauce, 16
   squid, stuffed, 16
   tomatoes stuffed with tuna fish, 15
   tomatoes, Trattoria stuffed, 39
   tripe, Borgotaro style, 24
   tripe, Friuli style, 25
   trout, pickled, *16,* 19
   veal, stuffed breast of, *16,* 21
   whitebait, marinated, 20
   zucchini, minted, 40
   zucchini, stuffed, 41
Antipasto sandwich, *188,* 192

Appetizers, *see* Antipasti
Apple(s)
   cake, 247
   cake, Mantua style, 246
Apricot(s)
   pie, latticed, *241,* 249
   sherbet, 264
Artichoke(s)
   bottoms, molded, 204
   Roman style, 28
   stuffed, *16,* 27
Arugola, 288

b

Bean(s)
   green, salad, 220
   soup, "for winter," 61
   and tuna fish salad, 229
Beef
   broth, 44
   fillets, Eva's marinated, *155,* 156
   fillets, Surprise, 155
   medallions in wine sauce, 155
   pot roast with Barolo wine, 158
   soup with little meatballs, 46
   steak and peppers, 159
   steak, pizzaiola, 160
Bel Paese cheese, 288
Black and white pudding, 234
Brains, calf's, sautéed, 168
Bread
   Italian, 73
   soup, Luigian, 46
   sticks, 74
Broccoli
   in oil and lemon, 29
   with pasta, 111
   soup, 47
Broth, *see* Soup
Bucatini, 288
   with bacon and tomatoes, 92

c

Cabbage
   rolls, stuffed, 205
   and sausage, 176
   soup, 48

e

Recipe index in Italian